Judith Wills has written more bestselling food and healthy lifestyle titles than any other British author. Her books have been translated into over twenty languages and have appeared in the bestseller lists across the world. Her previous titles include *The Food Bible*, which has sold over 275,000 copies and was recently revised for its third edition in January 2007; *The Children's Food Bible*, which is one of the most-borrowed non-fiction books in UK libraries; and the much-acclaimed *The Diet Bible*.

Judith is also a keen home cook and has written six cookbooks, including the bestseller *Slim and Healthy Mediterranean* and *Slim and Healthy Vegetarian*, and, in 2007, *Feeding Kids* with the Netmums organization.

Wearing her 'journalist' hat, Judith has written for most of the UK's major national magazines. She has made numerous television appearances and radio broadcasts and is now often known as the 'Diet Detective' (www.thediet detective.net), writing under this name for several magazines and websites. She also makes regular appearances at food fairs and literary festivals around the country, talking about food and health.

She lives on the borders of Herefordshire and Wales with her husband, Tony, and younger son Chris. Her main hobby is growing, cooking and eating good food, and she has an organic fruit and vegetable garden, greenhouse and orchard. She also enjoys interactive sudoku, and has a large collection of popular music from the 1970s. Indeed, she once took tea with Paul McCartney, and Keith Moon stole her lipstick.

TRANSWORLD PUBLISHERS
61–63 Uxbridge Road, London W5 5SA
A Random House Group Company
www.rbooks.co.uk

First published in Great Britain
in 2008 by Eden Project Books
an imprint of Transworld Publishers

A CIP catalogue record for this book
is available from the British Library.

ISBN 9781905811182

Designed by Nick Avery

All images courtesy of Shutterstock.

Addresses for Random House Group Ltd companies outside the UK
can be found at: www.randomhouse.co.uk
The Random House Group Ltd Reg. No. 954009

The Random House Group Limited supports The Forest Stewardship
Council (FSC), the leading international forest-certification organization. All our
titles that are printed on Greenpeace-approved FSC-certified paper carry the FSC logo.
Our paper procurement policy can be found at
www.rbooks.co.uk/environment

Printed and bound in Germany

2 4 6 8 10 9 7 5 3 1

JUDITH WILLS

THE GREEN FOOD BIBLE

eden project books

Contents

Introduction

Can you remember the days, certainly no more than ten years ago, when it was considered radical to buy organic produce? When the phrase 'ethical food' was almost unheard of, and no modern, fashionable dinner party was complete without seafood flown in from the USA, or a dish of strawberries from South Africa in midwinter?

What a change there has been since then in our attitude to food. Today millions of us are not only trying to improve our health by eating organic, healthy, additive-free food – but we are aware that it should be possible to shop and eat in a way that may also help improve our lives and our environment.

We realize that the food industry has come on a huge learning curve since the 1950s – and we have alongside it. After years of gladly embracing a cheap, fast-food culture, we now recognize that it is time to be intelligent and responsible in every food choice that we make. We have had our decades of experimentation and overindulgence. Now it is time to find simpler and friendlier ways to feed ourselves.

Such has been the swing in the past year or two towards attaining 'greenness' that for many people it is a bigger issue than, for instance, good nutrition. For many others, it is an issue that is rapidly increasing in importance, and it is one that sits naturally alongside our revived interest in home cooking and a more natural lifestyle.

More and more of us now see that our behaviour can prolong human, animal and plant life on this planet. What and how we eat, and cook, and how and where we shop, is a significant part of that behaviour.

So far, so good. But what, exactly, to put on our plates is not always clear. Just like all the conflicting nutrition stories one used to read in the press each day, we now have a similar problem with 'going green'. What really is the truth behind all the disparate reports? What really is the best way forward if one wants to eat responsibly and ethically?

This is what *The Green Food Bible* intends to do: offer a guiding hand through the conflicting and complicated maze that is eating today.

I have written this book because until quite recently I was the last person to consider green issues when choosing and preparing food. It was my younger son, Chris (who was always, I think, a closet Green), rather than any media, who, a few years ago, began to make me think that my wanton, wasteful, overconsuming ways were not habits to encourage in the next generation, not things of which to be proud, but negative traits I should try to alter.

And so I began. I am still only getting there, but as food has for many years been my profession, and one of my major loves, it was with food that I began to try to make my own difference. That is why everything you read in this book – the practical tips, plus the bits you may not, at first, want to read – comes from not only a great deal of research and consideration, but also from my own experience and learning curve.

The Green Food Bible is not an academic tome, nor a book for people who have been practising green eating for a long time now, but a practical book with the answers to the questions ordinary people like me will be asking.

I hope that with the help of *The Green Food Bible* you will more easily, surely and comfortably be able to take responsibility for what you buy and how you eat.

In other words, with this book in your kitchen I hope you will find 'eating green' a much more enjoyable and interesting journey than you may have imaged.

Judith Wills

1 What Does Green Mean?

IT'S THE LATEST BIG THING. FOR THE
FASHIONISTAS OF THE FOOD WORLD,GREEN
IS DEFINITELY THE NEW BROWN.

Their lentil-eating health fads have been all but replaced by
an intensive search for the ethically produced, the organic,
the seasonable, the sustainable, the local, the traceable. Truly
the fuel of good dinner-party conversation in the kitchens of
Hampstead and Chelsea.

It could be here to stay. It could filter down.

Well, in fact, it has already – a lot. But this time, when the
fly-by-night fashionistas have fled the scene because it's
become too 'mainstream', we need to stick at it.

With not only global warming to worry us, we also have
soaring world prices for our staple foods and speedily rising
obesity levels. We *need* to be concerned about the way food
is produced, where it has come from and how we obtain it.
If the food that we eat can be good for the planet as well as
truly good for our bodies, then so it should be. If the food that
we eat can help offer a good prognosis for how long life can
survive on earth, then marvellous.

And that is why *The Green Food Bible* is not a bible for the
fashionable, the cutting edge or the faddist – but a guide for
you and for me.

That G-word

Ethical food. It isn't always easy to define. What is 'green'? What is the difference between green and ethical? Does a product have to be organic to be green? Does it have to be local to be ethical? Or is a Fairtrade item from Africa greener than a local, mass-produced one? Is farmed cod green? Is wild salmon OK? Or should we go vegan to be truly virtuous? Which is more important – the number of miles a food has travelled or the amount of packaging it's wrapped in?

Is your head spinning? Is it me, or is this green thing confusing? The more you think about it, the more you come up with more questions than answers. These – and hundreds more – were the dilemmas that I began to uncover when I started to become more aware of, and interested in, green issues.

Choosing food, shopping, preparing meals, trying to offer our families a healthy diet – all this is hard and time-consuming enough without adding a long list of green concerns to our shopping trolley. And yet we are trying. And we want to try. And we should try.

Let's hope it's here to stay. But first let's try to sort out that big green question. The meaning of 'green'.

MY STRAW POLL

When I started work on this book, I did a straw poll of twenty people to find out what they understood by the word 'green' when referring to food. Here are the results, with the number of times each explanation was mentioned in brackets:

ethical (15)
organic (9)
local (9)
sustainable (7)
vegetarian (6)
in season (5)
Fairtrade (5)
no air miles involved (2)
short distance travelled (2)
supporting small producers (2)
no/minimal packaging (2)
minimal processing involved/simple (2)
home-grown (1)
not wasteful (1)

I then asked for a definition of the leading answer – ethical – from those who had given it, which turned up this:

Fairtrade (8)
no air-freighting (6)
supporting sustainable agriculture (5)
carbon neutral (4)
no cruelty to animals (3)
organic (3)

Not scientific, true. But my little poll shows up a couple of interesting points. One, that not all of these ideals are in harmony (Fairtrade and local, for example). Two, that people have different ideas of what 'green' does mean. Three, that 'green' and 'ethical' are, for most people, more or less interchangeable concepts.

I then asked twenty people (other than those already questioned) already committed to a greener lifestyle to list their own 'green food' criteria in order of importance to them. Here are the results, starting with the most important:

1 organic
2 local
3 minimal air miles/journey
5 in season
6 Fairtrade
7 sustainable agriculture
8 recyclable packaging
9 ethically produced
10 few production processes involved
11 energy-saving cooking method

So by now I had a picture of what people think green eating is, and what their priorities are.

Now skip several months. After much research, questioning, making a nuisance of myself and investigation, I think I have seen the green light, have found ways to reconcile the different green food issues, and can perhaps set them into some kind of sensible 'greenprint'.

In the remainder of this first chapter we will take an overview of all these foodie green issues in order to begin to discover a greener way of eating. First I'm going to take you back to a time when eating really was a simple affair.

Family food – then and now

GREAT BRITAIN, OCTOBER 1955

Here is a typical day in the food life of a family in the 1950s, Mr and Mrs Green and their children, Jane, fifteen, and John, thirteen.

8 a.m.

Milkman delivers milk in bottles. Bread is delivered from the local bakery. Family sits down at 8.15 to a breakfast of bread, home-made marmalade, boiled egg from the farm or the local grocer's store. Everyone leaves home to walk to work or school.

12.30 p.m.

Children have school lunch – minced beef and carrots with cabbage and mashed potato, all cooked by the canteen cooks from scratch, followed by stewed apples from a local orchard with custard made from Bird's Instant Custard Powder.

Dad has a sandwich of white bread, margarine, Cheddar cheese and pickle made at home, an apple, a slice of fruit cake made at home and a flask of tea.

Mum has a similar meal at home.

6.00 p.m.

The family sits down to a stew, made by Mum during the afternoon – a little 'scrag end' of lamb, dried haricot beans, plenty of carrots, swede, onions, sliced potatoes. Pudding is plum crumble and cream off the top of the milk.

To drink during the day, the family has tap water, tea and orange squash.

If Dad wants a beer, he may walk down to the pub and buy a pint.

At bedtime the family all have a hot milk drink and a digestive biscuit.

Food in the 1950s

By 1954, wartime rationing had finished in Britain, and families were beginning to enjoy items such as red meat, eggs, butter, cheese and sugar, all of which had been restricted during the war and post-war years. Virtually no one had a home fridge in the UK, although in the USA they were already widespread, and very few women drove or had access to a car, so food was bought regularly and taken home by foot or bicycle as needed, unless the local tradespeople delivered to your door – which was fairly usual.

All the vegetables bought at the local greengrocer's would have been sold loose and grown locally – otherwise, self-sufficiency or near self-sufficiency via an allotment was common. The meat came from the local butcher and was also local meat.

Only 30 per cent of married women went out to work – they became housewives and spent a good proportion of their time shopping locally for food and then preparing meals from scratch. Convenience foods were few (see p. 14). The concept of the supermarket was only just beginning – Mr Sainsbury had opened his first self-service store in Croydon in 1950 as an experiment, while Tesco's first self-service store opened in 1956 – and thus most foods were weighed out loose and packed, usually in a brown paper bag.

This is the meaning of green. This is the world that, within fifty years, had seemingly vanished for ever. Fast forward to 2005.

GREAT BRITAIN, OCTOBER 2005

Here is a typical day in the food life of a family in the very early twenty-first century, Mr and Mrs Black and their children Emily, fifteen, and Josh, thirteen.

7.30–8.30 a.m.
Various family members battle for the bathroom and the kettle. Josh grabs a cereal bar from a pack and a strawberry milkshake in a plastic bottle to eat/drink on the way to school; Emily has a black coffee.

Dad has some cluster cereal, milk from a large plastic container and some blueberries from South Africa. Mum grabs a latte in a plastic container from a chain coffee shop after her journey to work and picks up a blueberry muffin at the same time to eat in the office.

1 p.m.
Josh has a packed lunch containing cheese and breadsticks in a pack, blister-wrapped mini fruit, pre-packed mini bag of dried fruit, a bag of crisps and an orange drink in an individual tetrapak with straw. Emily nips out of school and down to the chip shop for a portion of chips on a polystyrene plate and served with a throwaway plastic knife and fork, and a bottle of cola – and spends the rest of her lunch money on a bar of chocolate and a lipstick. Mum has a supermarket Thai chicken salad in a plastic dish for lunch at her desk. Dad has a pub lunch – a reheated ready-meal curry and rice supplied to the pub by a catering firm and containing a variety of produce of untraceable origin. He has a glass of wine from South Africa.

4 p.m.–10 p.m.
The members of the family graze during the evening at various times. Josh helps himself to a frozen pizza at 5 p.m. and heats it in the oven, eats half of it and throws the rest away. Emily heats a ready-made chicken tikka masala in the microwave at 6.30 p.m., has an individual plastic tub of chocolate mousse and follows this with an apple from France and a kiwi fruit from Italy with a can of diet cola.

Mum and Dad order a takeaway when they get in at 8 p.m. – a Chinese delivered by scooter from 5 miles away and packed in non-biodegradable containers. They drink a bottle of wine from Australia.

BACK WHEN ... THE WESTERN WORLD IN THE 1950S

- **Kraft produced the first commercial packaged cheese – processed cheese slices.**

- **The average grocery store carried fewer than 1,000 different items.**

- **The first Kentucky Fried Chicken opened in the USA in 1952.**

- **The first broiler chickens for 'factory' farming were introduced into the UK from the USA.**

- **Birds Eye produced the first frozen peas in 1952 and the first frozen fish fingers went on sale in the USA.**

- **The first home microwave ovens went on sale in the USA in 1955 – but weren't available in the UK until 1974.**

- **Burger King first opened in 1954 in the USA. McDonald's corporation was founded in 1955.**

- **The first USA frozen ready-meal chicken dinner on an aluminium tray was produced in 1955.**

- **By 1954 chain supermarkets accounted for 40 per cent of retail food sales in the USA. The first Sainsbury's self-service opened in Croydon in 1950 as an experiment.**

- **By 1956, 80 per cent of US homes had a fridge – but only 8 per cent of UK households did, and virtually no homes in this country had a freezer.**

- **The population of England and Wales drank approximately 12 billion pints of milk per annum in the 1950s, virtually all of which were sold in glass bottles via doorstep delivery.**

- **In the 1950s, bottled mineral water for home consumption was virtually unknown.**

AND NOW … IN THE 2000S

- 30 million microwave ovens are sold throughout the world every year.

- Number of factory-farmed chickens sold in UK: 800 million per annum.

- 40 per cent of poultry sales involve heavy processing.

- Bottled mineral water sold in the UK in 2006: 2.17 billion litres.

- The average supermarket carries 40,000 different lines and nearly 90 per cent of the food that we buy is purchased in supermarkets.

- In 2004/05 each person in the UK produced, on average, 517kg of waste, of which 78 per cent was not recycled.

- 5 million tonnes of annual household waste is used packaging.

- Over 15 billion plastic bags are given out annually by the UK's six major supermarkets.

- 4 million tons of food packaging ends up in UK landfill sites every year.

- Nearly 50 per cent of the UK's total food purchases are imported. In 2004, the UK imported £19.1 billion worth of food and exported £8.9 billion worth.

- A billion pints of milk are delivered in bottles to UK homes each year, while over 6 billion pints per annum are taken home from shops in plastic containers.

- Food transport accounts for 25 per cent of all heavy-goods vehicle kilometres in the UK and 30 billion vehicle kilometres per annum.

At the weekend Mum or Dad may cook a 'proper' meal – a plate of pasta with Asian tiger prawns from the freezer, ready-made pesto from Italy and some bagged baby spinach from Kenya; or a rump steak from Argentina via Scotland, some new potatoes from Israel, mangetouts from Zimbabwe and baby corn cobs from Thailand; all purchased from the major supermarket 12 miles away.

They've heard of the word 'green' but the implications of trying to live a greener lifestyle haven't filtered through into their busy lives at all yet.

How did we get to this from that? Progress.

PROGRESS?

We've progressed so that we have more leisure time than ever before, yet we are somehow more busy, more rushed than ever before. There are far more items in the shops from which to choose, but in many ways we have less choice. We're cooking fewer meals at home, rarely eat *en famille*, our children have little idea of how to cook or even where basic foodstuffs originate (i.e. that milk comes from cows, that eggs come from hens or potatoes from the ground). The disposable age has filtered through to all areas of our lives, but thanks to global warming and the signs that the destruction of the fabric of our planet is gathering pace, we are getting the message that it can't continue. We can see that we should stop the 'progress' that the profit-motivated multinational companies and our own laziness want to continue. We recognize that we need

to find a new way ahead – a way ahead which will, at least in part, mean taking some steps back to those days fifty years ago when life was, indeed, much simpler.

What lessons can we learn from the Green family without causing so much disruption to our modern busy lives that it's all plain unworkable?

Well, we can take many – much of how they lived and ate is our 'new' definition of responsible living. It's a superb greenprint and perhaps it *is* workable with some tweaking, updating, redefining. Indeed, a recent report commissioned by Somerfield found that many of us want a return to the lifestyle and values of the 1950s.

But you can't go back, can you? Our new, large, cosmopolitan world knows too much, sees too much and enjoys its freedoms, its choices and its variety too much to want to go back to that enclosed, restricted, ordered existence of five decades ago.

And how important is it really to go green with our food choices, with the way we shop and prepare and cook and dispose of our food? Can it really be so urgent that we have to alter the way we do all this? Can any food changes we make really help save the planet? Aren't the doom-mongers just standing on a new bandwagon to further their own causes?

Well, let's see.

Food and climate change

The world is getting hotter. It has warmed by 0.74°C over the last 100 years and over half of this warming has taken place since the 1970s.

The three warmest years ever recorded have occurred since 1998, and nineteen of the twenty warmest have been since 1980. The most recent report of the Intergovernmental Panel on Climate Change (IPCC), published in 2007, concluded with 90 per cent certainty that human activities are responsible for rising world temperatures. 'Future global warming depends on the choices humans make now,' said the panel's co-chairperson, Susan Solomon.

According to the UK's Department for Environment, Food and Rural Affairs (Defra) in its report *Environmental Impacts of Food Production and Consumption*, published in December 2006, 'the main human influence on global climate is emissions of the key gases carbon dioxide (CO_2), methane and nitrous oxide. The accumulation of these gases in the atmosphere strengthens the greenhouse effect.'

At present, just over 7 billion tonnes of CO_2 are emitted globally each year through fossil-fuel (coal, oil and natural gas) use, and an additional 1.6 billion tonnes are emitted by changes in land use, such as deforestation. The concentrations of these gases in the atmosphere have now reached levels unprecedented for tens of thousands of years. In 2004, carbon dioxide accounted for 86 per cent of all greenhouse-gas emissions in the UK.

According to IPCC, temperatures are likely to increase by around a further 4°C – but perhaps by as much as 6.4°C – in the next 100 years if we can't find ways to halt the increase in emissions. Increases in greenhouse gases are also having other effects – for example, our oceans are becoming more acid because of the high amount of carbon dioxide they have to absorb, and this is reducing fish stocks, killing coral reefs and threatening the food chain.

Climate change will seriously damage or change worldwide food production, according to expert opinion. But conversely, our methods of food production, our eating and shopping habits also affect global warming. And that is why our own government, and governmental and other organizations such as the Food and Agriculture Organization (FAO) and the UN, are also devoting detailed thought and research to global warming and how to beat it (while mostly, nevertheless, still condoning anti-environmental practices such as increases in world trade and agribusiness).

On page 26 of its report, Defra states that: 'There is general agreement that the production, processing, transport and consumption of food accounts for a significant portion of the environmental burden imposed by any Western European country.' It goes on to say that food and drink consumption accounts for between 22 per cent and 31 per cent of global-warming potential.

Food contributes to global warming in various ways, outlined below.

METHODS OF FOOD PRODUCTION

The human quest for cheap food, a population explosion, and the growth in power of a handful of supermarkets and processed-food producers over the past fifty years have produced modern farming methods and practices that are bad for the environment and have disastrous long-term implications for our climate.

As CO_2 production increases, it is vital, for example, to retain the rainforests – as trees 'soak up' carbon dioxide. But vast areas of the world's forests have been destroyed and are still being decimated in order to provide land to grow plants that are deemed necessary for food production (and, ironically, now for 'biofuel' alternatives to petrol) – such as palm oil from Malaysia and Indonesia, or soya products from Brazil, which between them now figure in at least 60 per cent of the foods on supermarket shelves.

Indeed, all over the world small natural habitats and indigenous plants, shrubs, hedges and trees have been razed to make way for giant farms that grow only one kind of crop. And as 'old-fashioned' methods of crop rotation and soil management no longer apply, in time the soil loses its vitality, so nutrients are then applied via artificial fertilization. The vast increase in the use of nitrate fertilizers throughout the world is thought to be having an increasingly significant impact on biodiversity and to be one of the major causes of 'dead zones' in the world's oceans, as well as being the source of nitrous-oxide emissions.

As these modern farming methods increase global warming, so that warming is beginning to destroy the livings of many farmers across the world. For example, low-lying farming areas in Asia are subject to flooding and crop devastation because of the rise in rain and in sea levels, while in other areas of the world drought and higher temperatures mean that indigenous crops may fail.

TYPES OF FOOD THAT WE CHOOSE TO EAT

Modern Western families and individuals love fast food. Anything that is quick and easy – heat and eat. This type of food has usually gone through many processes in order to reach your shopping basket. The raw material (for example, the beef) is processed, usually in a factory which could be located anywhere in the world, into a dish (e.g. lasagne) with many components (tomatoes, onions, wheat) which, again, may have come to the factory from anywhere in the world where the ingredient could be sourced cheaply (partly with help from chemical fertilizers and pesticides). It is then packaged, often with two or even three different forms of packaging, including coloured print, photographs and so on. All this effort uses a great deal of energy at every stage.

We also love our 'luxuries'. Enjoyment of out-of-season foods, rare and expensive delicacies, treat-yourself foods, supper-party one-upmanship: this is all carbon non-friendly eating.

Various other food-choice factors affect our carbon output: meat and dairy use more energy in production than vegetable foods; large portions and supersize packages mean more energy use than smaller meals (and also, of course, mean a rise in obesity worldwide), as does the huge market for value-added drinks and alcohol rather than water from the tap.

FOOD MILES

While the air-freighted pack of out-of-season green beans from Kenya is now the cliché of the 'food-miles' debate, the food-miles issue is nevertheless extremely important. Here are some of the ways that the food on your plate can rack up unacceptably high mileage and energy wastage:

- Cost-cutting and production methods (see 'Types of food that we choose to eat' above) of processed foods usually mean that many components of each item on the supermarket shelves may have travelled thousands of miles before they are even put into the finished product.

- The finished product is often transported again by air, road or rail over hundreds or even thousands of miles to the shop where it is to be purchased. It often needs refrigeration during transport.

- Many non-processed foods, such as fruits and vegetables, meat and fish, are transported thousands of miles either because the cost of transport to the shop is more than offset by the very low cost of the product, or because of our demand for out-of-season, or new, or ethnic types of food.

- Many food raw materials are sent thousands of miles to undergo minimal processing which could be done near or nearer the point of origin.

- Food items that can be, and are, easily made in the UK are imported from other countries while similar UK-made products are exported.

- And you have to get to the shop, then get home again with your shopping. Few people walk to the shops any more – as 88 per cent of us shop at supermarkets which are mostly located outside town, this is hardly practical – and few people make time to plan out a week or two's shopping in advance to minimize the number of trips.

PACKAGING

Food and drink packaging is a major issue for us all – from the producer to the consumer and the waste manager. Packaging is big business and, while there are arguments for some packaging (for example, to prevent damage to goods, which in itself would be wasteful), our Western way of eating, shopping and home management produces nearly 30 million tonnes of household waste a year. Packaging is a factor in climate change because both making it and disposing of it use energy and resources.

WASTE

Research shows that in this country approximately a third of the food that we purchase ends up thrown in the bin or wasted – a fifth of the UK's household waste. For an average family's £100 weekly food shop, that means that each family in the land spends an average of £1,716 a year on food they aren't going to eat. This increases the need to return to the shops for yet more food, using up more resources. The extra waste in the bins, such as packaging, has to be disposed of somehow and this is another largely unnecessary use of energy.

From farm to shop to fork to bin – when we don't eat green we heat up the planet a little more.

FACTBOX

According to Christian Aid, a billion people – one in seven people on earth today – could be forced to leave their homes over the next fifty years as the effects of climate change – water shortages, sea-level crises, deteriorating pasture land, conflicts and famine – take hold.

Other ethical issues in choosing how we eat

While lowering greenhouse gases and carbon footprints are top of the agenda for many people, other issues can also have wide-ranging effects on our environment. The fate of the corner shop and the local greengrocer selling local fruits and veg in season may not, on the face of it, be as important as reducing fossil-fuel and energy use – thus saving future generations from a real roasting – but the implications are indeed serious.

BIODIVERSITY

Modern food choices are affecting biodiversity – the diverse elements of our planet including the varieties of plants and creatures and their natural habitats. Biodiversity is important for the soil, wildlife, local farming, small producers, our heritage and history, and for our free choice. Our planet is endlessly varied, fascinating and rewarding, yet the human quest for 'progress' and wealth reduces this diversity year on year. We can't always get back what is lost. Once a species is extinct, that's it; once a seed variety has gone, that's it.

The supermarkets have a long history of preferring fruit and vegetable varieties that are disease resistant, grow reliably, crop well, are of uniform appearance, and transport and keep well. Because of this, less profitable lines which may have a better taste, for example, can literally disappear.

And as the agribusiness producers of these supermarket-fillers thrive, our local small-scale farmers and local small-scale shopkeepers disappear.

SUSTAINABILITY

As the world's population grows, it is vital to choose sustainable ways of eating in order to retain biodiversity and provide ourselves with enough to eat.

Has the raw material been grown/caught/chosen/harvested in a way that ensures it won't run out for future consumers and that

FACTBOX
In 1950 the population of the world
was 2.5 billion.
In 2007 it was 6.5 billion.
By 2050 it is projected to be over
9 billion.

doesn't permanently damage the environment? The most obvious example is in our choice of fish and seafood – overfishing of certain species, non-ethical fishing methods, industrial pollution and contamination of our seas could wipe out cod, for example, while even fish farms can adversely affect wild stock.

The Western world's love affair with meat and dairy produce may also need to be re-thought, as animal products have a higher environmental impact than plant foods. In order to feed ourselves in the future, we will have to eat more green foods in every sense of the word. And while organic farming methods are, undoubtedly, better for the condition of the soil and preferable in other ways to mass industrial farming, the debate about organic food continues – which is why I have devoted the whole of Chapter 2 to organic and sustainable farming and food.

RESPONSIBILITY

While half the world becomes overweight and obese, the other half still struggles to find enough to eat. True, we have food aid: but the inhabitants of the poorer countries of the world, such as many areas of Africa, would prefer not to have to accept food parcels, food drops from the air and truckloads of leftover grain from North America. They would prefer to be able to grow enough food on their own land for themselves to eat. They would prefer to use their land to grow cash crops for export, and to receive a fair price. Thus 'fair trade' was born and thrives. So practical aid to help communities across the globe farm poor land or previously unfarmed land comes in part from the ethical choices we make as we shop. Feed the world. Even so – Fairtrade shopping choices need to be made thoughtfully.

ANIMAL WELFARE

Responsible ethical eating can also improve life – and death – for our food-chain animals. More and more we are realizing that cheap meat and dairy may be purchased at the expense of a decent quality of life for farm animals. The word 'farm' is hardly appropriate for the way much of our cheap animal and dairy protein is produced.

HEALTH

Because we need to be healthy and strong to be an efficient race with the will to change our planet and our habits, and because poor health in individuals can use up vital resources, health through good food is an ethical issue.

- **Obesity.** Conspicuous calorie consumption – pile it high, sell it cheap – has resulted in an obesity epidemic in the Western world and is a growing problem in developing nations such as China. Fat is an ethical issue in two ways: every calorie we consume that our bodies don't need is energy wasted and food wasted. Given that worldwide demand for staples such as wheat and dairy produce such as cheese is soaring and prices rocketing, it makes sense in every way to take a smaller slice of that pizza.

And eating to obesity can cause long-term ill-health, including diabetes, cancers, heart disease, which puts more pressure on the world's resources as we seek cures and fill hospitals.

- **Poor nutrient intake.** We need also to think about the nutritional content of food. We all need vitamins, minerals, protein, plant compounds and essential fats for health; there is much research linking various human ailments to a lack of the necessary nutrients. Much of what we buy today has a low nutrient to calorie ratio. That means we're buying calories but little else. Mass-produced and highly processed foods tend to lose nutrients as they proceed along the production line, while several research studies have shown that even vegetables and fruit have a lower nutrient content today than fifty years ago. I believe it is ethical to purchase only food which provides optimum nutrient levels for optimal calorie levels – that is, which give us adequate energy and optimal nutrient intake without making us obese. This is a subject we'll return to in Chapter 3.

- **Hidden and unwanted ingredients.** Lastly, it is well documented that modern food-production methods and industry are affecting our health in other, more insidious, ways. Pollutants in our food are many. We have growth-hormone and antibiotic residues in our meat and dairy. We have industrial pollutants affecting our fish and our fields. We have pesticides and herbicides in our grains, fruit and vegetables. We have artificial additives in our low-rent supermarket processed foods. All these 'hidden ingredients' or 'ingredients by stealth' in our foods may have serious long-term consequences. Infertility, behaviour problems, allergies, damaged immune systems – just some of the consequences of our modern food chain that have already been discovered.

Our food needs to be chosen with care.

Conclusion

Let us go back to our Green family. We need to find ways to emulate their unconscious and necessary green habits in the kitchen without giving up all that we hold important in our lives.

If you're currently more Mrs or Mr Black than Mrs or Mr Green but are considering a swap:

- You need to believe that you can make changes and that the changes you make will effect a difference. You can vote for this with your purse and your actions.

- You may need to embrace a new mindset over certain issues – deconstructing your current non-green foodie lifestyle to prepare the way for a new, truly modern one. This may be made easier by the knowledge that what you consider important today may not be so important to you in, say, a year's time.

- You need to know that not all changes you may make will be easy at first but that, before too long, you will feel better about yourself by making them.

- And before it all gets to sound too much like hard work, remember that the groundwork for many changes has already been done. You just need to build on it, bit by bit.

- Do what you can and what you want to do, week by week. If it's just a bit more than you did last month, last year – then that's OK. And there are dozens, hundreds, of people and organizations there to help, support, cajole, inform, provide, or even bully a bit (as you will see throughout this book and in the Resources section at the end).

- Be reassured that the green food world is not depressing or dull – or it certainly need not be so. I have made many changes myself over the past few years and, far from feeling deprived, I feel better about myself and I enjoy my food more than ever.

- A greener food life can be, I know, *more* enjoyable, *more* rewarding, *less* expensive, *more* healthy and *more* satisfying than any amount of conspicuous and disposable consumption as of old (i.e. yesterday). Just give it a go. Just do it.

2 Green, Greener, Greenest:
The Truth Behind Organic Food

'THROUGHOUT THE WORLD, THE OLD, TRADITIONAL WAYS ARE DYING OUT AND THE ANCIENT CONTRACT BETWEEN PEOPLE AND THE ANIMALS WHO SERVE THEM IS DYING.'

Jane Goodall, *Harvest for Hope*

Thirty years ago the words 'organic food' were hardly heard and people who sought it out – or grew/produced it – were usually thought of as hippies or 'weirdos'. Why would anyone, we thought, go to the trouble and expense of finding themselves dirty, misshapen carrots and pockmarked apples when it was now possible to buy low-cost, perfectly formed, pre-washed and packed versions from any supermarket?

Twenty years ago the organic movement had become a little more accepted and purchasers were seen as less idiosyncratic and peculiar. The Organic King was Prince Charles. And thus those hippies had morphed into middle-class professionals, buying organic because they perceived that it tasted better – and helped them to feel superior to the supermarket-loving masses.

Ten years ago the organic-food market had begun to become borderline mainstream with sales constantly rising – albeit organic still comprising only a tiny fraction of total food sales. Always first in line for a new opportunity to sell, around this time the supermarkets saw a main chance and began stocking organic lines in unprecedented quantity.

Now, in 2008, the average organic purchaser is likely to be – you and me. According to the major UK organic 'watchdog', the Soil Association (SA), nearly one in three shoppers buys organic food, with four out of ten people buying organic food at least once a month. Sales virtually reached the £2 billion a year mark for the first time during 2006, according to the SA's 2007 annual report. And the supermarkets sell three-quarters of all organic produce.

But the rise and rise of organic food, in Britain at least, has levelled off somewhat in the last few years. Why? Organic farmers just can't produce enough of the stuff to satisfy our demands – if it isn't available, we can't buy it. This is particularly true of organic grains and fruit. The gap is being filled with organic imports – around 50 per cent of our current organic purchases (including processed items) are imported.

Why we choose organic

So why do many of us so love organic? Over the years it has had a variable press – ranging from derision through to worship, depending on whom you read at what time. And, while the government supports organic farming methods, the official line has always been, 'Well buy it if you want, but it really isn't any better for you at all.' And in a recent major report, Defra actually came to the hotly disputed conclusion that some types of organic food, far from being better for the environment, actually contribute more to global warming and environmental damage than do non-organically produced foods of a similar variety – a conclusion we will be looking at a bit later in more detail.

Nevertheless, we are still prepared to pay up to a third more for organically produced fresh food, and the main reasons are that we perceive it to be free from 'nasties' such as pesticide residues, hormones, additives, and so on – thus it may be healthier than the non-organic version – and that it tastes better. There may also be a feeling that by choosing organic we are able to buy into a more wholesome lifestyle.

But is organic always as good as it sounds? Let's take a closer look.

What does organic actually mean?

'Organic farming involves using natural processes, including biodiversity ... rather than seeking to fight nature.'

Soil Association

'The main components of organic farming are avoiding the use of artificial fertilisers and pesticides, and the use of crop husbandry to maintain soil fertility and control weeds, pests and diseases.'

Defra

Organic farming uses natural ways to get the best from the land and to put something back. This means fewer chemical pesticides, herbicides and fertilizers. Organic farmers fertilize their land by using composted manure and by planting crops that naturally feed nitrogen into the soil. They beat pests by rotating their crops and using natural predators. Most organic farms are mixed – combining, say, sheep and cattle with crops facilitates the rotation process and helps create diversity. Farmland is less intensively used and wildlife is encouraged.

But if you think that all sounds quite vague with a lot of room for manoeuvre, in fact organic standards are quite rigorous. If a farmer wants to 'go organic', then it will usually take him two years to convert his land; he will also have to produce a detailed plan and show how he will carry it through. He's then inspected every year (and sometimes spot-checked) to make sure all is as it should be.

Organically produced foods or foods labelled as organic in the shops are also bound by strict rules, which aim to limit the amount of processing that is done and what is added to

WHO SETS THE STANDARDS FOR THE ORGANIC FOOD WE BUY?

In the early days of organic food there was much confusion about the precise meaning of the term, but this is now legally defined within the European Union (EU). Organic standards – the rules and regulations that define how an organic product must be made – are laid down in EU law and covered by the Organic Regulation, a 95-page paper, EEC document 2092/91. This original Regulation is due to be repealed on 1 January 2009, when a new version (EC document 834/2007) will immediately become law. Anything labelled 'organic' that is for human consumption must meet these standards as a minimum. The standards cover all aspects of food production, including animal welfare and wildlife conservation, and the banning of unnecessary and harmful food additives in organic processed foods.

Until 2003 standards were overseen by the UK Register of Organic Food Standards, which has now been superseded by the Advisory Committee on Organic Standards (ACOS). ACOS approves certifying bodies, advises the government, and does other work to ensure organic standards are maintained.

the foods during the production process.

It's worth taking a closer look at what is and what isn't allowed in certified organic farming and production. Unless otherwise mentioned, organic regulations referred to are detailed in EEC Organic Regulation 2092/91.

FERTILIZERS

Artificial fertilizers, such as manufactured nitrogen feeds, are not approved. The Soil Association says:

These kinds of fertilisers contain only the elements needed to make the crops grow – not all of those that are needed to ensure good health. They can also suppress the important soil microbes which deliver all the nutrients the plants need to be healthy ... Some studies estimate that only half the amount of artificial nitrogen fertilisers is actually used by the plants. The rest can 'leach' into rivers and streams, causing pollution. Nitrate levels are beginning to exceed levels set by European law – so it is important to use alternatives to chemical fertiliser, such as clover.

In place of artificial fertilizers, organic farming relies upon:

- Growing crops (such as peas and beans) that add nutrients to the soil and using crop rotation.

- Growing crops that are ploughed back into the soil (green manures which provide soil conditioning and humus as well as nutrients).

- Applying composts and farmyard manure – encouraging life in the soil. However, the amount of manure that can be used is restricted, so that high levels of nitrogen in the soil don't lead to leaching and damage to wildlife and rivers. See page 52.

- Applying certain mineral fertilizers and natural supplementary nutrients, the use of which is sometimes restricted. The Soil Association says that certified organic farms should have production systems that minimize the need for brought-in nutrients. Even some traditional fertilizers, such as blood and bone meal or hoof and horn, are allowed only in very restricted circumstances, where no cattle and sheep are present, to minimize the possibility of problems such as BSE and scrapie.

Most of these principles are how the majority of farmers in this country farmed their land as a matter of course as recently as fifty years ago – but they didn't use the term 'organic'. Crop rotation, for instance, is simply the commonsense idea (with which anyone who has an allotment or vegetable patch will be familiar) of alternating which crops you grow on which area of land year on year, a three-year rotation being traditional.

It is strange to have reached a situation where traditional farming methods are now labelled 'organic' and regarded as out of the ordinary, while mass industrialized farming is called 'conventional'. Agri-industry may now be the norm, but conventional, it really isn't.

For more on fertilizers, see page 57.

PESTICIDES AND HERBICIDES

The term 'pesticide' covers a wide range of chemicals used to control insect pests (insecticides), plant diseases (fungicides), weeds (herbicides) and other unwanted organisms in conventional farming.

Only a handful of chemicals are allowed in organic farming. Those permitted are based on natural substances; for example, copper is used as a pesticide (though its usage is highly restricted), as is sulphur, to control fungal diseases.

FACTBOX

Around 350 pesticides are permitted in conventional farming, and the Soil Association says an estimated 4.5 billion litres of them are used annually.

MORE INFORMATION ON PESTICIDES

If you want to know more about the health and environmental problems of specific pesticides, see if they are listed in PAN UK's (the Pesticide Action Network, see Resources) *List of Lists* of problem pesticides, or look them up on the pesticide database of PAN North America.

Organic farmers are allowed/encouraged to use a combination of the following measures to control pests, diseases and weeds:

- Growing appropriate species and varieties of crops and plants.

- Healthy soil, which helps prevent plant diseases, encourages growth and helps the plants to resist pest attacks.

- Appropriate crop rotation programme (see above), which helps avoid a build-up of one particular kind of pest.

- Timing cultivation to avoid certain pests.

- Mechanical cultivation procedures and hand, hoe and flame weeding.

- Protecting the natural enemies of pests by providing favourable conditions for them (e.g. hedges, nesting sites, release of predators).

For more on pesticides and herbicides, see page 49.

ANTIBIOTICS

The EC directive offers principles which should enhance the immune system of organic stock and strengthen their natural defences against disease, thus avoiding the need to use antibiotics. These principles and the similar advice given in the UK compendium of organic standards are, in précis:

- The selection of appropriate breeds or strains of animals, for example those which adapt to local conditions and which have natural resistance to disease or health problems.

- High-quality feed and regular exercise.

- Access to open-air areas and pastureland where appropriate.

- Avoidance of overstocking.

- Stock housing maintained in hygienic conditions.

If an animal does fall ill, first natural phytotherapeutic methods (using plants such as herbs and herb extracts), homeopathic products (e.g. plant, animal or mineral substances) and other approved trace elements should be used, but failing all else antibiotics can be used by a vet. After such treatment there is a 'withdrawal period' (the time between the last drug administration and the animal's meat, milk or eggs going on sale), which is at least twice as long as the statutory non-organic period and, in the case of the Soil Association standards, three times as long. This ensures drug-free meat and milk.

But, with exceptions for parasites, vaccination and compulsory EC eradication schemes, if an animal has more than two or three courses of antibiotics within a year, neither it nor its offspring or its milk can be sold as organic – i.e. it loses its organic status until it has undergone a standard 'conversion' period – normally six months in the case of sheep for meat production; nine months for cattle for milk production, ten weeks for poultry for meat production, and six weeks in the case of poultry for egg production.

For more on antibiotics, see page 51.

HORMONES

On this issue the EC directive says: 'The use of substances to promote growth or production, and the use of hormones or similar substances to control reproduction, or for other purposes, is prohibited. Nevertheless, hormones may be administered to an individual animal, as a form of therapeutic veterinary treatment.' For more information, see page 51.

GENETICALLY MODIFIED ORGANISMS (GMOS)

The genetic modification of human food and animal feed, led by the USA, is becoming more and more widespread throughout the world. GM technology involves the artificial insertion of a new gene, from a different variety or even species, into genetic material (e.g. a seed or animal DNA), producing almost immediate changes (in, say, taste, keeping qualities, disease resistance or cropping levels).

The GM lobby (consisting, in the main, of the multinational companies who own the patents for these technologies) say that this is little different from intervention through more traditional means – by selective plant or animal breeding. They also say that the benefits of genetic engineering for world food supplies are huge.

The anti-GM lobby say that long-term the effects – both environmental and otherwise – may be catastrophic. For example, via contamination of traditional crops in our fields, by the development of 'superweeds' near herbicide-resistant crops, and by the loss of traditional breeds of farm animals, the loss of natural evolution, by decreasing beneficial nutrients or increasing the chances of antibiotic resistance in humans and animals.

How much do we eat?

From the first imports of GM-containing tomato paste into the UK eleven years ago, already tests show that a surprisingly high percentage of the food that we eat contains GM material. One estimate is that over 60 per cent of our processed food contains GMOs – largely because of the soya that two-thirds of processed items contain. Half of the world's soya crops are now genetically modified and, usually, the non-GM crops are mixed together with the GM soya crops, thus making it nearly impossible for food importers and producers to avoid the GM element.

A recent test on American rice in the UK found that 10 per cent of grains contained GMOs; GM maize is also routinely used in processed food. Other foods that can contain GM are cheese (in rennet substitute). And in non-organic livestock production, 30 per cent of animal foodstuff can be GM food.

In truth, GM contamination may be present in much of the food that we eat.

GM and organics

The soon-to-be-implemented EU organic rules state that GMOs should not be used in organic farming or the processing of organic products:

It should not be possible to label a product as organic where it has to be labelled as containing GMOs, consisting of GMOs or produced from GMOs. GMOs and products produced from or by GMOs shall not be used as food, feed, processing aids, plant protection products, fertilisers, soil conditioners, seeds, vegetative propagating material, micro-organisms and animals in organic production.

This is broadly similar to the clauses in the still-current 1991 Regulation. However, it is becoming increasingly hard for organic farmers to ensure that their produce isn't contaminated. And once GM crops are allowed to be grown commercially in the UK (something that could be happening as this book is published in spring 2008 – as I write, the EU is fast-tracking approval of GM maize crops after being accused by the US government of blocking free trade) it will become even harder.

In the summer of 2006 the government published proposals for how GM and normal GM-free crops might 'coexist'. This would in effect allow routine contamination of any organic crops (mainly by airborne or bird-carried seed) which were unlucky enough to be near GM farms – especially as an original proposal for a 200-metre separation between GM and organic crops has been scrapped and replaced with one of only between 35 and 100 metres, depending on the crop – with no separation distance proposed at all for potatoes and sugar beet.

Organic farmers' organizations such as the Soil Association will be the first to do all they can to ensure contamination doesn't happen – but if GM crop growing becomes more and more widespread this task will eventually become near impossible.

In recognition of these problems, Defra has drafted a proposal to allow up to 0.9 per cent of 'accidental' GM contamination in British-produced organic foods. Although organic farmers will still be prohibited from knowingly using GMOs, protesters say that the higher threshold will, inevitably, lower standards in the campaign to keep organic produce truly GM-free. This 'genetic contamination', in the view of many, makes a mockery of the whole organic standard. Indeed, the recently formed UK Organic Trade Group and the Soil Association both oppose the proposal and believe there should be no GM in organic food.

There is also a provision for some GM content in organic seeds. The EU proposes to raise the threshold of allowable GM content to 0.3 per cent for rapeseed and maize, and 0.5 per cent for other crops. As the Organic Trade Group says, 'This will take away our ability to grow GM-free food. These genetically modified plants will continue to multiply unchecked and produce thousands of seeds. The effects of this remain unknown.'

If you disagree with GM crop growing or have other opinions on GM, you can help by joining GM Freeze (see Resources).

For more information, see page 51.

GMOs and organic food labelling

In June 2007, European agriculture ministers decided that organic foods can be labelled GM free even if they have up to 0.9 per cent genetically modified content (the same level of contamination that is acceptable in non-organic foods). The ministers supported EC commission arguments that setting a lower limit of 0.1 per cent – the lowest level at which GM

organisms could be scientifically detected – would make organic produce too expensive and 'would kill the sector'. See also page 141.

IRRADIATION

Irradiation of food is a process where fresh or dried food is 'zapped' with ionizing radiation to kill the micro-organisms that cause food to degrade and rot, and to kill food-poisoning bugs. It is a similar type of food preservation process to pasteurization, raising the food temperature a little. The process was made legal (under licence) in the UK in 1991 and the foods allowed to be irradiated in this country are currently herbs and spices, condiments, potatoes, yams, onions, garlic, vegetables and pulses, fruits, mushrooms, cereals, poultry, fish and shellfish. But due to strong public resistance against the process, all the supermarkets have since voluntarily banned almost all irradiated produce from their shelves, and only one UK licence, for the irradiation of a number of herbs and spices, has so far been granted. If irradiated food is sold, it should be labelled 'irradiated' or 'treated with ionizing radiation'.

There have been concerns that irradiation may decrease the nutrient content of foods or pose other problems, but the UK Food Standards Agency says that 'decades of research worldwide have shown that irradiation of food is a safe and effective way to kill bacteria in foods and extend its shelf life'.

Despite this apparent safety, in organic food production irradiation is not allowed – and this includes the treatment of organic feed and the treatment of any raw materials used in organic food. As there are several other permitted ways of preserving organic food when necessary (all the traditional methods) and ensuring its safety for consumption, this doesn't pose a problem for the industry.

ADDITIVES

The majority of additives that are allowed in non-organic foods – including artificial sweeteners and colours – are banned in organic products because of their health risks.

But to the surprise of many people, over thirty-five E-number additives *are* allowed and there is no organic regulation requirement for these to be organically produced.

Because organic processed foods can be labelled as such if they contain at least 95 per cent organic ingredients by weight, there is room for several non-organic additions and these include some spices and herbs, some fats, and fructose.

This may all sound like a cop-out until one discovers that non-organic food manufacturers can use over 400 food additives.

According to the new EC Organic Regulation, production of processed organic food should be based on the following principles:

- 'The restriction of the use of food additives, of non-organic ingredients with mainly technological and sensory functions, and of micronutrients and processing aids, so that they are used to a minimum extent and only in case of essential technological need or for particular nutritional purposes.'

- 'The exclusion of substances and processing methods that might be misleading regarding the true nature of the product.'

It continues, 'non-organic agricultural ingredients may be used only if they have been authorised for use in organic production ...'

The current permitted E numbers in organic food production are listed overleaf, but bear in mind that the 'approved' list is revised occasionally.

In addition to these E numbers, other organic additives/processing agents are allowed, with certain restrictions, including: ethanol, natural beeswax, carnauba wax, sulphuric acid, rice meal, tannic acid, egg white albumen, casein, gelatin, isinglass, kaolin, salt, pepper, nutmeg, activated carbon, bentonite (clay), diatomaceous earth, perlite, hazelnut shells, natural flavourings, yeast, lactic starter cultures, rennet, amylase, maltase, proteinase, sulphur dioxide (E220 for wine and cider only), tocopherol-extract (E306 as anti-oxidant in fats and oils), vegetable oils.

FACTBOX
Oxygen has an E number: E948. It is allowed under organic rules, and so are E941: nitrogen, and E938: argon.

E NUMBERS ALLOWED IN ORGANIC PROCESSED FOODS*

Approved by all EU member states at the time of writing:

E170	Calcium carbonates
E270	Lactic acid
E290	Carbon dioxide
E296	Malic acid
E300	Ascorbic acid
E322	Lecithins
E330	Citric acid
E333	Calcium citrates
E334	Tartaric acid (L(+) -)
E335	Sodium tartrate
E336	Potassium tartrate
E341(i)	Mono-calcium phosphate
E400	Alginic acid
E401	Sodium alginate
E402	Potassium alginate
E406	Agar
E407	Carrageenan
E410	Locust beam gum
E412	Guar gum
E413	Tragacanth gum
E414	Arabic gum
E415	Xanthan gum
E416	Karaga gum
E422	Glycerol plant extracts
E440(i)	Pectin
E500	Sodium carbonates
E501	Potassium carbonates
E503	Ammonium carbonates
E504	Magnesium carbonates
E516	Calcium sulphate
E524	Sodium hydroxide
E551	Silicon dioxide

A few of these are not permitted by the Soil Association whose standards are stricter than the basic EU regulations.

And these non-organic additives/processing agents, amongst others, are allowed: annatto (E160b, for traditionally coloured UK cheeses such as double Gloucester only), potassium nitrate and sodium nitrite (for curing meat), and some alcoholic drinks. And, of course, salt can be added.

Sometimes 'enrichment agents' are required by law to be added to food products and these include iron, thiamine (vitamin B) and nicotinic acid (vitamin B3) in white flour; retinol (vitamin A) and calciferol (vitamin D) in margarine; and various vitamins and minerals in different types of baby foods and formulas.

Phew! I think the message here is that organic or not, the less processing that a food goes through, the less likely it is to have been in some way altered or changed or added to by any of these substances. It's also wise to remember that just because a processed food is labelled 'organic', it doesn't mean it will necessarily be low in salt or sugar or fat.

A FEW WORDS ABOUT FISH FARMING...

In future years it may be that buying fish caught in the wild will be unusual, and that most fish will be farmed just as beef and pork are today. Already, a growing amount of the seafood that we buy is farmed in enclosed underwater pens in lochs and coastal areas of the UK (and elsewhere throughout the world).

There are various health, animal welfare and environmental concerns regarding fish farms. The fish are often fed on unsustainable feed

SOME ADDITIVES NOT ALLOWED IN ORGANIC PRODUCE

- artificial sweeteners of any kind, including aspartame
- monosodium glutamate
- all artificial colourings
- all artificial flavourings
- phosphoric acid
- trans fats

from the oceans, stocking densities are often very high, which can contribute to pen-water pollution and high levels of disease and parasites, and therefore use of antibiotics and chemical pesticides. Pens are permitted to be cleaned with toxic chemicals, and lack of exercise produces fish with much higher than normal levels of body fat and lower levels of healthy omega-3 fats and protein. Growth can be encouraged with growth promoters and artificial lighting. Lastly, escapees can, and do, breed with wild fish.

It's now possible to buy organic farmed fish (see page 108) – the Soil Association recently certified farmed organic salmon. The SA explains their decision on the grounds that if we are to continue eating fish (which the government says we should for our health), then responsible fish farming helps to limit the reliance on our increasingly depleted fish stocks.

The organic regulations for fish farming are broadly the same as those covering land-based organics. In organic farming, the problems outlined above are dealt with by offering the fish more natural living conditions with fewer stock per farm, in proper sea pens subject to tides which help to keep the waters clean and renewed, thus reducing the necessity for use of antibiotics. In cases of disease, only four drugs are allowed, under strict conditions, compared with 400 in intensive fish farming.

Feed may be the trimmings from fish factories or fish meal from other, generally sustainable, non-GM sources and organic plant foods. The use of artificial colouring in feed (which is used in non-organic farming to produce the deep pink colour in salmon) is not allowed; instead crushed prawn shells may be used. Soil Association regulations also do not allow farmers to use artificial lighting to manipulate the growth of fish – a common practice with non-organic farming.

However, just because fish feed is organic it may not necessarily be from sustainable sources. Good organic fish farms/suppliers will provide details of their fish feed, either on their websites or on their packs.

Organic farmed fish other than salmon is now available. For instance, farmed organic cod certified by the Organic Food Federation is also sold, but the SA doesn't endorse it, as artificial light is used in its production. Organic farmed sea bass and bream are also sold online by Graig Farms, certified by a French organic certifying association.

No fish or animal hunted or caught 'in the wild' can be described as organic, according to EU regulations. This is because organic standards can't be imposed on a wild creature throughout its life, nor organic testing imposed without a great deal of expense. Thus, says the EU, wild fish leading a natural life at sea are not organic – even though you could be forgiven for thinking that they may, indeed, be more organic than organic fish.

... AND ABOUT CHICKENS

The organic eggs that you buy, and the organic chickens, may both have come from non-organic chicks. Because of a national shortage of organically raised chicks, organic farmers are currently allowed, if they can't find any organic chicks to buy, to purchase chicks raised in a non-organic environment. The Soil Association states that, 'If the birds are to be sold for organic meat they must be brought in under three days of age and managed to organic standards for at least 10 weeks.'

Egg-laying birds may also not have been reared to full organic standards. If the farmer is not able to get hold of organic birds, other birds up to the age of eighteen weeks can be brought in and the eggs sold as organic as long as 'they [the hens] have been managed to our full organic standards for at least six weeks, and if they have already been reared to our organic standards with regard to feed and veterinary treatments,' the SA says.

The SA itself admits that this state of affairs is not good and that these government-approved concessions betray consumer trust in organic food. But until more organic farmers can be persuaded to hatch chicks organically (a specialist area), the problem will remain. This shortage is compounded, says Anna Bassett of the Soil Association, by the fact that most of the chickens in the UK are commercial hybrids, owned by the large companies. These companies are not duty bound to license their reproduction to small organic farmers. And, as Anna points out, to build up sufficient quantities of chicks from the other, traditional breeds will take a long time.

I think that eggs produced under the concessionary terms should be clearly labelled with a different symbol or flag so that consumers can make up their own minds about whether or not the eggs they are buying really are organic. In my book, that is doubtful.

Lastly, 10 per cent of the feed given to organic chickens is allowed to be non-organic, due to a shortage of organic feed.

How do I know if food really is organic?

To be labelled 'organic', 95 per cent of the ingredients by weight must be organically produced; that means without prohibited pesticides, fertilizers or additives.

There is a second recognized category with at least 70 per cent organic content but less than 95 per cent. Such products can be labelled: 'made with x per cent organic or organically produced ingredients'.

The new EC Organic Regulation 834/2007 states that: 'Processed food should be labelled as organic only where all or almost all the ingredients of agricultural origin are organic.' The same new regulation provides for a uniform EU organic logo to be used on all prepacked foods that are at least 95 per cent organic.

New tests are able to show whether or not much produce is organic – for example, meat can be tested for antibiotics and fruit and vegetables can be tested for prohibited artificial fertilizers.

In the UK, all organic products are certified by one of the eleven independent bodies that oversee organic production (the best known is the Soil Association, which certifies around 70–75 per cent of the organic foods in this country). They have strict standards that farmers must stick to, and they audit farms regularly to check. It is illegal to label products organic without this certification or without the certifying body's number (UK 2–15; see box overleaf). For example, the Soil Association is UK 5 and any foods certified by them should state on the label: 'Organic certification: UK 5'.

The certifying body's logo may also be used but isn't a requirement.

Imported organic foods must have been produced and inspected to equivalent standards. There must also be full traceability of organic ingredients back to the farmer. However, in recent years there have been several reported cases where food labelled as organic is found to be otherwise, and it leads one to ponder on how many cases have escaped the net.

Indeed, in the UK there is a growing number of cases of food being sold as organic when it

ORGANIC CERTIFYING BODIES

Code	Approved Body	Code	Approved Body
UK2	Organic Farmers & Growers	UK7	Irish Organic Farmers and Growers Association Ltd
UK3	Scottish Organic Producers Association	UK8	Food Certification (Scotland)Ltd
UK4	Organic Food Federation	UK9	Organic Trust Ltd.
UK5	Soil Association Certification Ltd	UK10	CMi Certification
UK6	BioDynamic Agricultural Association	UK13	Quality Welsh Food Certification Ltd

is nothing of the kind. For traders determined to cash in on the desire for organic produce, and with demand often outstripping supply, it isn't hard to do, particularly for fresh and unwrapped items such as fruit, vegetables, eggs, meat and poultry, in places such as local markets.

If you go to a market or small outlet and see fresh, unpackaged 'organic' food for sale, it is always worth asking for the UK certification body number (see box above) and a copy of the producer's organic-status certificate. If nothing can be shown, then there is no proof that what you see is indeed organic – however much mud may still be clinging to the vegetable leaves or straw to the eggs. If you have strong reason to think that a trader is trying to pass off non-organic food as organic, ask the local Trading Standards Officer to pay them a visit, and/or alert the Soil Association or another certifying body, in whose interests it is to make sure that inferior non-organic food doesn't dupe organic buyers.

Imported organic food

Now that organic food has become big business, and producers and sellers struggle ever harder to meet the demand from consumers, some of its green credentials have become diluted. This is most apparent in the subject of imports. Whilst many of us speak of organic food in the same breath as the words 'local, fresh and seasonal', much of the organic fruit and salad we buy – and a significant amount of other produce – is brought in from overseas, as supermarkets struggle to keep up with consumer demand.

While 66 per cent of the organic primary 'natural' produce sold in supermarkets is UK sourced – with dairy products most likely to come from this country and fruit and vegetables (especially in winter) least likely to do so – our organic food can be grown or produced anywhere. A large proportion of non-primary (processed, multi-ingredient) organic items are imported. While there are no figures for these, it is likely that the total figure for both primary and non-primary imported goods is around 50 per cent or higher.

The organic standard of imports should, according to the EC directive, be similar to that required within the EU. While there is no research to prove or disprove whether or not an imported organic food has an equivalent nutritional and environmental profile to a similar, UK-produced organic food, there has in recent years been a backlash from environmentalists against the mass importing of organic food. They rightly claim that the carbon footprint of such food – because of the miles it has travelled or the energy-hungry way it was produced – may negate the benefits of its organic status. Says US environmental activist Paul Hawken, 'if we are flying in raspberries in January and food from Chile, even if it is organic – it is stupid.'

The Soil Association is so concerned about the contribution to global warming made by air-freighted organics that in October 2007 it announced proposed changes to its standards to ensure that organic food is imported to the UK only if it delivers genuine benefits for farmers in developing countries, to take effect from January 2009.

The backlash has also come about because checks on the validity of imported organic foodstuffs have sometimes not been rigorous enough to prevent fraud. Importers are currently required by the EC Organic Regulation to 'inform the inspection body or authority of each consignment to be imported into the Community, giving any details this body or authority may require, such as a copy of the inspection certificate for the importation of products from organic farming.

On the request of the inspection body or authority of the importer, the latter must pass the information to the inspection body or authority of the first consignee', but perhaps the system is open to abuse until the words 'may require' and 'on the request of' are deleted, and the necessity to pass on details such as inspection certificates becomes the norm.

When the new Regulation comes into effect in 2009, the inspection system for imported organic goods will become tighter and should ensure that fewer 'rogues' escape the net.

IS ORGANIC FOOD FAIRLY TRADED?

Currently all Soil Association certified licensees (in the UK or abroad) must comply with the UN Convention for Human Rights and the core standards of the International Labour Organisation. The Soil Association also has its own ethical-trade scheme which ensures that the workers are treated fairly, the farmer receives a fair return and a positive contribution is made to the local community.

However, there is nothing in the EU organic standards regulations which says that organic food must be fairly traded, which would seem to give much scope for not applying fairtrade considerations.

Why is organic food more expensive?

1 To convert to organic farming is a costly and time-consuming process. Despite the rise in popularity of organic food, there is still a lack of UK farm conversions in the offing (as we have seen, this is usually a two-year process), meaning that demand is greater than supply – which always means prices are higher.

2 Organic food costs more to produce. Organic crop farming is less intensive, so yields are lower. Organic animal feeds are more expensive, and animals reared organically for meat tend to have longer lifespans, which also increases costs.

FACTBOX
Organic pigs cost 80 per cent more to rear than conventionally farmed pigs.

3 To top up the shortfall in UK-produced organic food, we import a lot – around 34 per cent of 'primary' (unadulterated) produce is imported. This may sometimes add to the cost of the food you buy.

It's worth noting, though, that the difference in price isn't the same across all products: some (such as organic chickens and meat) are often quite a bit more expensive, but others cost very little more than, or even the same as, conventional products.

FACTBOX
While many people go to their local farmers' market to buy healthy produce, there is only a small chance that it will in fact be organic. The National Farmers' Retailer and Markets Association (FARMA) estimate that only 10–15 per cent of stallholders at farmers' markets sell organic produce.

Are wholefoods and natural foods the same as organic?

No. While there is no legal definition of the word 'wholefood', it tends to be used to cover foods which are unrefined, unprocessed or minimally processed, so that they contain all the nutrients of the original food but no additives.

While many organic items in the shops may also be classed as wholefoods, they may not be – and while many wholefood items may also be organic, they may not be.

Natural means existing in, or produced by, nature. Foods in their 'nature' state – for example, a piece of fruit picked off the tree, a carrot dug up from the ground, berries picked from the bush or a fish caught from your local stream – might all be described as natural. But these may or may not be organic, and it would be an interesting debate to decide whether a fruit or vegetable or grain grown from hybrid seed, or an animal bred for food by man is, indeed, natural or not …

Does organic food actually taste better?

The best organic producers are committed to quality in all aspects of their food, including taste, and common sense might lead me to suggest that a vegetable, fruit, egg or animal which has been produced with care, time, traditional methods and so on might quite naturally taste better than a comparable mass-produced item which has been brought along as quickly and inexpensively as possible.

I can also say, as a small-time grower of my own organic fruit, salad and vegetables, that these often do taste better than their bought supermarket counterparts. And I find my neighbour's organic eggs probably 100 per cent better tasting than supermarket free-range eggs.

But because taste is an individual and unquantifiable thing it is nearly impossible to do any form of scientific trial comparing the taste of organic and non-organic products and so the only research that has been done gives consumer opinion.

In a recent Soil Association poll of consumers, taste was indeed a significant factor in people's decision to go organic. Fruit and vegetables scored particularly highly, with 72 per cent saying they taste better than non-organic. And 71 per cent said they preferred the taste of organic meat.

However, a 2006 blind taste test found that organic chickens scored poorly for succulence compared with battery-farmed meat (possibly because organic produce tends to have a lower water content than factory-farmed meat and organic chicken flesh tends to be firmer because the chickens are kept for longer and the protein content is higher).

It is certainly the case that carefully produced, conventionally grown food, or local, farmers' market non-organic food may well often taste as good as, or better than, mass-produced organic imports or produce from the organic farmers in the UK who perhaps take any short cuts that they can get away with. With processed organic products – such as biscuits, jars and cans – it may be harder to detect any difference in taste.

Is organic food better for us?

The Food Standards Agency's view is that organic food is no safer or more nutritious than conventionally produced food. The Secretary of State for the Environment (at the time David Miliband) also found in early 2007 that there is 'no conclusive evidence' that it is healthier. But these statements seem to me to be at best highly dubious and, at worst, clearly not the case.

RESIDUES

There are no records of our average daily intake of pesticides in food because it is too difficult or expensive to estimate. But should we be worried? The answer seems to be 'yes'.

Worldwide, at least 3 million people are poisoned and 220,000 killed each year from pesticide incidents, according to the World Health Organization. Farmworkers in developing nations are particularly at risk. In Europe in 2007, a study of 1,000 sufferers of Parkinson's disease found that people exposed to pesticides had up to a 41 per cent higher risk of developing the disease. Several studies conclude that daily consumption of tiny quantities of pesticides may result in damage to the developing brain and nervous system of small children. Indeed, the EC acknowledged back in 2003 that some residue levels found occasionally in certain fruits and vegetables – such as lettuce, apples and spinach – could pose a real health risk to them. And a 2007 Swedish report found that exposure to pesticide sprays doubles the risk of adults developing asthma.

The official line is that there is no risk to consumers from daily intake of pesticides when these are within the levels set by the British government. If you look at their residue-monitoring reports, they emphasize that two-thirds of our food does not contain residues. But every year, when fruits and vegetables are tested, a significant percentage have levels over the allowed limits. (And incidentally, safety levels are much higher in the USA.)

The last official UK residue report available as I write found that over 2 per cent of foods tested were above the maximum permitted levels of pesticides, and that 75 per cent of apples, 72 per cent of bananas and 28 per cent of potatoes (as examples) contained residues.

Much more scientific research and monitoring needs to be done, especially in the light of current nutritional thinking. The government mantra is that we should all eat more fruit and vegetables ('at least five a day'), which has given rise to the completely sensible thought train that, while residues in a certain product (e.g. a lettuce) may be at acceptable levels, if you multiply that severalfold in getting all your 'healthy' fruit and veg, suddenly you are ingesting a whole lot more. No one knows what this cumulative effect may be.

There is also, of course, the accepted nutritional advice that a healthy diet includes plenty of wholegrains. Unfortunately, research carried out by PAN UK (the Pesticide Action Network) and published in 2007, shows that flour and bread are two of the foods likely to contain the highest levels of residues – in the latest check 84 per cent of UK wheat samples tested contained residues.

Until we know more about the effects of pesticides on our long-term health, if you aim to follow a healthy diet it might indeed be prudent to swap at least PAN's worst 'top ten' of fruit and vegetables and other foods (based on an analysis over five years) for organic alternatives.

UNWANTED ADDITIVES

Over the years a number of so-called 'safe' additives have later been found to be harmful to humans and banned (e.g. the recent Red 2G or E128, just banned in the EU because it can

WORST FOODS FOR RESIDUES *% of samples contaminated with residues*

10 worst vegetables and salad		10 worst fruits		10 worst other foods	
celery	67	citrus fruits*	83–100	oily fish	67–98
pre-packed salad	40	pear	70	cereal grains	79–91
potato	38	strawberry	69	flour	73
peas (edible podded)	38	apricot	61	cereal bars	68
beans (green and speciality)	38	cherry	60	dried fruit	58
plantain	36	raspberry	57	bread	33–56
lettuce	36	banana	57	herbs	53
sweet potato	35	apple	56	chips	48
tomato	30	melon	56	crisps	45
cucumber	30	grapes	54	rice	45

* Courtesy Pesticide Action Network, UK, July 2007

cause cancer), while certain E numbers – E102, 104, 124, 110, 122, 129 and 211 (artificial colourings and preservatives) – are definitely linked to behavioural and other problems in children, including asthma and rashes. A new study from Southampton University funded by the Food Standards Agency confirms this and no doubt in time these E numbers, too, will be banned.

Why wait for years until so-called 'safe' items are discovered to be harmful and removed from our food? As we've seen, organic food should contain minimal additives, and those that are in the food should, with few exceptions, be natural.

ANTIBIOTIC AND HORMONE RESIDUES

There is widespread concern about the use of antibiotics in intensive poultry units. The British Medical Association is concerned that the 'risk to human health from antibiotic resistance is one of the major health threats that could be faced in the twenty-first century'. The use of antibiotics in organic farming is strictly controlled.

And pregnant women who regularly ate beef from American cattle treated with growth hormones had sons with average 24 per cent lower sperm count, research has found. Although in the EU these hormones have been banned since 1988, it supports the theory that increasing levels of hormones and similar chemicals in the environment – from items such as fertilizers and pesticides – are

linked to falling fertility levels. Organic farming doesn't allow growth-promoting hormones to be used.

GM

There may be health risks in eating GM potatoes – and potentially all other GM foods. A Russian study by Monsanto revealed in 2007 that feeding rats GM potatoes actually damaged their internal organs. Ken Hayes, the Soil Association's standards researcher, said, 'I think [the public] are very much right to be concerned because there just isn't the research done into the potential risks of GM on our food.' And, says Friends of the Earth, most testing is carried out by the very biotech companies that have the most to gain from results that say GM food is safe.

FOOD SAFETY/FOOD POISONING

Because organic food doesn't contain artificial preservatives, it can have a shorter shelf-life than non-organic foods. Items such as bread and meat may therefore need eating up more quickly.

There has in recent years been much debate about the amount of food-poisoning bugs present in organic chickens. Some research has found high levels of harmful campylobactor in organic birds. The Veterinary Laboratories Agency carried out recent research on bacteria levels at organic and non-organic farms and found that even on farms which hadn't used

In the USA, research published in 2005 in the *Journal of Food Protection* found that 31 per cent of free-range chickens and 60 per cent of organic chickens tested positive for salmonella, and concluded that, 'Consumers should not assume that free-range or organic conditions will have anything to do with the *Salmonella* status of the chicken'. Earlier research from the United States Department of Agriculture (USDA) food-safety service reported that conventionally produced chickens had a salmonella rate of 9.1–12.8 per cent.

As you will see in the section 'Animal welfare' on page 60, some poultry farms producing chickens labelled as organic may have less than ideal conditions, with crowding and large flocks, and may be little better than conventional chicken houses. Such conditions tend to predispose to disease.

Conversely, according to Belgian research also published in the *Journal of Food Protection*, organic poultry farms with good management – for example lower stocking rates and smaller flocks – provide a reduced risk of cross-infection. The researchers also found that poultry products derived from broiler chickens running free in woods until slaughtering age (12–13 weeks) had a significantly lower *Salmonella* contamination rate than poultry products from enclosed broilers slaughtered at the age of 6–8 weeks.

What does the Soil Association, the UK's largest representative of organic farming, say? 'We believe the heavy drug use and crowded conditions of [factory farming] ... increase the susceptibility of the poultry to new diseases,

antimicrobials (antibiotics) for years, 'Some resistant *E.coli* [bacteria normally associated with beef rather than chickens] not only persisted but also proliferated in the absence of antimicrobial use'.

'Organic foods grown in soil fertilized with manure are at greater risk of being contaminated by mycotoxins, or fungi. Fungal toxins are a particular problem in organic foods because all effective fungicides are synthetic in origin and prohibited for use by the Soil Association. Copper sulphate and sulphur, which are used, are far less effective.'

Dr Brian Iddon, House of Commons Hansard Debate, 16 October 2007

which may increase the risks to human health.'

What does this all mean? Basically, organic or otherwise, 'risk' foods such as eggs, meat, lettuce and soft cheeses should all be treated with respect, stored in suitable conditions, eaten in peak condition and cooked properly – in the case of meat and poultry, thoroughly, to reduce the risk of food poisoning.

NUTRITIONAL CONTENT

Although the UK Advertising Standards Authority has, in accordance with the line taken by the FSA and the British government, banned organic producers from making health claims about their food, the evidence that they are wrong is mounting.

An EU four-year project which ended recently has, indeed, found that organic food *is* more nutritious and health-promoting than conventional food. The results of this project may even persuade the FSA, which is reviewing the new evidence, to change its tack.

Here is some of the evidence to date:

- Naturally grown tomatoes are 79 per cent higher in quercetin and 97 per cent higher in kaempferol (flavonol anti-oxidants that help to prevent heart disease) than non-organic tomatoes, a ten-year US study has shown. The University of California team who did this research say that the difference may be accounted for by the absence of fertilizers in organic farming.

- Research in Europe has found that organic tomatoes, peaches and apples contain more vitamin C and anti-oxidants than conventionally grown ones.

- Organic cow's milk has been shown to contain up to 68 per cent more of the healthy omega-3 fatty acids than normal milk. New research shows that organic milk, cheese and yogurt can all protect young children against allergies, eczema and asthma. This is believed to be due to the fatty acid ratios, while higher levels of vitamins A and E may also be a factor.

- An American study found that organically grown food contained much higher average levels of minerals than non-organic food. For example, 63 per cent more calcium, 73 per cent more iron, 125 per cent more potassium and 60 per cent more zinc.

- The meat from organic rare-breed lambs from Wiltshire has been found to contain higher omega-3 levels, less fat and cholesterol and more protein than common breeds used in conventional farming.

- The meat from traditionally farmed beef cattle contains more omega-3s than intensively reared beef.

- Organic kiwi fruit has been shown to have higher levels of vitamin C, polyphenol anti-oxidants and 'all the major minerals' than non-organic kiwi fruits grown in the same environment.

THE DECREASING NUTRIENT LEVELS IN OUR FOOD

In 2006, the independent campaigning charity the Food Commission published its analysis of the mineral content of food in the UK today compared with sixty years ago (using official government figures). It found, for example, that levels of iron in many basic foods are severely depleted. Rump steak contains 55 per cent less iron, milk 60 per cent less, and Cheddar cheese 47 per cent less. Levels of calcium and magnesium have also dropped.

Defra's own figures show that trace-element levels have dropped by up to 76 per cent in our fruits and vegetables.

I believe – as do many environmentalists – that modern farming methods, which pay scant attention to proper soil fertility and structure, have brought about this blanket reduction in the nutrients in our food. I believe that the organic farming movement reproduces most of the traditional farming methods of sixty years ago, and this is why organically produced food is superior.

- Organic potatoes and green vegetables are higher in vitamin C.

- In a 2001 review of forty-one studies, organic crops were all shown to have higher levels of vitamin C, magnesium and phosphorus.

- Recent studies show higher levels of omega-3 DHA fatty acids, vitamin E and beta-carotene in chickens raised on pasture, and the meat contains more protein and less fat percentage than factory-farmed chickens.

- Organic eggs from birds who spend most of their time foraging for food outdoors may be as high in omega-3 fats as special non-organic 'high omega-3' eggs in the supermarkets.

So why might organic food be more nutritious? Several reasons may come into play.

- The Soil Association says: 'Using chemicals to fertilise the soil [as in conventional farming] often only provides crops with the three basic elements that they need to grow, rather than providing them with all the nutrients they need to actually be healthy. These three elements are nitrogen, phosphorus and potassium (NPK fertilisers). While these are essential to enable the crops to grow, plants actually need a minimum of 13 different nutrients and minerals.'

- Because organic meat and produce usually takes longer to mature, it has a lower water content and this can increase its nutrient to weight ratio.

- Organic meat is from animals which are allowed regular access to land rich in organically fertilized grasses and herbs. This may naturally produce meat higher in healthy fats and lower in saturates than conventionally produced meat.

- One theory is that certain plant chemicals (e.g. the flavonoid compounds in the tomato study above) are produced in the plant as a defence mechanism. Non-organic produce tends to be grown with high levels of added nitrogen-rich fertilizers to help them thrive, and so they don't have the need to produce so many flavonoids, whereas organic produce may rely on what nutrients it finds in the soil.

And how do these extra nutrients in organic food affect our health? Well the plant chemicals such as flavonoids, polyphenols, carotenes, indoles and so on are linked in many scientific papers with protection against cardiovascular disease and many forms of cancer. The higher levels of omega-3s in some organic produce, which boost health in many ways – for example, they can help prevent heart disease and stroke, may boost brainpower and help beat depression – and are usually provided in the diet by oily fish, may mean we could eat a little less fish, and this in turn could help to protect endangered species.

The fact is that when we're talking about fruit, vegetables, salads, plant produce, eggs, milk, meat, fish – organic food not only often contains fewer of the items that may harm us, but also may have definite nutritional, and therefore health, benefits. Whatever the FSA may try to tell you.

HOWEVER …

Just because something is organic, it doesn't mean it meets all the healthy-eating criteria. An organic muffin, for example, can be high in fat, sugar and calories and low in some of the 'good for you' things. A diet rich in organic butter, cream, chocolate and sugar may not make you particularly healthy. And some organic foods are too highly refined to be classed as particularly 'good for you'.

No doubt some sellers think of trendy labels such as 'organic', 'eco-friendly' and so on as temptations to buy, and excuses to charge more. Green credentials are to food today what health claims were ten years ago.

Things may get a little better in 2009 when the EU's current Organic Regulation comes into force. Among its generally tighter requirements, it will say that 'Organic processed products should be produced by the use of processing methods which guarantee that the organic integrity and vital qualities of the product are maintained.' It further says that organic food should mean 'the processing of food with care, preferably with the use of biological, mechanical and physical methods'.

Obviously, these are words of advice and hope rather than a strict set of rules and thus there will no doubt be much room for bending of the intention. But, hopefully, they may help 'junk food organics' disappear from the supermarket shelves. We will have to wait and see.

Is organic food better for the environment?

Can organic eating help prevent global warming? Is it better for the planet in any other ways? Let's look again at some of the main rules of organic farming and how they work with the environment, in comparison with non-organic farming methods.

The current EC Regulation on organic farming requires that farmers pay close attention to their environmental footprint and the new 2009 regulation is even more direct. Mixed farming is encouraged and, indeed, most organic farms in the UK are mixed – i.e. they have both livestock and crops, which is, environmentalists agree, more sustainable than monoculture (large farms which concentrate on one end product only).

Soil fertility is maintained by the use of renewable natural resources such as livestock manure and green 'manure' crops.

The number of animals on organic farms is limited, which should minimize pollution of the soil and water, overgrazing and erosion, and improve animal welfare.

Preference is given to indigenous breeds and strains — livestock and crops which are local to the area tend to thrive and be more hardy than imported breeds and strains, thus perhaps making a lower carbon footprint (for example, they may need less energy to help them grow than imported varieties).

And the cropping and stockfarming system should contribute to the development of sustainable agriculture.

To sum up, the new Regulation will state: 'All (organic) production techniques used shall prevent or minimise any contribution to the contamination of the environment. Organic production shall use tillage and cultivation practices that maintain or increase soil organic matter, enhance soil stability and soil biodiversity, and prevent soil compaction and soil erosion.'

Compare that with the regulations for 'conventional' farming. There is *no* requisite to improve the soil's organic matter, *no* requisite to enhance soil stability and biodiversity, *no* requisite to utilize renewable natural sources, *no* requisite to contribute to the development of more sustainable agriculture, *no* more than basic provision for animal welfare, *no* preference for indigenous breeds and strains … I could go on.

FERTILIZING THE LAND

It takes a lot of energy to manufacture and transport artificial fertilizers (as well as artificial herbicides and pesticides); many of them are produced overseas and thus also require high levels of oil or gas to transport them, creating a large carbon footprint.

Because it is easily washed away from the surface of the soil, artificial fertilizer may easily run off and pollute rivers and streams, causing environmental damage. We saw earlier that some studies estimate that only half the amount of artificial nitrogen fertilizers added by non-organic farmers is actually used by the plants. No wonder that nitrate levels in UK rivers are beginning to exceed those set by European law.

As we have seen, organic farming not only bans artificial fertilizers but also severely limits the amount of manure that can be used, as it, too, may pollute water with high nitrogen levels. The EC directive limits the amount of manure that can be spread on the land of organic farms to 170 kg of nitrogen per year per hectare of land. But, according to Gundula Azeez, Policy Manager for the Soil Association, 'Organically managed soil is estimated to absorb twice as much water because of its better structure and higher organic content. This reduces water run-off.'

FACTBOX
It costs us about £120 million a year, which we pay through taxation and higher water bills, to try to tackle water-supply pollution, largely caused by artificial fertilizers.

PROTECTING WILDLIFE

It is well documented that modern industrial farming and monocultures are destroying (or have destroyed) the habitats of our wildlife, and are harmful to biodiversity. According to the Soil Association, organic farms have 44 per cent more birds in their fields, and over five times as many wild plants. This is because organic farmers work with nature to provide habitats for natural pest controllers such as spiders, beetles and birds.

These working methods include:

- The avoidance of pesticides and herbicides. Industrial pesticides don't differentiate between 'good' and 'bad' pests and thus they kill natural predators (e.g. the ladybirds that would normally eat greenfly).

- Mixed farming, with a variety of crops grown on one farm, and crop rotation also encourage diversity of wildlife and plants.

- Some weeds are 'allowed' to remain in cultivated areas, providing valuable ground cover to protect the soil, a microclimate and homes for insects that will feed on pests that might otherwise damage the crops.

- Under-sowing – the sowing of grass or clover under a cereal crop so that it exists at low levels while the crop is there. This increases the level of wildlife in the cropped area and ensures food and habitats for wildlife all year round.

ENERGY AND LAND USE

The new 2009 organic Regulation will encourage organic farmers to rely on renewable and local resources, such as manpower and windpower, to minimize the use of non-renewable resources (such as petroleum) and to recycle farm waste and by-products to return nutrients to the land.

But in terms of volume of produce per hectare, organic farming often cannot compete with industrial farming. The conclusion of Defra's December 2006 report *Environmental Impacts of Food Production and Consumption* says:

> The land use requirements of organic agricultural technique, were they to be widely applied, can be seen as a major environmental issue. What we might ... say is that, for organic agriculture to offer an approach to food production that is better than conventional agriculture, yields need to rise and methods need to be developed (or if they exist, adopted) that reduce releases of nitrogen compounds, particularly to the water environment.

However, the Soil Association strongly dispute many of Defra's findings on organic farming, which they say are based on non-existent models. Gundula Azeez, SA Policy Manager, says the Defra report was based on a method of organic farming which is used by no more than handful of farmers in the UK – its model was a farm without livestock and with a third of its land out of production at any one time. She continues:

In reality, almost all organic farms are based on integrated crop and livestock production and rotation, avoiding the need for land out of production. Also, the study didn't include data for soil carbon (organic matter) levels, an important aspect of organic farming which reduces greenhouse gas emissions.

While there is no UK data for the overall global warming impact of organic farming, there is now data on energy use from Defra-funded studies in 2000 and 2006. These show organic farming is overall more energy efficient than non-organic farming. This is mainly because it doesn't use nitrogen fertilisers, which are produced from petro-chemicals in an energy-intensive process. Typically organic farming is about 30% more energy efficient for producing the same quantity of food.

Only in four areas of production does organic farming use more energy than non-organic [see table below].

Energy use for heated glasshouse tomatoes is higher because yield is less than with non-organic tomatoes. The Soil Association advises people to buy seasonal vegetables, and encourages all farmers using heated glasshouses to use 'green' sources of electricity.

Organic production is also less energy efficient for poultry production and eggs than non-organic farming, because of the slower growth rates of organic systems which are less intensive and genuinely free-range.

ORGANIC ENERGY USE/TONNE IN COMPARISON WITH NON-ORGANIC ENERGY USE *Soil Association*

Vegetables	%	Livestock	%
leeks	58% less	beef	35% less
wheat	29% less	lamb	20% less
carrots	25% less	pig meat	13% less
oilseed rape	25% less	eggs	14% more
onions	16% less	chicken	32% more
potatoes	2% more		
tomatoes (long season)	30% more		
milk	38% less		

Organic farming and animal welfare

The EU lays down strict rules about animal welfare for organic producers, covering the animals' diet, housing, transport, reproduction, hygiene and medical care. For example:

- Tail-docking in sheep and trimming of birds' beaks must not be carried out unless, with authorization, for safety reasons.
- After 2010 keeping livestock tethered will be forbidden except in rare cases.
- Livestock loading, transporting and slaughter must limit stress to the animals.
- Housing conditions should include easy access to feeding and water, suitable heating, ventilation and natural light, and adequate freedom of movement and comfort.
- Calves must not be kept in individual boxes after the age of one week.
- Laying hens should have at least eight hours of 'nocturnal rest without light'.
- Poultry must have access to an open-air run which must be mainly covered with vegetation.

FACTBOX
75 per cent of the UK's (non-organic) pigs live all their lives indoors.

POULTRY

The table below compares housing conditions for organic birds with other types. Here are some additional notes:

Barn hens: About 7 per cent of the eggs sold in the UK are 'barn eggs'. These are from hens kept in huge sheds called percheries which can house tens of thousands of birds. Percheries must provide perches, litter and nests. New percheries built since 2002 must provide 1100 cm^2 of floor space per hen (which equates to nine birds per square metre) while older percheries are allowed to provide as little as 830 cm^2 per hen (twelve birds per square metre). The 'deep litter system' allows only seven hens per square metre. Barn housing doesn't apply to table chickens.

Caged hens: For caged table chickens, the Defra recommendation is seventeen birds per square metre, while the chicken industry's own limit is nineteen. In 1999, the Council of the European Union decided that battery cages are to be banned across the EU but not until 2012. However, the EU will still permit the use of 'enriched' cages after this date, which must provide 750 cm^2 per hen as well as limited perching, nesting and scratching facilities.

The Lion Quality: has additional standards for barn and free-range hens producing its Lion Symbol eggs.

POULTRY HOUSING – organic versus free range and 'factory' farmed

	Indoors, laying hens Birds per sq m	Indoors, table chickens Birds per sq m	Perch area cm per bird	Outdoor area sq m per bird
Organic*	6	10	18	4
Free range	9–12**	13	15	1
Barn	7–12	n/a	15	none
Caged	18	17–19	none	none

* Soil Association standard.
** Maximum density reduces from 12 to 9 after December 2011.

WHY ORGANIC CHICKEN WELFARE STANDARDS MAY NOT BE ALL THEY SEEM

- Chickens reared to the current EU Organic Regulation often live in huge flocks – with up to 9,000 birds in a single shed – and are then sold as organic. In large flocks, chickens are more likely to block the doors and this means that many birds may never go outside. A large number of chickens which are bought by the consumer as organic will have come from such flocks.

- In order to maintain the best possible animal welfare, the Soil Association normally permits flock sizes of no more than 500 birds, with 2,000 as a maximum. Many experts believe that smaller flocks help to reduce the risk of serious suffering for chickens.

  Compassion in World Farming agrees with the SA that smaller flock sizes increase the potential for higher welfare.

- Some organic egg-laying chickens have space in their houses equivalent to only one sheet of A4 paper, compared to Soil Association organic egg-laying chickens who have around three times the space.

- Other UK organic certifying bodies vary in the parameters they set. Bodies with similar standards to the SA include the Biodynamic Agricultural Association (Demeter), Irish Organic Farmers' & Growers' Association, Organic Trust, Quality Welsh Food Certification and the Scottish Organic Producers' Association (SOPA) .

Other non-industrial farming methods

Biodynamic agriculture is an ecological and sustainable system of agriculture, producing food that respects all creation. It is based on the ideas of the Austrian philosopher Rudolf Steiner, whose teachings became known at the start of the twentieth century.

Biodynamics includes many of the principles of organic farming, such as crop rotation and composting – indeed, the Soil Association says that it 'is a type of organic farming' – but also uses special plant, animal and mineral preparations and the rhythmic influences of the planets and stars – for example, planting to coincide with phases of the moon. It has sometimes been described as 'super-organic' or as 'holistic farming'. Biodynamic farmers should be totally self-sufficient, buying in no fertilizers or feedstuffs. Neither are they allowed to use antibiotics if animals become ill, whereas this is permitted in organic farming.

Sustainable agriculture is similar to, but not the same as, organic farming. Whereas organic is a specific set of legal standards, sustainability is more of a philosophy or a way of life. One definition of sustainable agriculture is that it is a farming method which can produce food indefinitely without causing irreversible damage to the ecosystem.

Both organic and sustainable agriculture aim to preserve the land for generations to come and have many similarities, but the main difference between them is that organic food production must be certified yearly by an independent authorized body, whereas sustainable food has no independent certification process – i.e. there cannot be a label on any food saying 'sustainable'. A sustainable food system takes into account economic, social, cultural and technological considerations, and systems of food distribution and consumption. It also uses practices that are resource-conserving, socially just, humane, economically competitive and environmentally sound.

Proponents of sustainable food often prefer that you shop locally and source your food carefully rather than worrying overmuch about whether it is certified organic. For example, in the USA, even though organic food production is certified by the USDA, large corporations have found ways to raise dairy cows in confinement, use massively large acreages to plant crops, and ship food thousands of miles to sell. These practices are not considered sustainable.

Of course, because neither biodynamic nor sustainable farming has any recognized pathways enabling you to buy food produced by these systems, if you are interested in doing so you will need to do some detective work. And as with organic farming, food produced following biodynamic or sustainable farming ideals will almost certainly be more costly.

Currently these farming philosophies are much more prevalent in the USA than in the UK.

Conclusion

It seems clear to me that, for the most part, organic food production is compatible with the ethical ideals of sustainable food production – but the movement is not without practical problems and ongoing issues, which may need to be addressed and rationalized.

If we all decided tomorrow to go organic and purchase only organic food, then the whole thing would implode. We would go hungry. Millions of industrial farmers and other companies and workers would be unemployed.

Organic methods, while comparing well on an energy-use basis, produce less food per hectare than non-organic methods and so a completely organic world food production system is unlikely in the foreseeable future to provide enough food for the world's increasing population unless major changes in what we eat, and how much we eat, and waste, take place.

World governments need to legislate for greener and healthier ways of producing food which will provide enough for us all to eat. Scientists need to do much more research on how to increase production within the boundaries of all the environmental considerations, and food producers need to find compromises that will enable them to meet these criteria.

Meanwhile we, the consumers, need to recognize that one big – very big – thing we can each do for our planet and to help our food feed us all – is to eat a little less. Fatness, as well as food, is an ethical issue.

And we need to be more mindful of what we purchase. The next chapter looks at all the many branches and issues of ethical eating and helps you decide your priorities.

3 Ethical Eating

'THE ERA OF THE MERE CONSUMER IS OVER,
HE IS THE PRIMARY ACCOMPLICE IN THE
DESTRUCTION BEING DONE TO THE EARTH.'
Carlo Petrini, founder of the Slow Food Movement, June 2007

While human food needs account for only around a quarter of total global-warming potential, what and how we eat is nevertheless a significant contributing factor to our worldly problems. Chapter 1 explained how our food habits have changed over the past fifty years or so and why it's important that we call a halt to some of the habits that are having a negative effect on our lives and our planet. Chapter 2 looked at how organics and other sustainable methods of producing our food may help. In Chapter 3 I aim to sort out some of the confusion that surrounds the green food choices that you may have to make.

Adopting 'food awareness'

WHY DO WE EAT? YOU MAY AT FIRST THINK THAT THE ANSWER IS SIMPLE: WE EAT BECAUSE WE NEED FOOD TO LIVE. BUT IT ISN'T THAT STRAIGHTFORWARD.

A study by Tara Garnett at the Centre for Environmental Strategy recently looked into our reasons for consuming:

People's basic motivations [for consumption] may be distilled into the following:

- Consumption to meet our needs – a means of surviving, reproducing and staying safe.
- Consumption to communicate with others the social, psychological and cultural dimensions of our lives.
- Consumption as routine: consuming is just something that we do because we always have and everyone else does too.

These three basic drivers are particularly true of food. Food sustains us; what and how we eat says a lot about us; but much of the time we eat without much thinking about it.

Ethical eating involves all of these motivations. If you eat ethically you sustain yourself and help keep yourself, your descendants and the planet safe. By eating ethically you are telling others a lot about yourself and your beliefs.

'But much of the time we eat without thinking about it.' To make changes we need first to be aware of what we do, and then to be aware of what needs to change, and why. Any new habits we adopt may not bear much relation to what everyone else does, or indeed to what we have always done before.

Chapters 4–7 will help you adapt to new food choices until they do become routine. But the hardest part is altering your mindset. You want to be sure you know what you're going to do, and why. Choosing food takes enough time anyway in our busy lives – and for many people I've talked to, having a whole extra level of concerns to decipher may sometimes be one burden too many. Some of the green food issues are seemingly in direct conflict. Some seem too hard, or too precise, or too vague to take on board. In ethical eating a little knowledge can indeed be dangerous, but too much knowledge can be confusing. Doing nothing, however, isn't an option.

Let's get on. Here is a list of the issues we're going to cover in this chapter:

- **Local food versus food miles.**

- **Cheap food versus expensive food.**

- **Fair trade versus local food.**

- **Local non-organic versus elsewhere organic.**

- **Seasonal eating versus out-of-season luxuries.**

- **Convenience foods versus home cooking.**

- **Carnivore versus vegetarian or vegan.**

- **Healthy eating versus endangered fish.**

- **Portion control versus pigging out.**

- **Tap water versus other drinks.**

And when we've talked all that through, I'll attempt to give you a relatively easy 'ethical eating blueprint' of just a few lines, which I hope will help you make the right food choices without too much trouble.

Local food versus food miles

'On one level there is absolutely nothing wrong with importing goods and services to meet our needs; but our eyes are bigger than our planet. If the whole world wanted to copy our levels of consumption, we would need the resources of more than three planets like Earth. And we only have one.'

Andrew Simms, Policy Director, New Economics Foundation, UK, 2006

Climate change is the most pressing environmental concern we face today. The Intergovernmental Panel on Climate Change warns that we need to cut greenhouse-gas emissions from human activities by 60–80 per cent by 2050 in order to avoid the worst impacts, but if we are to achieve this goal, everyone across the globe – from large and small businesses to each individual – will have to play their part.

Methods of agricultural production and processing, packaging, storage, cooking and waste disposal are all key considerations – and so is food transport, which in the UK alone is calculated to be responsible for 2.5 per cent of the country's total CO_2 emissions, or 3.5 per cent if individual shopping trips are included. If you then consider the transport of food by air, sea and land to and from other countries, you can see that our eating habits are responsible for significant quantities of greenhouse gas.

And thus in recent years the term 'food miles' has been coined. Food miles are the distance that food travels from 'field' (where the food is actually grown/reared/produced) to 'fork' (where it is consumed).

Global trade is inevitable, and has a history going back thousands of years. For the past century Britain has become increasingly dependent upon food imports – partly through necessity, partly through trader profit motivation, and partly through the consumer need/greed/want for different, new, exciting food opportunities. Indeed, if these imports now ceased (assuming that our food exports continued at the current level), it would create almost immediate food shortages.

Nevertheless, there are some areas of the import/export trade that beggar belief.

- **Why**, for example, in 2006 did we import beer worth £370,065,000 and export beer worth £408,088,000?*

- **Why** in the same year did we import chocolate worth £624,968,000 and export chocolate worth £306,125,000? And import sweet biscuits worth £224,952,000 while we exported £214,150,000 worth?

- And, given that fish is one of our major imports, **why** did we export almost as much fresh or chilled fish in 2006 (£274,115,000) as we imported (£425,374,000)?

Latest figures from Defra overseas trade data system.

There are dozens of examples like this. Over the years we've been so spoilt for choice that we don't consider the food miles, instead choosing the brands we think we prefer – and often they are brands from abroad, although we could get fundamentally the same thing here. Why can't we just eat our own produce and other countries do the same, when the products are broadly comparable and the import/export figures are too? The reason, of course, is that there is a lot of money to be made in food trade.

There are also ludicrous food miles racked up in the name of economy. For example, some foods that start out in this country travel thousands of miles before arriving back here to

FACTBOX

Domestic and international transport for the UK food market produces 19 million tons of carbon dioxide and costs more than £9 billion a year all told. *Defra, 2005*

FACTBOX

- In 2005, the UK imported nearly two and a half times as much food as it exported.
- The average annual worth of UK food, feed and drink imports between 1995 and 1997 was £16,904 million; by 2005 that figure had increased to £23,429 million.
- Meanwhile, during that period, exports hardly increased – in 1995–7 they were worth an annual average of £9,903 million; in 2005 they were worth £9,942 million.
- Both imports and exports, by weight, have roughly tripled in the last twenty years.

be sold. Prawns caught off the coast of Scotland are being shipped to the Far East to be shelled and then returned to the UK, and nuts are being grown in France, then sent to Italy to be packaged before being returned here. Why? The food companies concerned say it saves them money and thus it saves us, the consumers, money. We will return to this debate later (see page 80).

Sadly, until packaging labels are required to list such travels we can have little way of knowing what is happening.

Since the 1950s there have been huge changes in the food production and supply chain in Britain. One of the most significant has been the globalization of the food industry, with an increase in imports and exports as well as wider sourcing of food within the UK itself. Another important factor has been the growth in the power and popularity of a small number of large, often global, food retailers and manufacturers. This concentration of the food supply base into fewer, larger suppliers has meant major changes in delivery patterns, with most goods now routed through regional distribution centres.

Centralization and superstore shopping, often many miles from people's homes, has meant a switch from frequent food shopping (on foot) at small local shops to weekly shopping by car. All these factors have led to a large increase in the distance food travels. (Food miles from the shop to your home are discussed in Chapter 4.)

However, the method and efficiency of the transport, and the efficiency of the food-production system at farm level are usually taken into account when considering the significance of food miles for any particular food.

Air transport has a very high climate-change impact per tonne carried, whereas sea transport is relatively efficient. While around 90 per cent of the UK's food imports arrive by ship (after a road journey in the country of origin), air freight has increased significantly in recent years. Rail is efficient but very little used for food transport – less than 1 per cent of our food is carried this way. Road travel within countries and continents is the most frequent method of internal transport, and the current

dominant system of food supply in the UK and EU involves large HGVs travelling long distances between suppliers and shops via the distribution centres. This system enables very efficient loading of vehicles, which reduces the impact per tonne of food, and a real effort is being made by food suppliers, transporters and supermarkets to organize an integrated 'backhauling' system so that trucks don't return from a journey empty – instead they pick up supplies from the local area, or on the way back to base

The impact of food transport can be offset to some extent if food imported to an area has been produced more sustainably than the food available locally. For example, a case study showed that it can be more energy efficient to import tomatoes from Spain than to produce them here in heated greenhouses outside the summer months. Another case study showed that it can be more sustainable to import organic food by sea than to grow non-organic food in the UK.*

The previous six paragraphs are largely based on information in The Validity of Food Miles as an Indicator of Sustainable Development, Paul Watkiss et al., for Defra, 2005.

Now let's take a closer look at the shops where we buy our food. The appeal of the supermarkets lies in their ability to supply consumers, wherever they live, with a wide range of consistent products, all year round – at reasonable, often low, cost. This is possible because they source from around the world, thereby overcoming seasonal or geographical variations and shortfalls. In turn, this depends upon reliable transport and, for perishable goods such as fresh fruits and vegetables (one of our major food imports), and meat and dairy, upon speed and/or refrigeration or temperature-controlled storage during transport. Refrigeration units in transit tend to be less energy efficient than stationary ones and so this is another significant factor in greenhouse-gas production caused by transport.

The other appeal of the supermarkets is the wide range of composite, ready or convenience foods which are new, exciting, ethnic, multi-ingredient and so on. The majority of the British population now relies upon these items on a regular basis. So a meal that might contain six ingredients (if you were cooking at home from scratch) may contain thirty or forty. Each of these ingredients may have come its own hundreds or thousands of food miles.

THE CASE FOR IMPORTING

As the Factbox on page 71 explained, we import nearly 2.5 times as much food into the UK as we export. This makes it sound as if, were imports to cease, the majority of us would go hungry. In fact, we can produce around two-thirds of our food needs ourselves

FROM FARM TO FORK
– typical journey of a processed food

1 Raw ingredients are taken from the farm or source to their place of primary processing. This might include washing and cutting.

2 The various ingredients and the packaging are transported to the manufacturing plant where they are processed (turned into the finished dish/product) and packed. This can involve a number of journeys. The more ingredient-heavy the end product, the more transport is likely to be involved.

3 The finished product may be taken to a centre where it is consolidated with other goods destined for a number of retailers.

4 This load can travel on to a regional or national distribution centre. Direct deliveries are not usually made from regional centres to nearby shops.

5 A full load from the distribution centre travels on to stores.

'Any significant reduction in the levels of food imported into the UK, would mean reduced consumer choice. A significantly reduced range of foods would be available, with some foods only being available very briefly on a seasonal basis. This could cause severe nutritional problems, as some foods which are relied upon to provide a balanced diet may not be available. It would also significantly disadvantage, in particular, many ethnic minority consumers, whose recipes will often require or demand foods which are not commonly grown or produced in the UK.'

The Food Standards Agency, 2001

'From a transport perspective at least, a reduction in overseas imports is perhaps the most significant challenge we have to address and as such we should concentrate on this rather than on the final thirty miles or so.'

Tara Garnett, Wise Moves – Exploring the relationship between food, transport and CO_2, for Transport 2000 Trust

'...We need to get more carbon literate and move swiftly past this phase of crisp-packet labels and air-freight stickers. We need to start setting out a vision for a truly sustainable low-carbon food system, and the steps to achieve it.'

Kath Delmeny of Sustain, writing in Food Ethics magazine

– though at present we prefer to export a substantial amount of it.

If we were to reduce our national food-miles tally by eating our own indigenous food, that would represent around 65 per cent of our national energy (calorie) needs. In addition to this we could import foods that we now regard as staples (such as rice, tea, coffee, bananas, oranges, spices) which are hard or impossible to grow here; that would, at an educated guess, account for another 5 per cent of our calorie needs. Then, because we are as a nation overweight (with two-thirds of adults either overweight or obese), we could reduce our collective calorie intake by, I estimate, 10 per cent with no negative health effects and probably real benefit.

So that leaves a shortfall of 20 per cent. Therefore, although over the years ahead we might perhaps find ways of increasing our food productivity, on a national and an individual level, we will undoubtedly still need to import some of our food. What we must do is, as far as possible, limit what we import to items that are least damaging to the environment, both in the way they are produced and in their method of transport here, and make sure that what we import is what we really need. As, ultimately, what we buy in the shops is reflected in what the shops buy in for us, we do have a say in this. At the end of this section you will find some suggestions on what you can do to help.

A LOOK AT IMPORTED FRUIT AND VEGETABLES...*

- More fruit and vegetable produce is imported than any other food commodity with the exception of fish and some alcoholic drinks.

- The long-distance transport of fruit and vegetables requires mobile temperature control, which is highly energy intensive.

- Air-freighting of foods has an overwhelming negative environmental impact, and fruit and vegetables are the largest air-freighted food sector by volume. The signs are that the proportion of fruit and vegetables transported by air is likely to grow.

- It is uncertain whether technological change – such as 'cleaner' or more aerodynamic vehicles – will by itself be able to compensate for the overall continuing growth in food miles and the increasing use of air for the transport of foods.

- In general, the long-distance transport of food is growing. As such the problem is likely to increase rather than lessen in importance.

...VERSUS LOCAL FOOD

'Large agribusinesses are concerned with maximizing profits and minimizing waste. This leads to job loss, intense pesticide use or reliance on genetically modified plant strains,

*With thanks to Tara Garnett of the Centre for Environmental Strategy, University of Surrey, whose working paper Fruit and Vegetables & UK Greenhouse Gas Emissions was produced for the Food Climate Research Network.

and less biodiversity as big firms grow only those crops that suit economic concerns. Instead of a farmer who is part of the community, agribusiness is run by managers and vice presidents who are loyal to the corporation, not the land and local community.'

US *National Geographic*

At first glance it seems like a 'no-brainer' – it is obviously best to eat food which has been produced as near to home as possible rather than food which has come from the other side of the world. But buying all our food locally isn't always an option.

For one thing, in recent years local shops have been closing at an alarming rate. According to the Institute for Grocery Distribution, around 2,000 small shops are closing every year. In 2005, that represented 7.4 per cent of the total of local shops.

For another, there just isn't enough food produced in your local area or mine to feed us all. As we've just seen, we need to produce at least 20 per cent more food in the UK even to come near to producing enough to feed us all. And, of course, half the UK population lives in cities where local food purchasing doesn't present quite such an easy option, nor as enticing a picture as that of the village dweller cycling to the local farm shop for eggs, chicken and veggies produced on their green and pleasant acres.

And it isn't always easy to tell how truly 'local' the food you buy near home really is. Locally sourced or local food is defined as food whose main ingredients are 'grown, processed and sold' within a given radius.

Shopping at your local high-street food shops (what is left of them) is no guarantee that you are 'buying local' except in the sense of the last of those three terms. Your local independent grocer (if he has not been bought out to become a small-town outlet for one of the big four supermarkets) is just as likely to stock food grown and/or processed in all corners of the world as is your nearest superstore and, because the small, local shopkeeper has not received the favourable prices that the large shops command, the goods may be more expensive. So while in this case local shopping may help your local community's purse and

FACTBOX

Up to a quarter of the 'local' loose potatoes that you buy may, in fact, be no such thing. In 2007, a quarter of so-called new Pembrokeshire potatoes were found by local inspectors to have come from places such as Italy, while another scandal found that Israeli and Cyprus potatoes were also being sold as British.

viability, it goes no further than that.

But even when you can find food labelled 'local', there is a debate about what does constitute 'local': is it 5 miles, 30 miles, 100 miles, or even anywhere in this country – a definition that is not unusual? The Campaign to Protect Rural England and Waitrose restrict this radius to 30 miles; others may adopt a less defined limit, or even a countrywide one – in other words, if it isn't imported it counts as local! Currently there are no laws covering this issue.

And 'locally grown/produced' food sold loose by vendors in 'movable feast' markets or even local shops – or indeed, even chain stores – has been found, time and again, not to be from the local area at all.

If you are aware of these problems it may be easier to avoid them.

A good local alternative

There isn't yet a legal 'local' label that has the same trustworthiness as, for example, the Fairtrade Foundation's symbol or the organic certification, but farmers' markets and other local outlets, such as Women's Institute markets (now called Country Markets), pick-your-own shops and farm shops are a good

FACTBOX
The Americans have coined a name for consumers who prefer to shop locally: locavores. A locavore prefers to buy only food which has been harvested within a 100-mile radius of his or her home.

bet. There are currently over 550 farmers' markets in Britain, where farmers sell their own produce direct to the public, thereby keeping food miles to a minimum. Many, although not all, of these are certified by Farma, the National Farmers' Retail and Markets Association, which can also certify farm shops, pick-your-own establishments, and home-delivery box services. Other farmers' market associations are listed in the Resources section. Because the supply chain has been

A NOTE ON MILK

Milk at farmers' markets can be pasteurized or unpasteurized. Raw, or unpasteurized, milk (often in green-top bottles and considered by some to be superior both nutritionally and tastewise, as well as being less energy-intensive than pasteurized milk) can be sold to the public in England and Wales only direct from the farm via a farm shop, farmers' market or a farm's own delivery. Raw milk has to be labelled to state that it has not been heat treated and may contain organisms harmful to health. It has been banned in Scotland since 1983, regarded as unsafe to drink.

reduced and overheads are lower, the price of the food is sometimes (but not always) more competitive than in your local supermarket.

To sell at a Farma farmers' market, the stallholder selling meat, poultry, eggs, fruit and vegetables, milk, game and fish must themselves have grown, reared or caught the produce they are selling. Prepared foods, such as preserves, cakes, breads or pies, can contain stallholder-produced ingredients or, if this isn't possible, must contain at least 25 per cent ingredients bought from local farms. (Bread is an exception – a minimum of 10 per cent local ingredients can qualify.)

In addition the stall has to be staffed either by the farmer or members of his or her team who can answer questions about the produc-tion process. There are also limits on how far the stallholder has travelled – in rural areas this should be no more than 30 miles, while in urban and coastal areas it can go up to 50 miles.

I suggest that if you are going to shop at farmers' markets, pick-your-own or farm shops, or get local deliveries of box schemes, then check that they are Farma certified or that any other farmers'-market networks have guide-lines with which you are happy.

Supermarkets and local food

Several of the big supermarket chains are now realizing the customer-pleasing, local-community-pleasing potential in 'getting back to basics' and are doing business with local suppliers near to the individual stores, so it is more and more likely that you will find truly local produce in your local superstore. Whether or not you want to give your cash to them rather than to a truly local shop is food for thought.

BUT IS LOCAL A REAL SAVER OF FOOD MILES?

Several researchers have come to the conclusion that local shops (as compared to regional or national) don't actually save as many carbon emissions as you might think. This is for several reasons, including the fact that smaller deliveries are less efficient than larger ones: local deliveries are more likely to involve half-empty vehicles as, by necessity, deliveries may be small. This boils down to what is described as 'logistical inefficiency'. Tara Garnett, the respected researcher on food and the environment from the University of Surrey, suggests that for perishable foods, including fresh produce, the advantages of shopping on foot at local stores may outweigh these disadvantages of greater inefficiency. She says that a regional approach offers more CO_2-reducing potential than either globalized systems or very local ones – an idea I find truly commonsensical.

The consensus seems to be that we should aim for 'two-tier' shopping – buying our non-perishable goods at further-away large stores infrequently (say once a month), and our perishable items at local stores, shopping on foot, three times a week or as often as necessary.

WHAT TO DO

- Accept that importing much of our foodstuff will continue for the foreseeable future – while a decrease in imports can be achieved, the degree is unlikely to be great. Meanwhile, make your wishes known with your purse and purchase imports discriminatingly, then hopefully retailers will get the message.

- Buy truly local food when you can.
  If you can't find a 'made locally' product, then source it from elsewhere in the UK. Even if it isn't from down your road, it will not only help British food producers and businesses, but also our trade deficit. Items that you should be able to buy produced in Britain include meat, poultry, eggs, dairy, fish, vegetables, bread, sugar, chocolate, alcohol, indigenous fruit (like apples, plums, pears), all the foods in season on the list on pages 92–3, and items such as pet food.

- If something doesn't grow or isn't made in Britain and you consider it a staple, then you will have to go for imported – oranges, bananas, coffee, tea, spices, rice.

- If you can, choose imports from the nearest EU countries (e.g. France, Scandinavia, Spain) rather than the USA, China or Australia, for example.

- If you're buying something which is coming a long way, choose Fairtrade if possible.

- Imported items to consider leaving on the shelf include any imports that require air-freighting. Personally, if I know or suspect that an item has been air-freighted, I avoid it. Other imported items to be wary of are heavy goods, such as glass-bottled mineral water and meat, and goods that have been chilled/frozen in order to get here, such as dairy produce, fish and meat. Both result in a larger carbon footprint.

- Also remember that some UK-sourced foods may not be as green as similar items that have travelled from abroad. This is likely to be particularly true of British hothouse products versus Mediterranean-sourced non-hothouse products. However, it is also important to emphasize that where it appears to be 'better' to source from far away, it may be preferable not to source that product at all. Bringing winter lettuce in from the continent may use less energy than a hothouse lettuce grown here, but eating a reasonable alternative – such as a cabbage and carrot coleslaw – might be a more responsible choice. See seasonal eating, page 87.

- Lastly, consider that even locally produced foods can rack up food miles if the word 'local' is interpreted rather liberally.

You will find more information on supermarkets, what they are doing to reduce food miles and how to make the right choices when you shop in Chapter 4.

Cheap food versus expensive food

CARLO PETRINI, FOUNDER OF THE SLOW FOOD MOVEMENT, SAYS, 'FOOD IS NOT TOO EXPENSIVE, IT IS TOO CHEAP'.

In the UK, food accounts for only 10 per cent of household spending – a lower percentage than ever before. We expect our food to be cheap, but in fact we pay too little for it. This emphasis on driving down costs has implications for how and where our food is sourced, produced, processed and delivered.

The main factors that help the major supermarkets give us cheap food are:

- Cheap production – often by sourcing and/or processing overseas.

- Quick maturation (e.g. meat, cheese, chickens), thus encouraging factory-farm practices.

- Purchasing power and clout, making the farmers work harder and harder to produce more and more for less and less income.

While sometimes some of the supermarkets do offer a fair deal, it seems to be too easy for them to put the squeeze on their producers and suppliers in order to offer the customer the cheap prices they seem to want. Thus the scenario for the small shopkeeper is that he or she must pay more than the supermarkets for similar goods and this in turn is a major reason why small local shops are shutting down with alarming frequency all across our land.

But cheap food for all has other downsides apart from the immediate environmental concerns such as food miles and animal welfare. Hundreds of British farmers sell up every year or diversify into tourism or other sidelines because they cannot earn an income from growing or rearing our food. The massive purchasing power of the supermarkets and their decisions to purchase abroad in order to keep costs down is doing immeasurable damage to our rural economy – not only the farmers, but also agricultural workers and service providers, and their dependants, are all affected.

IT'S TIME TO THINK

Most of us don't think about why our food is cheap or where the food is coming from.

I could fill a book with the way that livestock is abused in this country in the name of cheap food, but I won't. I'll only say that next time you look at a pack of cheap chicken breasts think of the football-pitch-sized sheds where they may have been kept in a 'flock' of 150,000 or more birds; where they may have been farmed from birth to slaughter in as little as forty days (twice as fast as thirty years ago); kept in artificial light with no outdoor access; living with no room to move around and in their own excrement ...

Or with the way that the importers of 99p pineapples or 35p bunches of bananas exploit workers, demanding long hours for low wages and risking their health through high exposure to pesticides.

The probable cause of BSE – 'mad cow disease' – which was rife in the UK in the late 1980s and early 1990s was cost-cutting cattle feed which contained infected animal matter. Even when we have a large disaster – such as the recent turkey-farm bird-flu outbreak in Norfolk – and get a rare insight into the conditions in which some of our food is produced, the effect is short term. We shun that product in horror for a few weeks but soon it's all forgotten and, helped by a good PR or advertising campaign, we're buying again.

When you buy cheap food, there is always a reason, and the reason is often not what you'd really want to hear.

As with most consumer goods, you get what you pay for – and it should be time to regard cheap food not as a blessing but as a problem. If we value true choice, quality, diversity, animal welfare, and our heritage and communities, we need to pay a realistic price for our food.

It is time to stop feeling pleased with ourselves to find a £2 chicken or a 99p pack of minced beef.

WHAT TO DO

- Be a responsible customer: put the cheap pack back on the shelf. Keep to the same food budget but buy less, of better quality.

- Save money in other ways (e.g. on transport or by buying lower-cost types of fruit and vegetables, such as cabbage). Think about picking your own blackberries as an exercise activity, or growing some blackcurrant canes at the bottom of the garden, rather than having to pay £2.99 for a 150g pack of imported blueberries.

- Frequent supermarkets that value quality over cheapness – in the UK, Waitrose is probably the best example, with perhaps Marks & Spencer second.

- Frequent local greengrocers, fishmongers and delis which stock quality food (not all of them do – you may enjoy shopping around the local alternatives until you find the ones where the produce seems to be best in terms of freshness, quality, taste). The food here will be dearer, but you'll save on petrol.

- Eating a little less is a good way of not spending too much more (see page 110).

FACTBOX

There are approximately 20 million caged hens in the UK, which produce 63 per cent of the 10 billion eggs we consume each year.

Fair trade versus local food

'With more than seven out of every ten pounds spent on food shopping in the UK going through supermarket tills, Britain's leading grocery retailers now serve as the main gatekeepers for developing country food exporters to the UK market.'

Julian Oram of ActionAid, in *Food Ethics* magazine, summer 2007

WHAT IS FAIR TRADE?

'Fairtrade' with its blue-and-yellow symbol on a black background, is a registered mark – for a product to display this symbol it must meet the Fairtrade standards of Fairtrade Labelling Organisations International (FLO). The Fairtrade Foundation is the licenser in the UK. Under this banner, food producers in the developing world are certified and then receive a minimum price for their product/s, which covers the cost of sustainable production, and an extra premium that is invested in social or economic development projects. They are also offered contracts that allow for long-term planning and sustainable production practices.

Fairtrade may cover small farmers working in co-operatives, or large plantations, whose employers pay fair wages and offer decent working conditions. The extra premiums may typically be spent on building schools, hospitals, irrigation systems or housing.

So Fairtrade helps poorer countries, workers and producers to make a living and be self-supporting – an ethic to be encouraged.

FACTBOX
In the UK, the Co-op was the first supermarket to offer Fairtrade produce, selling Cafédirect coffee back in the early 1990s. But still around 99 per cent of the coffee that the world drinks is not fairly traded.

Foods from suppliers who aren't part of a Fairtrade scheme may have involved, for example, child labour; twelve-hour days or more; unfair prices offered by the buyer to the producer, thus preventing development and any standard of living for small farmers, and ensuring that larger producers pay only minimal wages to their plantation workers; and the use of dangerous pesticides, leaving hundreds of thousands of workers in ill-health.

Some of the foods you are most likely to find 'fairly traded' in your local shop are bananas (for example all Waitrose and Sainsbury's bananas are Fairtrade), pineapples and coffee, but you can find other Fairtrade

FACTBOX
The market for Fairtrade products is expected to grow by up to 150 per cent in the next five years. Currently UK Fairtrade sales total around £300 million a year.

foods and drinks, including cocoa, chocolate, wine, dried fruits, fresh fruits and vegetables, honey, juices, nuts and seeds, and nut and seed oils and spreads, quinoa, rice, tea, sugar and spices.

While Fairtrade is a social concept, Fairtrade produce has much in common with organic and sustainable food. Environmental conditions are important in Fairtrade – producers must implement environmental improvement plans, and the use of dangerous chemicals is banned. Says the Fairtrade Foundation, 'While many producers use organic practices, Fairtrade doesn't require them to do so. This is because many of the most disadvantaged cannot meet organic standards, and not all will be able to sell their crop as organic, so they won't be able to benefit from the premium prices.' However, some Fairtrade products labelled and certified as organic can be found – for example, organic Fairtrade pineapples are in Sainsbury's, Waitrose and Tesco, and in many online stores (see Resources).

The Fairtrade scheme has some detractors. Some feel that it doesn't go far enough, while others say that most of the Fairtrade profits go to retailers rather than the farmers. Another criticism is that the system may encourage farmers to produce one crop rather than diversifying. But, for the time being, Fairtrade is the best hope the developing-world producers have.

FAIRTRADE AND FOOD MILES

Some people who are trying to avoid too many 'food miles' and to shop locally, are rightly concerned that they are contributing to greenhouse-gas emissions by adding Fairtrade products to their trolley. Typically, Fairtrade goods come from places such as Africa, South America and the Caribbean – thus their air-freight or shipment isn't green.

A real dilemma. If we all avoid buying Fairtrade products we are depriving poor countries, and those countries' people, of a way to a better future and independence.

FACTBOX
Currently pineapples are being sold in some UK supermarkets for as little as 99p each. In Costa Rica, the world's leading producer of pineapples, workers on a typical plantation have to pick 5,000 pineapples a day in order to make the 'superior' pay, equivalent to £4.50 a day.

OTHER FAIRLY TRADED LABELS

The Fairtrade name and logo is registered, but there are a few other similar schemes around. Some food companies and outlets have their own fairtrading schemes. Starbucks, for instance, runs a Coffee and Farmer Equity Practices scheme.

All these schemes have differing standards. And some products simply state on their labels that the food inside has been 'fairly traded' – without an explanation or code of conduct, this could mean anything.

The Rainforest Alliance: You may see this name on some food labels – coffee and bananas, for example. While the New York-based RA has some similarities to a fairtrade organization, its mission statement is to 'ensure long and healthy lives for people, for wildlife and for the planet by establishing sustainable ways of working the land'. As such it is not a 'fairtrade' organization, but their remit does cover worker protection. They sold £500 million RA products in 2006.

'Climate change challenges some of our most treasured hopes for an ethical food system. We may need to accept this, but we also need to decide where the buck stops. Where do we say that some objectives, such as fair trade or animal welfare, are non-negotiable, even if it means sacrificing some carbon efficiency?'

Kath Delmany, Sustain, the alliance for better food and farming

WHAT TO DO

- Buy some Fairtrade in amongst your other shopping and try to ensure that it is shipped not flown in.

- If you are going to buy a product that comes from abroad anyway, and it's a choice between Fairtrade or very cheap non-Fairtrade, buy the Fairtrade version. A Costa Rica pineapple or mango not labelled Fairtrade may have been planted or harvested by a worker experiencing any of the difficulties listed above and is best avoided.

- If Fairtrade organic is available, buy that – but don't avoid fairly traded items that aren't labelled as organic, as many of them will have been produced to organic or near-organic standards.

Local non-organic versus elsewhere organic

As organic food becomes bigger and bigger business, some of its green credentials can become watered down, as we saw in Chapter 2.

Currently British farmers manage to produce only around half of the organic food that we want, and so the rest is imported. Of this, by far the most damaging form of transport with the most global-warming potential is air-freight, volume of which has doubled since 1992. It is responsible for 11 per cent of the CO_2 emissions from UK food transport, generating 177 times more greenhouse gas than shipping.

Thus the Soil Association, after a wide-ranging one-year consultation, announced in late 2007 that it proposes changing its standards to ensure that organic food is air-freighted to the UK only if it delivers genuine benefits for farmers in developing countries. This means that from January 2009, air-freighted organic food will have to meet the Soil Association's own Ethical Trade standards or the Fairtrade Foundation's standards – and licensees will also be required to develop plans for reducing any remaining dependence on air-freight.

Other options are for foods to be labelled with the number of air miles they have travelled, or a requirement that the producers/importers pay for flights by carbon offsetting.

In my view, sometimes UK non-organic options may be preferable to imported organic options, whether or not they have been air-freighted. As we saw in Chapter 2, sometimes supermarket organic produce has been produced on large farms which, if you were to visit them, you would hardly recognize as practising organic ethics; this may be especially true of table chickens and eggs.

Instead, for example, a lot of local markets (farmers' markets, WI markets) in your area will be selling food from small producers who, while not registered organic (often because this is a time-consuming and fairly costly exercise), nevertheless follow the spirit of traditional and organic farming and help to conserve locality and diversity in what we eat. It is always worth investigating what you can buy locally before resorting to organic imports. Similarly, a lot of family butchers sell meat reared in the area, often from their own farm and one or two others.

All that said, if we do all shun organic imports, whether air-freighted or not, we will be helping to deprive hundreds of thousands of small farmers in Africa and other developing countries of their living. In time, perhaps our food labels will let us know every detail about the place where the item was farmed – and we can then choose sensibly between all the options.

FACTBOX

According to the Slow Food Movement:

- **75% of European food-product diversity has been lost since 1900**
- **93% of American food-product diversity has been lost in the same period**
- **33% of livestock varieties have disappeared or are near to disappearing**
- **30,000 vegetable varieties have become extinct in the last century, and one more is lost every six hours**

WHAT TO DO

- If you must buy organic food from abroad, avoid air-freighted goods. Check the labels – they may provide information on this.

- Avoid out-of-season organic – this frequently involves imports.

- Choose Fairtrade imports, which are often produced to near-organic standards and which benefit the local communities (see the Fairtrade discussion on pages 82–4). Sometimes Fairtrade imports will also be certified organic.

- Check out your local farmers, high-street greengrocers, butchers, fishmongers, local adverts, markets, WI, etc., and source 'almost as good as' produce instead of organic imported.

Seasonal eating versus out-of-season luxuries

What a great and green idea to eat only what is in season! Why don't we all do it, all the time?

Buying fruit and vegetables when they are locally in season can be a positive choice, as they are unlikely to have been transported long distances or heated during production. And buying them direct from producers is a good way to source fresh produce and reduce packaging.

So – no air miles; you support local, natural, traditional ways to eat; and you avoid the need to heat greenhouses.

However, seasonal eating – sourcing from the UK only – can sometimes be more difficult to achieve and more time-consuming than you might at first think. It takes more thought to plan out meals for a family. It may take more sourcing to find the seasonal produce. It can sometimes be less expensive but often it is more, as at certain times of year (and if the weather is inclement) local seasonal produce may be in short supply.

For busy multitaskers – the typical 'doing it all' parent/career person – it can seem too hard to bother with. For health-conscious people, it may be hard to go without anti-oxidant-rich blueberries in winter. And for foodies used to their luxuries, it can seem too austere. But take heart – fruit and vegetable producers in the British Isles are finding ways to prolong the growing season of many favourites by breeding. For example, in 2007 the earliest-ever crop of English strawberries went on sale – in March! We should soon also have extended-season raspberries, cherries and plums.

And, for times when you choose non-local seasonal items, the government helps you to feel less guilty by saying on its consumer website: 'If food comes from a long way away it doesn't necessarily mean it has big climate change effects. Long distance transportation of produce by boat – for example, bananas and apples – or food imported when in season [in its native country], can have lower climate change effects than food produced out of season or stored for long periods.'

If you can't find what you need (rather than want) – say, plums in August because of a poor British season – then try to choose the same item from the nearest possible country. The season for fruits and vegetables grown without extra heat can be longer in Mediterranean countries, which have more reliable pollination, germination and ripening – but drought can cause its own problems.

If you can't find what you need in a nearby country either, then go the government-suggested route and choose further-away

foods, like bananas, harvested and shipped to us immediately. This saves the energy cost of storage and, in the case of some fruits, such as apples, cuts out the need for freshness-prolonging treatments.

Also don't forget that some British-grown items can be stored for several months quite naturally, if a little care is taken. Apples, pears, quinces, root vegetables, squashes and pumpkins, onions, garlic and shallots should all last from weeks up to many months in the right conditions (for more on storing fruits and vegetables yourself, see Chapter 5). So you can buy in bulk in season if you have a suitable storage facility. And don't be too suspicious of these items for sale in your local shops seemingly out of season: if they've been stored in natural conditions you can buy without feeling unethical.

We also need the government to put more funding into researching strains of fruits and vegetables that will grow in this country during the colder months and we need more land set aside for market gardening rather than for livestock if we are ever to become any more self-sufficient in our fresh produce.

Lastly, don't forget that being a 'frugal foodie' can score you many brownie points and create envy amongst your foodie friends.

WHAT TO DO

- Try box schemes (see Chapter 4). Do a meal-planning session after the box arrives.

- See what you can source at WI and farmers' markets in the way of bottles and jars of preserves, fruits and pickles which were made from seasonal produce.

- Consider buying loads of fruits when they are in season and bottling them yourself. You can also buy vegetables in bulk and store them (potatoes, squashes, carrots, onions) if you have a cool, dark space, or freeze them. For more on the energy consumption of frozen foods, see Chapter 5.

- If you are going to buy out-of-season imports, make sure they carry the Fairtrade label; make sure that they were not grown using extra heat (i.e. that they were seasonal in their country of origin); and make sure that you really feel they are necessary to your diet and well-being. If the label informs you of non air-freight, go for that too.

- Research shows that indigenous British fruits such as blackcurrants, and vegetables such as cauliflower, are just as rich in anti-oxidants as imported luxuries like blueber-ries and baby sweetcorn. Buy in bulk when fruits and vegetables are in season and freeze. Other research shows that out-of-season imported fruits and vegetables actually contain fewer nutrients than the same product grown in the UK and eaten in season (or frozen). Imports tend to contain less vitamin C.

- At some times of the year it will be much harder to find seasonal food that suits than at others. Plan for these 'lean times' with plenty of stocks in the freezer and larder.

- And I suggest that foodies missing their out-of-season soft fruits and so on should spend some of their money on some of the cookbooks on seasonal foods which provide endless recipes so that they can never get bored or feel deprived.

- For menus and recipes for seasonal food, see Chapter 6.

FACTBOX
One well-recognized way of reducing energy use in greenhouses is through the use of a system called **Combined Heat and Power (CHP)**, which nearly doubles the overall efficiency of fuel use in glasshouses. Currently 25 per cent of tomato-growers make use of CHP.

FOODS IN SEASON

The seasonal foods listed here are based on UK produce unless otherwise stated, and are grown without additional heat. I have tried only to include mentions of foods from other countries when that food is not grown here, but is a staple or frequently eaten and nutritionally important item for most of the British population.

Seasons for fish and game apply to wild rather than farmed food. I have only included fish which is on the Marine Stewardship Council (MSC) approved lists. Several types of fish are now farmed and much of what you find in the shops from these species won't be wild. These include salmon, oysters, rainbow trout and, increasingly, cod, scallops and mussels. These will be available for much of the year. If buying farmed fish, try to ensure that it is organic and UK produced. Other types of fish from other parts of the world are sustainable (e.g. albacore tuna) but may have travelled a long distance to get here and may be included under the umbrella of 'imported luxuries', as it will need to be shipped in cold storage or frozen.

Remember, when buying seasonal produce it may in fact be from other countries of the northern hemisphere which have similar seasons.

Spring

(March, April, May)

Fruit:
cherries (late spring); oranges (from Spain and other Mediterranean countries); rhubarb.

Vegetables:
asparagus (late spring); Brussels sprouts (early spring); cabbage; carrots; cauliflower; celeriac; chard (baby leaves); kale; leeks; lettuce and baby salad leaves (various types, late spring); mint and other fresh herbs (late spring); morel mushrooms; nettles; radish; rocket (late spring); samphire; spinach (baby leaves); spring greens; spring onions; purple sprouting broccoli; swede; watercress.

Meat and game:
spring lamb; duck; rabbit.

Fish:
clams (early spring); brown trout; John Dory; lobster; red mullet (early spring); sea trout.

Summer

(June, July, August)

Fruit:
apples, dessert (late summer); avocado (from Spain and other Mediterranean countries); blackcurrants; blueberries; cherries; damsons (late summer); figs (late summer); gooseberries; greengages; oranges and lemons (from Italy and other Mediterranean countries); peaches (usually from France and Mediterranean countries); pears; plums; redcurrants; raspberries; rhubarb; strawberries.

Vegetables:
asparagus (early summer); aubergine (mid to late summer); basil; beans – broad, dwarf, runner, and all beans for drying and storing; beetroot (late summer); cabbage; carrots; cauliflower; celery; chard; chillies; coriander leaf; courgettes; cucumber; dill; fennel; garlic; globe artichokes; kohlrabi; lettuce and salad leaves (various types); mangetout; marrow; mint; peas; peppers (late summer); potatoes (new); purple sprouting broccoli; radish; rocket; samphire; shallots; summer squash; spinach; sweetcorn (late summer); tomatoes; turnip; watercress.

Meat and game:
Welsh lamb; hare; rabbit.

Fish:
brown trout; crab (midsummer onwards); haddock; herring; mackerel (late summer); meg rim (Cornish sole); mussels (late summer); pollack; queen scallops; sea bass (late summer); sea bream; sea trout.

Autumn

(September, October, November)

Fruit and nuts:
apples (dessert and cooking); blackberries; elderberries; figs (early autumn); lemons (from Italy); pears, plums; raspberries; hazelnuts; walnuts; chestnuts; cobnuts.

Vegetables:
beetroot; broccoli; cabbage; carrots; cauliflower; chard; courgettes; cucumber; garlic; kohlrabi; lettuce and salad leaves (various types); marrow; field mushrooms and other edible fungi; Jerusalem artichokes; lamb's lettuce; onions; peppers; radish; rocket; potatoes; spinach; squash; sweetcorn (early autumn); tomatoes (early autumn); turnip.

Meat and game:
autumn lamb; goose; partridge; wood pigeon; venison; grouse; guinea fowl; partridge; teal; pheasant; rabbit; hare.

Fish:
Clams; cockles; crab; gurnard; haddock; John Dory; king scallops (late autumn); lemon sole; lobster (late autumn); mackerel; megrim; mussels; native oysters; pike; pilchard; pollack; red mullet; sardines; sea bass; sea bream.

Winter

(December, January, February):

Fruit:
apples (stored); pears (stored); bananas (from southern hemisphere); pomegranate (from Mediterranean countries); Seville oranges (from Spain).

Vegetables:
beetroot; Brussels sprouts; cabbage; cauliflower; celeriac; celery; chicory; chives; Jerusalem artichokes; kale; laverbread and dulse seaweeds; leeks; maincrop potatoes; rocket; swede.

Meat and game:
duck; wild duck; goose; guinea fowl; hare; partridge; venison; wood pigeon; turkey; pheasant; rabbit.

Fish:
clams; cockles; crab; gurnard; haddock; John Dory; king scallops; lemon sole; lobster; mackerel; mussels; pike; pilchards; queen scallops; red mullet; sardines; sea bass; sea bream.

Convenience foods versus home cooking

In 2007, researchers from the University of Wales Institute, Cardiff (UWIC), developed a 'low ecological footprint' diet. They had to consider various factors, including food miles, energy consumption, processing and packaging. In the words of the project leader:

Our study was to investigate how much impact a diet has, starting right from the beginning to the time that it is eaten – what has had to be grown, bred or produced, the processing of it, and the miles it travels to the shops. Most people would be quite surprised that the biggest environmental impact of food is not the food miles, but because of the processing it goes through.

Only around 20 per cent of us regularly cook ourselves meals from scratch at home – and even when we do, we call meals such as pasta with a ready-made sauce, or rice and chicken with a pour-over curry 'home cooking'. People who work spend on average 40 per cent less time cooking than those who do not. Nearly two-thirds of households buy ready meals and around 10 per cent of us eat them more than once a week.

When weighing up the greenness of a ready meal compared to a properly home-cooked one, several factors need to be considered:

- Where the ingredients in the ready meal came from. Often the labels don't give you proper information on this, but a check of the ingredients list will help. Items such as out-of-season vegetables or prawns, for example, are likely to have been shipped or air-freighted from abroad.

- How many ingredients are in the meal (the more ingredients, the higher the environmental impact is likely to be because each item will have its own carbon pathway). American food expert Steve Ettlinger, author of *Twinkie, Deconstructed* (see Resources section), describes his journey to discover the origin of the ingredients and additives in our food and found that 'some of the processes involved in producing food require enough energy to fuel a small town'. He found that, in the USA, processed foods, including even organic ones, contained ingredients from many different countries.

- Animal produce in a low-cost ready meal is likely to have been mass-produced, the eggs battery, chicken meat non-free range. Food manufacturers who process items into composite meals containing lots of added flavourings, colours and so on, know that they can get away with inferior-quality meats and poultry.

- Packaging. You may have a container for the food, surrounded with a see-through pack or a plastic top, and then a cardboard label or box round that. If you're adding extras – a sachet of ready-cooked rice and a bagged salad – your packaging tota will be very high. For more on packaging, see Chapter 4.

A LUNCH SNACK COMPARISON

A typical ham and chutney sandwich bought from a supermarket costs around £2.50 and contains: malted brown bread (39%), tomato (18%), sweetcure smoked formed ham (18%), leaf mix (9%), fruit chutney (7%), mayonnaise (4%), butter. Malted brown bread contains: wheat flour, water, malted wheat flakes, wheat bran, yeast, salt, malted wheat flour, malted barley flour, wheat protein, spirit vinegar, emulsifiers (mono- and di-acetyltartaric esters of fatty acids), vegetable oil, flour treatment agent (ascorbic acid). Sweetcure smoked formed ham contains: pork, sugar, salt, preservatives (sodium nitrite, potassium nitrate). Leaf mix contains: lettuce, lollo rosso 19. Fruit chutney contains: sugar, pear, plum, red wine vinegar, tomato, onion, water, date, tomato purée, cornflour, garlic powder, colour (plain caramel), cayenne pepper, nutmeg, black pepper. Mayonnaise contains: vegetable oil, water, egg, spirit vinegar, cornflour, egg yolk, sugar, salt, white pepper.

Total: 35 different ingredients

PROS AND CONS OF READY MEALS VERSUS HOME COOKING

Ready meals – pros
- Cooked in large quantities in energy-efficient ovens.
- Waste kept under control (to reduce costs to the producer).
- Only one final set of packaging.
- Only finished product transported home.
- May be heated in microwave, thus saving energy over oven cooking.

Ready meals – cons
- Little knowledge of provenance, or quality of contents (e.g. additives, low nutrient value).
- Likely to contain a long list of ingredients, thus increasing carbon footprint.
- No leftovers to use for another meal.
- Pre-set portion sizes may not suit all.
- May not be convenient for families – e.g. microwave heating mainly suitable for one person.

Home-cooked meals – pros
- More knowledge of where ingredients have come from and their nutritional value.
- Can batch cook and save energy/money.
- May be leftovers to use in other dishes.
- Likely to contain small list of ingredients, also saving energy in production/transport.
- May produce vegetable waste (e.g. peelings) useful for composting.
- Encourages interest in and affinity with food and its origins.

Home-cooked meals – cons
- Some cooking methods and recipes can be high in cooking energy costs.
- Several different ingredients may mean more packaging and more bulk to transport home and dispose of.

A home-made ham and salad sandwich costs around £1 and might contain: organic bread (contains wholemeal flour, salt, oil, yeast), organic butter, ham, organic tomato and lettuce slices, dash of pumpkin seed oil or balsamic vinegar.

Total: around 9 different ingredients

It is quite obvious that the home-made sandwich uses a lot fewer resources than the shop-bought version. There is no way of telling where all the ingredients in the bought sandwich have come, from so it's not possible to consider 'food miles' accurately, although in all likelihood many of the ingredients will have been imported. The bought sandwich contains 'ham formed from selected cuts' – i.e. it has gone through an additional process rather than simply being sliced cured pork. The bought sandwich contains a third of your day's recommended salt intake.

The home-made one is considerably lower in salt, fat, sugar and artificial additives, and will also be pesticide free.

The bought sandwich is wrapped in both cellophane and card. If you take the home-made sandwich to work, you can take it in a re-usable container.

A SUPPER COMPARISON
A typical ready-meal roast chicken dinner costs around £2 and contains: potato (28%), chicken (17%), chicken stock, chicken bouillon, water, tomato purée, vegetable juices from concentrate, onion, stuffing ball (3%), carrot (3%), swede (3%), chicken fat, cornflour, wheat flour, chicken gelatine, salt, malt extract, pepper, bay leaf. Chicken bouillon contains: chicken stock, chicken fat, carrot juice, mushroom extract, onion extract, sugar, salt. Chicken stock contains: chicken, water, salt, cornflour, sugar, onion, nutmeg, parsley. Vegetable juices from concentrate contain: carrot, celeriac, lettuce, parsley, beetroot, spinach. Stuffing ball contains: water, rusk, hydrogenated vegetable fat, dried onion, salt, wheat flour, dextrose, soya protein isolate, sage, yeast, nutmeg, coriander, black pepper.

Total: 35 different ingredients

A home-made roast chicken and vegetable supper costs around £2.25 (see note) and might contain: Chicken-leg portion roast in a tray with chunks of potato, onion, carrots, sweet potato, garlic, oregano, lemon juice and olive oil until everything is tender and cooked through, served with local steamed spring greens.

Total: 10 different ingredients

The ready meal contains hydrogenated (trans) fats, which are not a healthy ingredient, and the total amount of chicken it contains is 51g (less than 2 ounces) of the total meal, which weighs 300g. The total vegetable content, excluding potato, is (if you include the tomato purée and the onion mentioned but not given a weight) approximately 10 per cent, or 30g (just over an ounce). The meal also contains soya protein, which unless the pack states otherwise is likely to contain GM.

The 250 calories that the bought chicken supper contains is very little for a single serving – weighing approximately half that of the home-made supper. The protein content, at less than 20g, is also low for a main meal. The vegetable content of the bought supper provides only around a third of a 'portion', while the home-made version provides at least two portions (greens, one, and onion and carrot the other – potato doesn't 'count' as it is a starch).

In addition, if you make the home-made roast meal using a leg from a whole chicken you can get several meals out of the rest of the chicken (or you could roast the whole chicken and use the surplus in various other meals, snacks and soups – and you could do a similar thing with the vegetables).

The cost of the home-made meal is an approximation, based on using a portion from an £8 organic chicken, which will make six meals (thus your chicken portion costs £1.33), and on buying local vegetables in season.

Cooking energy costs: The home-made meal will use up approximately 100 per cent more energy in cooking compared with heating the ready meal (in a conventional oven), but energy costs can be kept down by 'one tray/one pot' methods.

WHAT TO DO

- Try to cut down buying ready meals and convenience foods to occasional use.

- When you do buy them, try to choose good-quality, additive-free ready meals. Several small companies now provide these – and farmers' and WI markets often sell home-made ready meals, sauces, pies and so on (see A–Z for more ready-meal information). No doubt the supermarkets will be following this lead. As I write, of the major supermarkets Sainsbury's, for example, has a range containing 'totally natural and healthy ingredients' – but where these are sourced is hard to tell.

- Look at the ingredients list: if it is very long, think twice.

- Think of all the quick-to-prepare items that are fresh or marginally processed rather than highly processed. Think eggs, yogurt, bread, fruit, nuts, seeds, pasta, cheese – if you want a quick meal or snack, base it around these.

- When you have a less busy evening or day, spend some time cooking your own 'ready meals' and freeze them. If you use a freezer anyway, this won't use extra energy.

- When buying for home cooking, try to choose items in minimal packaging (see Chapter 4). When cooking, always make more than you need and freeze the surplus.

- See Chapter 5 for plenty of ideas on cooking quick, easy food that's also green.

Carnivore versus vegetarian or vegan

All the signs indicate that it is important for our planet that we drastically cut the amount of meat that we eat. The British government-linked Environment Agency says: 'The potential benefit of a vegan diet in terms of climate impact could be very significant', while a European Commission report – Environmental impact of products (EIPRO), May 2006 – reaches the conclusion that 'food accounts for 31% of global warming potential. Of this, meat and meat products (including meat, poultry, sausages or similar) are singled out for their high environmental importance.' The report estimates that the meat, poultry and sausage contribution to global warming potential is 38 per cent of the food category. The second most important group is dairy products, at 14.5% of the total food category.

- Between 7 and 8 per cent of total UK greenhouse-gas emissions are from farming – particularly meat and dairy farming.

- Friends of the Earth calculates that if world demand continues to grow at its current rate, we will soon need two more planet Earths in order to grow enough animal feed. Livestock currently accounts for 70 per cent of agricultural land use and one third of the Earth's land surface.

- Each day every cow in Britain emits up to 200 litres of methane (the second most important greenhouse gas after CO_2, accounting for 14 per cent of all greenhouse gas emissions) – and the UK has around 10 million cattle. One estimate likens the global-warming impact of one cow to that of a four-wheel-drive car in average use for a day.

- The typical Western diet, containing 25–30 per cent animal-source food, produces 1.5 tonnes more carbon dioxide per person per annum than the equivalent vegan diet. Beef-eating accounts for 3–4 per cent of a typical UK resident's carbon footprint.

- The average amount of meat eaten worldwide is 100g a day, though people in the richest countries eat about ten times as much as those in the poorest. Britain would need to cut consumption by about 60 per cent to eat no more than our fair share.

In this country, meat for dinner is often seen as a right rather than a privilege, whereas back in the 1950s, a plate of chicken or beef was usually a special Sunday treat. And in the past forty years, worldwide meat consumption has rocketed – from 56kg to 89kg a head each year in the UK; from 89kg to 124kg in the USA; from 4kg to 54kg in China. Continuing economic and population growth across the world means that the amount of meat reared will increase in the years ahead – by 2016 it is thought that 30 per cent more beef, 50 per cent more pork and 25 per cent more poultry will be needed just for developing nations.

We don't actually need all this meat – we can get the protein, vitamins and minerals we require from smaller amounts, and/or from other foods. But we have become used to it.

However, whether meat is mass farmed, organic, biodynamic, imported, local or whatever – the fact is that to produce meat is much more wasteful of energy and resources than to produce non-animal food.

So is meat red for Stop and are vegetables green for Go? Well – nearly. Let me list the reasons why.

Beef cattle have each to eat around 7kg of food to produce one quarterpounder beefburger for us to eat. Around 30 per cent of the surface of the world's land is taken up in providing food for the livestock that we eat. Half the world's wheat and 80 per cent of the corn that is not grown for brewing or biofuels is for livestock feed. According to United Nations research, in addition it takes nearly 20 litres of drinking water to produce that quarterpounder. And it takes 35 calories of fossil fuel to produce one calorie of meat. Thus it seems clear that it is much more efficient to use land to grow crops directly for humans to eat.

Meat and dairy production also cause huge environmental impact through soil erosion (due mainly to overgrazing and hooves), water pollution and other factors. The world's livestock (including 1.5 billion cattle) cause 18 per cent of total greenhouse-gas emissions – partly due to their production of methane and nitrous oxide (from front and rear ends), which amounts to more than all the world's cars, planes and other transport put together. Methane has twenty times more powerful a global-warming impact than carbon dioxide. In the UK, agriculture accounts for 67 per cent of nitrous oxide and 37 per cent of methane emissions.

The production of pork meat, it has been found, uses less energy than beef (no. 1) or lamb/mutton (no. 2), chicken and eggs uses less again – but even so, these animal products still require more energy and land and have a greater environmental impact than plant sources of human food. Indeed, fish caught from the seas can be an energy-intensive food – fish caught by beam trawling being the worst method.

The message is that, across the world, and especially in Western and fast-developing countries, we need to cut back on our meat and dairy consumption.

NUTRITION AND MEAT

- Your daily protein requirements can be met with a bowl of lentil soup, two slices of wholemeal bread, a handful of nuts, a portion of peas and a selection of other grains and green vegetables.

- Plant protein can be of as good a quality as meat or dairy protein. Plants that provide protein also provide other valuable nutrients, including essential fats and fibre.

- A high red- and processed-meat intake can be a contributing factor in health problems, including osteoporosis and cancer. Vegetarians live longer and are less likely to suffer from obesity.

WHAT TO DO

- Eat much less meat – particularly beef – and dairy, less chicken and fewer eggs, and eat more plant foods, such as pulses, nuts and seeds, and a moderate amount of fish. Some vegetarians eat a great deal of dairy produce which, as we've seen, is less environmentally friendly than a diet which contains more plant sources of protein and calories and a little meat/fish.

- 1–2 medium portions of meat a week is a good goal for which meat-lovers could aim. Another idea is to have 2–3 small portions a week as a constituent of composite meals such as casseroles, stir-fries or curries which also contain vegetables/pulses/grains/nuts/seeds. The recipes in this book will give you ideas.

- When you do buy beef, lamb or mutton, try to buy meat from pasture-grazed animals. Grazing can help support the biodiversity of the land. Organic livestock is often allowed to graze the fields and can eat no more than 40 per cent concentrated feed; and Welsh lambs (organic or non-organic) will usually have a traditional diet of grass for much of the time. If we all did this, as well as eating much less meat altogether, demand for grain-fed livestock would be reduced and a much higher percentage of the world's remaining livestock could be raised on grass, thus drastically reducing soil erosion and the need for artificial fertilizers. Grain, pulses and vegetables could then be grown for humans on the land previously used for livestock feed. As a further benefit, meat from pasture-fed livestock and the eggs of free-to-roam hens contain higher levels of vital omega-3 fats (found today mostly in oily fish) and would be a useful source to take the pressure off the world's fish stocks; it also contains less saturated fat and less cholesterol.

- If you have a garden and love eggs and chicken, consider having laying hens and table birds of your own.

- When increasing the amount of fruits and vegetables that you eat, choose with care – eat more root crops and brassicas, indigenous fruits such as apples and pears, and try not to increase your consumption of hothouse fruits and vegetables or luxury imported soft fruits which don't store well. Imported bananas, apples and citrus fruits are a better choice.

EXPERIMENTS IN ECO-DIETS

Experimenters at the University of Wales Institute, Cardiff, set about trying to design a diet to be as environmentally friendly as possible. Said Dr Ruth Fairchild, food and consumer science programme director at UWIC's Cardiff School of Health Sciences, 'We devised a vegetarian diet ... [but] we decided not to go further with this as we found that [it] had a higher ecological impact – due mainly to the amount of cheese in the diet.' The 'ecodiet' that the team finally devised – high in plant foods (but nevertheless containing some chicken, eggs, milk, yogurt and alcohol) and low on packaging – managed to reduce the total domestic footprint figure by almost 40 per cent and the total food and drink footprint by 26.1 per cent.

And in one Swedish report for *Food Policy* journal, researcher Annika Carlsson found that a meal containing both meat and indigenous vegetables was less greenhouse-gas intensive than a fully vegetarian meal made up of 'exotic' (imported) vegetables.

- Because vegetables and fruits are one of the largest food imports into the UK, it is important to try to encourage vegetable-growing in your area – support your local markets; press councils for more allotment space and get one yourself; dig up the flowerbeds – if you grow your own, you exercise your body naturally without having to use up both resources getting to the gym and energy while you are there.

- As a population, perhaps we also need to persuade the government to put more funding into schemes to help people start up market-gardening enterprises, or convert from livestock to fruit-growing, for example.

ORGANIC PRODUCTION AND ENERGY USE

Research carried out by the Soil Association using MAFF/Defra studies has found that organically produced British beef uses 35 per cent less energy than non-organic, while organic sheep use 20 per cent less energy and pig meat 13 per cent less. Organic poultry production, however, uses 32 per cent more energy and organic egg production 14 per cent more.

Healthy eating versus endangered fish

We are told we must eat more fish – especially oily fish – for our health and in order to live a longer life. But if we all obeyed the edict to get around 2–3 portions of fish a week, the seas around the British Isles would pretty soon run out of stock.

Our waters are so overfished, particularly of certain species such as cod, that we need to conserve our wild seafood, not eat it all up. No wonder there has been a tremendous growth in the amount of farmed fish that we eat: around a third of fish and seafood eaten worldwide is now from fish farms – but these can also have a negative environmental impact.

WHAT TO PUT ON YOUR PLATE

The following list, based on information from the Marine Conservation Society (MCS) and Greenpeace, provides a guide to the 'greenest' types of fish to choose, on environmental and health grounds, and to those species you should try to avoid.

MSC = Marine Stewardship Council

Green-light fish:

best choices

White fish
Line-caught Pacific cod
Line-caught Cornish sea bass
Oily fish
MSC-certified herring from British waters
MSC-certified Alaskan Pacific salmon
Shellfish
Pot-caught Devon brown crab
Clams
Welsh cockles
Sustainably harvested or rope-grown
	mussels
Sustainably harvested or farmed native
	oysters
MSC-certified Californian or Australian
	lobster
Dive-caught scallops

Amber-light fish:

next best choices

White fish
MSC-certified Alaska or walleye pollock
Cornish or Welsh sea bream
Farmed, organic Atlantic cod
Coley
Dab
Flounder
MSC-certified line-caught Pacific halibut
Cornish line-caught pollock
Red mullet (other than from
    Mediterranean)
Farmed tilapia
Whiting from English Channel

Oily fish
Line-caught MSC-certified Cornish
    mackerel
Traditionally harvested European sardines
    or pilchards
Organic farmed Atlantic salmon
Organic farmed brown, sea or rainbow
    trout
Dolphin-friendly handline- or troll-
    caught albacore, yellowfin or skipjack
    tuna

Shellfish
Sustainably harvested or farmed scampi,
Dublin Bay prawn, langoustine from
    north-western UK waters
Pot-caught spider crab
Hand-picked winkles

Red-light fish:

avoid these types

White fish
Wild Atlantic cod
Dover sole
European eel
Haddock
North Sea brill
Southern European hake
Wild Atlantic halibut
Greenland halibut
Trawl-caught sea bass
Monkfish
Plaice from overfished stocks
Shark
Skate/ray
Snapper
Swordfish (except from US-managed
    fisheries)
Wild North Sea turbot
European hake

Oily fish
Bay of Biscay anchovies
Wild Atlantic salmon
Herring from depleted stocks
Whitebait

Shellfish
Scampi, Dublin Bay prawn, langoustine
    from northern and north-western
    Spain and the Portuguese coast
Tropical farmed and wild prawns (tiger
    prawns)

For more detailed and current information on species, depleted and overfished stocks, visit www.fishonline.org

The MCS also suggests that we should:

- Avoid eating deepwater species such as monkfish, Atlantic halibut and ling, as they are slow to mature and especially vulnerable to overfishing.
- Avoid eating fish during their breeding season (see the chart on pages 92–3 listing fish in season).
- Avoid eating small, undersized fish which have not yet reproduced.

While the MCS endorsements/suggestions are very helpful, they do point up one or two new dilemmas. Is it always best to try to go for fish caught around the British Isles to reduce the food miles your supper has travelled, or is it a good idea to choose fish and shellfish from sustainable fisheries in the waters off countries such as Canada, Australia, South Africa or from the South Pacific? These catches will involve thousands of food miles before they reach your local fish counter, but every time you choose a fish from across the world, you may be helping to increase our own fish stocks.

The answer? A balance of both local (wild and farmed) and imported fish is probably the best solution for the time being.

There is one other problem, which is that it isn't always possible when buying your fish and seafood to find out exactly how it was caught. A glance at the MCS lists shows words such as 'line-caught', 'dive-caught', 'rope-grown' and other terms which are meaningless if you can't find out from asking the fishmonger or reading the label whether or not they apply to the fish you are thinking of purchasing.

Fishing methods which are the least sustainable are beam trawling (used for flat fish like plaice and sole) and dredging (for shellfish on the sea floors). If you can't find out how your fish was caught, the purchase is probably best avoided, as retailers today will almost always use a positive selling point (such as green credentials) to persuade you to buy, if they can. If they're keeping quiet, it's more than likely that the product is not environmentally sound. The price is another way of telling: if it seems inexpensive, give it a miss. These days, if we want good sustainable fish we have to pay for it.

Farmed fish

The problem with fish farming – unless it is managed carefully, responsibly and sustainably (which some fish farmers certainly do) – is that it can pose its own threats to the environment; see page 38. There is also an animal-welfare problem with fish farming, particularly in the case of salmon – fish which in nature don't shoal and spend much time travelling long distances at speed. Farmed cod may be a better bet in this respect, as cod are naturally shoal fish. However, the cod-farming industry in the North Sea has come in for criticism because the fish spend their lives in almost permanent artificial light – a system that ensures they keep feeding and thus grow more quickly. The system also uses more power for the lights than might be considered ethical, and because of this the Soil Association doesn't endorse any farmed cod as organic, even though they may be certified by other organizations.

The fact is, if we want to eat more fish, farming will probably be our only option in the long term; but we need an official watchdog to ensure that farming systems are ethical.

WHAT TO DO

- Choose your fish from the MCS list on pages 106–7.
- Vary your choices as much as possible.
- Have recommended portion sizes (see page 110).
- Avoid small whole fish which are likely to be too young.
- Buy organic, sustainably farmed fish sometimes.
- Farmed mussels, oysters and dive-caught, hand-gathered scallops are good, low-impact produce.
- Instead of wild or farmed salmon, think of getting your healthy oils from herring or mackerel in season.
- Also, get omega-3s from other sources such as leafy green vegetables, flax seeds and oil, hempseed and oil, eggs, pumpkin seeds.
- For more information on reading the labels on fish produce, see Chapter 4, and on where to find good 'green' fish, see 'Fish' in the A–Z.

FACTBOX

The Food Standards Agency recommends that 'people should consume at least two portions of fish a week, of which one should be oily'. If we all follow this recommendation, the UK's fish consumption would rise by more than 40 per cent and our consumption of oily fish would increase by at least 200 per cent.

Portion control versus pigging out

Carlo Petrini of the Slow Food Movement, wise man, says, 'I am a gastronome, not a glutton. Being a gastronome can actually mean eating less, but better.'

Jonathon Porritt, chairman of the British government's Sustainable Development Commission, says, 'On a planet with 9 billion people and really serious constraints on the amount of carbon dioxide and other greenhouse gases that we emit, it's almost inevitable we will learn to have more elegant, satisfying lives, consuming less. I can't see any way out of that ...'*

*From interviews with David Smith and Jasper Gerard of the Observer, *2007*

Eating less is such an easy thing to do and it will actually rid two-thirds of us in this country of the need to stare in the full-length mirror every day and say, 'Oh I'm so fat – I wish I could lose a bit of weight.' If you eat less, you lose weight if you need to. If you're already thin, you're probably not overeating anyway so this section isn't for you (unless you're living on small amounts of rubbish food – in which case, read on).

If you want to eat green – eat less. It makes sense. Food takes resources and energy to produce and creates greenhouse gases. If you eat less food, we save more resources, use less energy and create less greenhouse gas.

A slimmer you weighs less and thus it takes less energy to transport you around by car,

bus, train, plane. You also take away some of the food barons' profits – but never mind. They can afford it. And if their profits begin to plummet then they will put their minds to offering us better-quality food at a fairer (higher) price – and less of it.

If you spend your money on slightly more expensive food where it will do most good – local food, Fairtrade food, organic food, small producers' food – you are ensuring the employment and livelihoods of people following sustainable practices and you are ensuring that the biodiversity of the planet continues. Producing good quality, ethical food takes more manpower, not less (think of the farmhands up to well into the twentieth century who tended the farmer's fields in their dozens to produce the grain; now it takes only one machine to do the old work of hundreds of people) – so anyone Mr Baron makes redundant should find a job in the local community.

And a healthy natural diet should leave you healthier too – which could save our National Health Service a lot of energy and resources, thus helping with greenhouse gases in another way.

WHAT TO DO

- Cut out the rubbish first – the overproduced, mass-market, additive-ridden, unfairly traded, industrialized 'food' whose production often robs the soil and pollutes the rivers. I'm thinking cheap meat and eggs and chickens too – the animals that 'lived' to provide you with this food probably did not live an enjoyable existence and their production used up more energy than you would care to think about.

- Cut out stuff that we know contains few nutrients – the sugar, the mass-produced cakes, biscuits, pastries, pots of desserts, giant bottles of rubbish soft drinks, and so on. This isn't just a healthy-eating issue – it really isn't. You need to feed yourself less food, so you need to make sure that what you do eat has a high nutrient:calorie ratio.

- Choose wholefoods – wholegrains, pulses, vegetables, fruit, nuts, seeds. Add to that small amounts of the animal proteins and then very, very small amounts of what you fancy – maybe wine, chocolate, coffee, tea, home-made cake ...

- Buy organic or carefully produced food whenever you can for its likely higher nutrient content (see Chapter 2).

- Relish your food – enjoy finding or growing it, prepare it with care and love, eat it slowly and savour it. Good food is a gift.

- If you are overweight, also walk or cycle more if you can – that way you will save the planet's energy at the same time as getting fitter and burning off more calories.

Water versus other drinks

The UK's Chartered Institution of Water and Environmental Management says 'Branding and bottling of water where there already exists a wholesome and safe supply of mains drinking water cannot be seen as a sustainable use of natural resources, and adds to the overall levels of waste and pollution to be managed in modern society.'

FACTBOX
- In the UK, bottled-water sales rose 5.8 per cent to 2,275 million litres, in 2006, worth £1,700 million retail. Consumption in 2006 reached 37.6 litres per person. This is a 16 per cent share of the UK soft-drinks market.
- 56 per cent of adults in the UK regularly drank bottled water in 2006 compared with 40 per cent in 2001.
- Britain imports about 30 per cent of its bottled water. (Defra)
- Fewer than 20 per cent of plastic water bottles are recycled.

Zenith International, UK Bottled Water report

While water is the best drink you can choose both for the environment and for your waistline, bottled water is, environmentally, pretty much a disaster. This is because of factors including the energy cost of getting it out of the ground, making the bottles, bottling it, transporting it, then disposing of the bottles (for more on packaging materials, see Chapter 4).

It's also a rather depression-inducing fact that the water-bottling industry is largely controlled by multinationals – so the vast profits from selling bottled water are unlikely to be felt much at the water's source.

Some 'ethical' waters are distributed by smaller players and help developing nations – for example One, a bottled water whose sale buys playpumps in developing villages to collect water. But these schemes still encourage the purchase of bottled water – and that, whichever way you look at it, isn't good.

Tap water in the UK is among the safest and purest in the world – and often has quite a nice taste, especially if cold. An average cost comparison by Yorkshire Water of a litre of bottled water with a litre of tap water finds that bottled water costs up to 10,000 times as much.

ALTERNATIVE DRINKS

- Making hot drinks uses energy to boil water.

- Keeping drinks cold uses energy; making ice cubes uses energy. Although neither you nor I is going to give up our hot or our ice-cold drinks, bear in mind the energy-saving principles outlined in Chapter 5.

- Coffee – only a small percentage of the coffee bought worldwide is Fairtrade.

- Tea – buy Fairtrade tea: loose tea is less energy-intensive than teabags. As an alternative, try British-produced teas using indigenous herbs such as lemon balm and mint.

- Sugary drinks, such as colas and squash, contribute a high amount to greenhouse-gas emissions and have also been linked with obesity, dental and other problems. Best to avoid.

- Juice – it takes around sixteen oranges to produce a litre of pure juice, and 22 litres of water in production. It also takes around 900 litres of water for irrigation. Eighty per

FACTBOX
Most water bottles are made of polyethylene terephthalate (PET), and 27 million tonnes of plastic are used each year worldwide to make water bottles. Every year 22 million tonnes of bottled water are transported between countries, resulting in many thousands of tonnes of greenhouse-gas emissions.

cent of orange juice drunk in Europe comes from Brazil. For every tonne consumed at least 25 tonnes of materials are used up. The whole fruit plus a glass of tap water would probably be a better idea.

- Alcohol – European wine producers are throwing away up to 15 per cent of all the wine they produce, while we import new world wines from Chile, Australia and so on. What kind of sense does that make? Beer and whisky – we know how to make it in the UK; if you can, seek out small local producers.

For more information on individual drinks, see the A–Z.

WHAT TO DO

- Make your own blackcurrant juice or elderflower cordial (see recipe on page 199). If you drink bought juice, look at the label and try to buy British-made juice, such as blackcurrant or apple.

- Drink tap water when you can. If there's room in the fridge, you can chill it during the summer if you like.

- Using a water filter may improve the flavour and take away any worries (probably unnecessary) that you have about impurities.

- Fill up a re-usable lightweight waterproof container with tap water and take that with you when you go out and about. The same with children's lunch boxes.

- If you must buy bottled, buy from a local spring/company and recycle or re-use the bottles.

- If there is no other choice available, buy an 'ethical' brand such as One.

- Limit your consumption of hot drinks and buy Fairtrade chocolate, coffee and tea.

- Buy local alcohol for preference – cider, beer, British perry and wine. In many areas of the UK you can find truly local drinks – local farm cider or perry, and beers from local breweries (often sold in health-food shops, local delis and off-licences). But note that beers from the major brewers who control much of the UK market may have travelled up to 24,000 miles in production and transportation. Otherwise, choose European wines from France, Spain or Italy rather than from the southern hemisphere or California, and beers from Scandinavia or Germany rather than from Japan or India.

Conclusion

In her report *Wise Moves*, Tara Garnett comments:
'We are paying less and less for environmentally damaging food that we have less and less time to eat. A low carbon food system will ultimately look very different from the one we have at present, and will require us all to rethink many of our core assumptions about shopping and consuming. Eventually, however, change we must. The existing system cannot deliver the greenhouse gas reductions that we desperately need to achieve at the rate we need to achieve them. And despite the quality, the diversity, the abundance and the affordability of the vast range of foods on offer it may be that the system as it stands does not, ultimately, fulfil our needs.'

SORTING OUT PRIORITIES

This is a code devised by me which is similar to, but not the same as, the one used by 'locavores' (see page 77).

- If you can, buy seasonal, organic, local food.
- If not, buy seasonal, organic food from other areas of the UK.

- If not, buy seasonal, local, non-organic food.

- If not, buy seasonal, non-organic food from other areas of the UK.

- If not, buy local non-organic food.

- If not, buy fairly traded imported organic.

- If not, buy non-hothouse, shipped, imported organic, in season in the country of origin.

- In general, buy imported products only if they are not available here and are things that you regard as a vital part of your larder (e.g. most spices, citrus fruits, lentils, bananas, coffee, tea).

If you can, follow this code at least most of the time – then you can forgive yourself for the out-of-season, non-Fairtrade berries that somehow slipped into your shopping basket.

4 Ethical Shopping

'EACH TIME WE PURCHASE FOOD, WE ARE NOT ONLY DECIDING WHAT PRODUCTS WE BUY, BUT WE ALSO SUPPORT A FORM OF AGRICULTURE WHICH AFFECTS OUR HEALTH, OUR WELLBEING AND THE FOOD INDUSTRY ITSELF.'

Jeanette Longfield, co-ordinator of Sustain, the alliance for better food and farming, 2007

Reading the media you'd think that many of us had already forsaken the supermarkets to shop in local artisans' stores and farmers' markets. And there's even research to back this up.

Over 50 per cent of Britons are becoming ethical shoppers, paying more attention to where their food comes from, according to the latest shopper research from food and grocery expert IGD. Ethical shopping covers products such as Fairtrade, organic, free-range and environmentally friendly.

The biggest group of ethical shoppers – 33 per cent – buys products that support their beliefs, 15 per cent boycott products they feel strongly about, and 4 per cent buy ethical products because they think it's fashionable.

The ethical proportion of the average shopping basket has been growing, and sales of ethical products are increasing at 7.5 per cent per year, compared with 4.2 per cent for conventional products.

But although the number of people visiting the smaller outlets is growing by a few per cent a year, and when surveyed consumers say that this type of shopping is a good idea, around 95 per cent of us still shop regularly at the supermarket – a fact borne out by research conducted by YouGov for Farma (see right).

In the IGD research, only 16 per cent of adults had visited a farmers' market in the past year, only 21 per cent a farm shop, 21 per cent an organic or health-food store, and only 46 per cent a greengrocer.

According to IGD, 36 per cent of adults visit a supermarket more than once a week. And according to ActionAid, every week in Britain 32 million people shop in supermarkets.

The figures mean that what we feel and think is not the same as what we do. When we do choose to buy 'green', we still prefer to use the supermarkets to *do* it.

*The facts and figures in this section come from the IGD report Tomorrow's Shopping World, 2006.

WHERE DO WE SHOP FOR FOOD?

SUPERMARKET 98%

CONVENIENCE STORE 31%

VILLAGE SHOP 25%

FARMERS' MARKET 12%

HOME DELIVERY 10%

DELICATESSEN 9%

Main shopping and other shopping; YouGov poll for Farma

How green are the supermarkets?

But can the supermarkets ever be green – or is small-shop local shopping the only way to go? Let's take a closer look.

Tom McMillan, editor of *Food Ethics* magazine, has questioned the ability of the supermarkets to become truly ethical:

'The big players are cleaning up their act, but can they do enough? Could we ever shop loyally at a supermarket chain – and be the kind of customer they need us to be – yet also buy on fair terms for workers and live within the planet's means?'

Meanwhile Alla Heeks, (of the box-scheme pioneers Abel & Cole, comments: 'All businesses exist to meet consumer demand as best they can with the resources available. Supermarkets have done this brilliantly for some time. Now the nature of the demand and the resources available are changing dramatically. Supermarkets are badly positioned to handle these changes. Their supply chains and infrastructure have evolved to serve a different purpose, in a different context.'

For several decades, supermarkets have relied on an energy-intensive supply chain which has largely disregarded environmental concerns – from the industrial agriculturalists with which they have done business to their methods of transport. But in response to the consumer wish for greener shopping (and also to the fact that a trendy green image makes excellent sense for business and profits; for example, ASDA's savings on energy will save the store £500,000 per annum), the supermarkets are finally falling over themselves to provide us with a more ethical experience when we buy our food. We like this because we can salvage our green conscience without having to drag round dozens of different local shops and without having to pay too much in the way of premium prices.

And it is true that, used in the right way, the supermarkets' powerful position should allow them to help make very positive changes in how and what we eat, and to educate us to make the right choices naturally. Their position in the marketplace should enable them to bring sustainability to all consumers, not just to the well-off, enlightened few. Tesco, for example, says that customers 'want our help to do more in the fight against climate change'. But can we truly trust the supermarkets to police their own environmental footprint?

Some of the ways in which the big stores are addressing the green issues are: offering more Fairtrade products; reducing food packaging and plastic bags; labelling foods with air/food miles, or at least saying if they are air-freighted; offering more local produce for sale;

offering 'seconds' that might otherwise have been dumped; offering a good choice of organic produce; selling only sustainable fish. Behind the scenes they are using renewable energy, recycling materials and so on, and making sure through ads and PR agencies that we all know about it.

All our major UK supermarkets increase the amount of organic food they stock each year, and also so far have managed to increase the proportion of British organic that they sell – so much so that, for instance, both Waitrose and M&S managed to source 89 per cent of their organic food from UK producers, and Sainsbury's 86 per cent, according to the latest Soil Association shopping survey.

There is also an abundance of labels offering some kind of promise of decent food – Freedom Food, LEAF, Red Tractor; for a breakdown of what these actually mean, see page 139.

THE TOP SUPERMARKETS – WHICH IS GREENEST?

So it's 'green wars' as each retailer battles to be first to wear a carbon-neutral halo. Which supermarket should you choose? Let's have a look at some of the things each company is doing ...

Tesco

● In March 2006, Tesco outlined a ten-point Community Plan and in January 2007 set out their plan 'to deliver a revolution in green consumption'. This basically covered issues from carbon-footprint labelling on foods, to cuts in their own CO_2 emissions, wider choices of 'green' foods, energy savings on packaging and use of CHP (see page 89) for in-store energy.

- They have also promised to encourage more organic production from their suppliers, to source more locally, to restrict air transport to less than 1 per cent of products and increase rail haulage.

- They pledge to reduce the carbon footprint of their existing stores and distribution centres around the world by 50 per cent by 2020.

- They have their own 'nature's choice' farm management and environmental standards scheme which covers all of their 12,000 growers.

ASDA

- In October 2005 Wal-Mart and their UK subsidiary, ASDA, committed to initiatives that included sending zero waste to landfill by 2010, sourcing all their energy from renewables, and selling more sustainable and local products.

- They have an internal cardboard-recycling league table and have promised to cut packaging on own-label food and sell more loose food. They are trialling a scheme to provide bins in the shop foyers for custom-

ers to dump surplus packing, and give suppliers advice on how to reduce their packaging.

- They have been working to develop their rail-freight capacity, and for three years have been using rail to move food from south-coast ports to northern depots, which, they say, saves 4.5 million road miles a year.

- Wal-Mart announced in 2006 that it would switch to sourcing all its wild-caught fish from MSC-certified sources over the next 3–5 years.

Sainsbury's

- In 2007, Sainsbury's were voted greenest supermarket in the Independent Greenest Companies awards, and ranked seventh greenest company in Britain, for work on organic produce, commitment to sustainable fishing and local sourcing. They also won an Ethical Award from the *Observer* magazine for the launch of compostable packaging.

- Sainsbury's has made big sustainability commitments and said in 2007 that environmental and ethical issues are core business drivers for them.

- They describe themselves as the UK's leading Fairtrade trader. All their bananas are Fairtrade. In 2007 they launched Fair Development Fund with £1 million over four years to help producers in some of the world's poorest countries to join Fairtrade.

- They removed all carrier bags from the checkouts for a day and promoted the use of re-usable bags by giving them away free to customers.

- They have various initiatives to promote British organic farming, such as 'Farm Promise' milk, helping British farmers convert to organic standards.

- In 2007, they announced plans to convert 20 per cent of their online delivery fleet to green electric vehicles.

Waitrose

- Waitrose pledged in summer 2007 to sell only organic or LEAF Marque (see page 140) fresh and frozen produce by 2010.

- All their beef, pork and chicken is British.

- They came joint top on the MCS's league table because of their commitment to sourcing fish from responsibly managed fisheries.

- In 2006 Waitrose started selling Class 2 fruit in its stores – that is, produce that is perfectly edible but because it is misshapen, the wrong colour or size does not qualify as Class 1. For years this produce has not been available in any UK supermarket.

- They stock over 1,300 organic product lines and are committed to sourcing organic products, whenever possible, from within the UK.

- They sell only Fairtrade bananas.

- Waitrose say they have reduced packaging consumption by 33 per cent relative to sales since 2000.

- They have introduced customer recycling points for plastic bags in all shops.

Marks & Spencer

- In March 2006 Marks & Spencer published their green 'Plan A', which includes a commitment to tripling sales of organic food, cutting waste, selling significantly more Fairtrade and organic products, and making the company carbon neutral within five years. In the same month they switched all their tea and coffee to Fairtrade.

- In January 2007 they committed to sell only MCS-certified fish by 2012.

- They have launched air-freight labels on fresh produce and keep GM out of the ingredients in their products.

- They signed up to take 10 per cent of total energy from renewable sources from April 2004.

- They have cut packaging and use only free-range or organic meat.

Morrisons

- Morrisons works closely with British farmers and growers in supplying their fresh food. When in season, 100 per cent of carrots, broccoli, swede and cauliflower are British, as are 90 per cent of onions, potatoes and mushrooms.

- They support a variety of local and small suppliers. For example, in Welsh stores there are 230 locally sourced products.

- They 'seek to ensure our own-brand products and the ingredients that go into them are produced as responsibly as possible, and we have specific policies that cover raw materials, sustainable seafood sourcing and animal welfare.'

- In 2007 they introduced a labelling scheme (Recylopedia) to help increase awareness of what can be recycled and where.

- In 2007 they opened the first of their environmentally friendly BioEthanol E85 filling pumps at Morrisons petrol stations.

Co-op

- This group has, arguably, been the UK's biggest supporter of fair trade since 1992 – the year the Fairtrade Foundation was established and the Co-op began retailing Cafédirect coffee.

- Voted greenest high-street retailer in 2007 by *The Money Programme*, releasing £324 worth of carbon for every £1 million turnover, compared with £1,194 for the worst retailer.

FISH FROM OUR SUPERMARKETS

Waitrose and Marks & Spencer are placed jointly at the top of the annual MCS League Table. Both companies are strongly committed to sustainability and have a reputation for selling only fish from responsibly managed fisheries. Tesco and Sainsbury's are placed third and fourth respectively.

Marks & Spencer, Waitrose and Morrisons all have the distinction of not selling any fish from the MCS list of fish to avoid. Waitrose sells the greatest number of fish from the MCS fish to eat list (26 species), followed by Morrisons (22 species) and Tesco (20 species).

The Marine Conservation Society Sustainable Supermarket Survey, 2007

- During 2005, 98 per cent of the electricity supplying the Co-op was sourced from renewable sources – wind, hydro and biomass technologies. This makes the Co-op one of the largest purchasers of green electricity in the world.

- The group introduced Britain's first degradable plastic carrier bag in 2002 and was subsequently the first retailer to introduce these materials into mainstream grocery packaging.

- Has won the Queen's Award for Sustainable Development for initiatives including its eco-friendly packaging, Fairtrade principles and recycling.

From that little list, it seems obvious that each one is making a huge effort to outgreen all the others and it's hard to choose a clear winner. But not everybody is convinced of the true greenness underlying these pledges and claims. One obvious problem is that most of the promises are just that – promises which just might not all come true. And another is that, although there is fanfare about the issues each supermarket is dealing with, the fact that there is still much room for improvement may be easy to overlook.

Anyway, let's have a look at the issues that are clouding the horizon ...

A DIFFERENT KIND OF SUPERMARKET...
US-owned Whole Foods Market has, with its wholefood superstore in west London, begun an assault on the UK market. Started in 1980 in Texas by a cooperative of farmers, it now has 43,000 workers and sales of £2.8 billion per annum.

Despite the claim that they source locally whenever possible, research carried out in 2007 by the BBC revealed that many of their items have travelled hundreds or even thousands of miles. Also, despite the perception that everything they sell is organic, that isn't the case.

A QUESTION OF CHOICE...

While there is much more choice in the average supermarket than anywhere else, some people say that, in fact, by holding a virtual monopoly, they really take away our freedom of choice and this is not a particularly green attribute. There is a feeling that, should their power be allowed to grow even more and if eventually there really are no small shops left, then we would have *no* choice but to shop for food with them. The only ways we can prevent this from happening are by supporting the small shopkeeper and by the government and local councils intervening to stop, for example, more massive out-of-town stores.

But on the subject of choice itself, there has been a recent backlash: how ethical is it to have too many foods to choose from?

Tara Garnett, in her *Wise Moves* report on food transport, writes:

Curbs on the consumers' right to choose are seen to be not just uncommercial, but undesirable. The truth is, however, that if we are to see major reductions in greenhouse gas emissions from our food system, then something will have to give and that something is likely to be the dazzling array of choice that we currently enjoy. But while a little bit of what we fancy does us good, we might question whether more is better still. Measures to discourage 'season creep' might be helpful, and only a minor infringement of the Inalienable right of everyone to eat anything, anytime, anywhere.

Some of the ways she proposes to achieve this are to price foods to reflect the environmental damage they cause – meaning that the supermarkets would need to increase prices on some of the very items that are currently the cheapest (cheap meat, cheese, imports from the Far East, for example); informing people of the environmental and ethical issues (the supermarkets do this up to a point but could certainly do a lot more);

FACTBOX
In 2007, Tesco 'localchoice' milk was found to come from up to 150 miles away. Sold in Hereford, the 'Heart of England' milk had been produced in Lincolnshire and Derbyshire.

making it attractive for people to eat more responsibly (again that is happening up to a point, if attractive equals being made to feel good about one's purchases); providing sufficient quantities of lower-carbon foods so that they are readily available to buy (again, inroads are being made but there remains much, much more to be done).

CHOICE AND THE SUPERMARKETS

'An influential report called *I will if you will*, published in 2006 by the Sustainable Consumption Roundtable, concluded that the supermarkets need to make the right choices much easier for people to take. In this spirit, they are doing more and more 'choice editing' on fair trade, organics and climate change.'
Tom Berry, in *Food Ethics* magazine, 2007

In the meantime, a visit to any large British supermarket reveals, before you are even halfway down the first aisle, that Choice is still king. But most of this is not the choice between, say, an ethical coffee and a non-ethical coffee, or even two brands of ethical coffee – but plain old choice between fifty different kinds of biscuit just because we still like to have the option of oat cookies with choc chips, oat cookies with sultanas, oat cookies with cherries, oat cookies with almonds, oat cookies with hazelnuts, or oat cookies plain. And then we like a choice of oat cookies cheap, oat cookies medium priced, and oat cookies 'the very best' (and therefore the most expensive).

Try to count all the different lines of cakes, or chilled desserts, or jars of sauces ... it's nearly impossible.

Remove all the packaging and brand names and you would probably be hard-pressed, in all honesty, to tell the difference between a lot of them.

The supermarkets have long realized that the more choice we have, the more we will eat and the more we will buy, and it remains to be seen whether or not they will go down this particular ethical route and narrow our choice for the sake of the planet.

We, the manufacturers, the retailers – we are our own vicious circle. And actually, in this case, I think that the first move could well come from us, the consumers. We have to recognize that we don't need all this choice and all this plenty. It's not doing us any good.

A smaller range of products in each food category would mean less energy consumption in every way: in the food growth, manufacture, transport, packaging, and in our energy too.

So much choice can create, literally, a 'spoilt for choice' mentality that has us ever seeking more new lines and trying different brands, flavours and formulas. Barry Schwartz, US author of *The Paradox of Choice,* believes that too much choice actually makes us more dissatisfied, not less.

And many people are realizing that they find too much choice problematic. Like too much information, it's 'one more hassle' in their lives – myriads of small decisions to be made, even before you can have a cup of tea. Breakfast? Afternoon? Green? White? Black? Indian? China? Ceylon? Loose? Bag? Large box, small box, two for one or just the one, half price? These decisons are, let's face it, unimportant at every level. Looking back at the 1950s and 1960s, or before that – or even after that – I don't recall everyone wearing long faces and having suicidal tendencies because they couldn't find asparagus in the middle of winter, or because there were only four different sorts of biscuit on the shelf. Let's stop worrying about food choice or hankering after it. Behavioural research shows that humans easily adjust to new circumstances and if less choice is available, I feel certain, we won't all become miserable human beings; we'll simply adapt.

ETHICAL TRADING

While the supermarkets are keen to promote their Fairtrade ethics, all may not be quite as it seems on that front. The international anti-poverty campaigning charity ActionAid, in its report *Who Pays?*, describes several scenarios where food workers still have atrocious working conditions and pay, including Costa

Rican banana-plantation workers on 33 pence an hour and cashew-nut processors in India on 30 pence a day. The report comments:

> While there are isolated examples of good practice, it is increasingly clear that supermarkets will not deliver the widespread improvements that are needed unless they are given more of a push by government. We want to see an independent regulator established to monitor the relationships between supermarkets and their suppliers, ensuring that supermarkets do not abuse their dominant position.

> If more of the millions of pounds we spend every day in supermarkets flowed back to the workers who produce what we buy, the very act of shopping could become a tool for poverty reduction.

Sadly, for all the supermarkets' ethical talk, 99 per cent of the coffee and bananas that we buy are still not fairly traded.

Back in the UK, where supermarket/suppliers wars have been well documented for years, not everyone agrees that the supermarkets are not improving. Andrew Fearne, Director of the Centre for Supply Chain Research, Kent Business School, University of Kent, wrote in 2007:

> the reality is that ... the unethical abuse of buying power ... is rapidly becoming the exception to the rule in many, if not most, of our supermarket supply chains, as supermarkets finally wake up to the damage that behaviour of this kind does to their business and the benefits to be gained from developing strategic relationships with key suppliers.

> The fact is that supermarkets are a dominant force in retail food supply chains the world over and the behaviour of supermarket buyers in many countries leaves a lot to be desired – they're no angels! However, the best UK supermarkets are light years ahead of the best in other countries in terms of how they work to develop collaborative relationships with suppliers who are willing and able to invest in building strategic relationships with them. We shouldn't confuse a few cases of unethical behaviour, with a systemic abuse of power designed to rip the heart out of British agriculture – after all, supermarkets have a vested interest in building a sustainable food and farming industry in this country.

So which point of view is correct? Well, they both are. There is still a lot of room for improvement – and again, the sooner we consumers realize that cheap food from abroad and from home pays its price, the sooner we will be happy to pay more for our food ... on condition that the supermarkets make their profit margins transparent so that we can see that it is they, as well as us, who pay. And how could supermarkets still make their healthy profits while selling fewer goods? Well, if we pay more for less, they will make as much on less.

WASTE

Just as too much choice leads to overconsumption, overconsumption leads to waste. And there is much evidence that just as we waste a third of the food that we buy, the supermarkets waste a lot of the food that *they* buy – or, at least, earmark. This can happen because, of course, much food by its nature is perishable and doesn't last for ever. While the buyers in the head offices and branches of all the supermarkets receive an excellent salary for attempting to minimize overordering and for anticipating exactly what the consumer will want to buy tomorrow and next year, the fact is that they do make mistakes and so a huge amount of food gets wasted.

And the waste starts right at grower/producer level.

The Food Climate Research Network found that:

> growers overproduce so that they can provide supermarkets with continuity of supply. The surplus is often left in the fields and this evidently represents a waste ... clearly the underlying cause of the waste is our and/or supermarkets' expectation that products should be consistently and ubiquitously available. This means that supply has to be able to meet demand whatever the fluctuations and vagaries of that demand and of other factors. In other words, the waste has less to do with technology than with today's marketing, retailing and consumption systems.

Anyone who grows their own produce at home knows that there will always be a proportion of the crop that is less than perfect, but most of the supermarkets demand from their suppliers consistency of appearance in, for example, fruit and vegetables. They blame us, saying that we expect uniformity and for our purchases to look nice. Pre-packing is another reason for demanding uniform size. If apples, for example, are sold in a tray of four, they obviously have to fit the tray, not too large or too small. And with pre-weighing it's a similar story.

Thus the 'runts, misshapens and misfits' never make the shops (though see page 122 for Waitrose's policy on Class 2 fruit). The rejects may be left on the ground or tree to rot, as producers/growers find that attempting to find alternative buyers for such produce is more costly in terms of time and effort than it is worth – although occasional use may be found for them by local shops and factories. Harvesting by machinery, and then washing and polishing by machinery (usually carried out by the supermarket contractors) also damages a high proportion of produce, creating yet more waste. But *when* did we ever go to the supermarket bosses and demand perfectly formed produce all of exactly the same size? I can't think of one person who would do that. I think it has always been more to do with convenience and marketing ploys for the stores themselves.

In direct-marketing systems such as box schemes, farmers' markets and so forth, waste levels are very low and the amount of produce grown that is actually sold is very high. This mainly reflects a greater acceptance of imperfections by their customers, and a higher use of hand labour for harvesting.

While fresh fruit and vegetables are an obvious example of the way supermarkets waste food, because of their fragility and perishability other foods are lost every day in several ways:

- 'Sell by' dates mean that food has to be discarded even if it is actually still perfectly edible. The habit of 'freeganing' (raiding supermarket waste bins at the end of the day for free food) has gained popularity because of this. While some supermarkets have a 'reduced-price' corner or shelves to sell off as much of this produce as they can, others, such as Marks & Spencer, don't, feeling that cut-price goods aren't the right image for them. Some stores try to offload nearly out-of-date food on local charities, which is at least something.

- Damaged in transit. High food mileage means food spoiling is inevitable and, ironically, if packaging (which helps to protect food) is reduced this may increase the problems.

- In-store difficulties such as fridge and freezer breakdowns, breakages, damage and so on inevitably cause waste.

Obviously small shops get waste too, but in green terms supermarket waste is a bigger issue simply because it is virtually an accepted part of the system and its costs can be absorbed by the stores. For smaller outlets waste has a more direct impact on profit and so may be controlled more tightly.

Supermarket or the small shop?

'It seems far-fetched to expect from [the supermarkets] any form of green or ethical strategy that will seriously dint their profits. They'll just cherry-pick the bits that work for their own bottom-line, and that ultimately isn't enough. So it's up to us to by-pass supermarkets in favour of the rewards and pressures of alternative ways of food shopping. In effect, we need to shop as citizens, not just as consumers. That's a tricky juggling act, but shifts in transport policies, planning and economic regulation could make it a whole lot easier.'

Kate Soper, Professor, Institute for the Study of European Transformation, London Metropolitan University, 2007

'A supermarket can fill its shelves with products whose embedded carbon, natural resource use and pollution footprint have not been considered. But so can a small, local shop.'

Alan Knight, in *Food Ethics* magazine, 2007

Whichever way you look at it, the huge national and global power of the supermarkets has changed the way we shop and the way we live – and probably there is no way back even if we want there to be.

For example, fifty years ago there used to be a large network of wholesale markets in the UK, at which small retailers would purchase their supplies. Now, because the supermarkets and their regional distribution centres purchase direct from 'their' suppliers, the number of wholesale markets has shrunk and looks set to continue to shrink. Without them,

it will be hardly possible for the independents to access supplies and survive.

And as we have seen, as the buying power of the supermarkets is so great, the independents can't possibly compete on price (or on choice – though that may not be such a bad thing).

Twelve thousand independent food stores have either been closed in the past six years or bought out by the big supermarkets, according to Competition Commission figures. All we can do is try to keep alive the best of the small shops and producers that we still do have, not just by appreciating them, but actually by patronizing them regularly – practising 'localism'. As we saw at the start of this chapter, what we feel and what we do too often seem to be two very different things.

If we don't use our local independents, this, according to the Parliamentary Small Shops Group, is what might happen:

- The vast array of skills demonstated by specialist retailers will be lost to the UK economy.

- The environment will suffer in terms of increased road and air miles, resulting in greater congestion, additional need for road-transport infrastructure, noise pollution and air pollution accelerating climate change.

- Regular social contact will be lost for certain members of the community, thereby entrenching social exclusion.

- Access to affordable, healthy food will deteriorate as the geographic spread of shops becomes more concentrated.

- Lower earners and immobile people will suffer the most, with a widening of inequali-ties in terms of health, low access to important products, and fewer local employment opportunities.

- Local economies will be severely damaged across the country as consumer spending by residents goes to national retailers rather than to local businesses.

And the supermarkets – having realized that there is indeed a growing interest in local products – are unlikely to miss another opportunity to plug a gap in the market; indeed they are already plugging it. A survey for the Guild of Fine Foods, which represents 25 per cent of delicatessens and farm shops in the UK, revealed that two-thirds of the store owners considered Waitrose to be more of a worry than any other retail chain. The Guild's director, Bob Farrand, said: 'Waitrose actively mimics delis and farm shops with speciality and locally sourced foods, but often at lower prices because of its buying power.' Waitrose is currently planning to double annual sales from £3.7 billion to £8 billion and open more stores across the country.

If the measures the supermarkets are taking do, indeed, help decrease their, and our, carbon footprints, then whatever their motives, it doesn't really matter. What matters is results. But whether increased sales – or increased turnover – can ever marry with true environmental savings is another story.

SMALLER SHOPS – THE PROS AND CONS

If small shops can't compete with the supermarkets on price, what can they offer to the committed green buyer, or indeed to the committed self-interested buyer?

They may sell local produce – but

sometimes it is hard to tell where produce has come from even in a small, one-off local store. Shopping locally isn't the same as sourcing locally. Sourcing locally helps producers, while shopping locally helps the shopkeepers and community.

Local specialists may sell foods you just can't find anywhere else – for example, local cheeses or pies and cakes baked on the premises from locally sourced ingredients.

They may sell better-quality goods – but that isn't necessarily the case. I have found several instances of local shops stocking out-of-date food of all types, fruit and vegetables that were so old that they would have been unlikely to contain any vitamin C, and fish that looked, and smelt, stale. Local is *no* guarantee of quality, so you need to get to know your area, winkle out the good places by asking around, and don't go back to places where the food isn't up to standard.

Local shops may save food miles as far as your shopping trip goes and will be even more ethical if you shop on foot or by cycle and cart. Shopping locally may also save you time – but some researchers have found that it actually takes longer as you may have to go to many shops to buy what would have all been under one roof at the supermarket. And if the food you buy is, indeed, locally sourced, then you will save many food miles. But, as we saw in Chapter 3, research shows that local shops are wasteful of food miles when it comes to deliveries because of smaller loads, non-full vehicles, and other factors.

Local, independent shopping supports the local community. Every £10 spent with a local food independent is worth £25 to the local economy, compared with just £14 when the same amount is spent in a supermarket chain. *

So, the sad truth is that while your small local shops may offer you a selection of delectable, fresh, locally sourced, locally made, carbon-friendly, ethical foods ... they may not. If you are prepared to find and use the best ones, and to spread the word – more customers means not only more income but also more security – then most of them will, hopefully, survive. They also need to help themselves – forming regional cooperatives, perhaps, to organize new supply systems and suitable wholesalers. And they need to stay in tune with changes in the way we eat and shop. The new website localfoodshop.com has recognized both these needs.

Because if the large supermarkets are their major competition – and are likely to remain so – other competitors are snapping at their heels too.

* *Nick Baker MP,* How Green Is Your Supermarket *report, 2004*

Box schemes

Having started little more than a decade ago with just a few forward-thinking local traders delivering boxes of surplus produce to early organic converts, there are now hundreds of box schemes both at local and national level. The best known is probably Able & Cole, no longer a little ethical retailer but a company with a £20 million turnover and a staff of over 200. They – and other box-delivery schemes – now cover not just vegetables and fruit, but also items such as wine, coffee and breakfast cereals. The future Tesco of the green world? Indeed the parameters between 'box scheme' and 'your groceries delivered' are becoming very blurred.

Downsides? Well, some basic vegetable boxes still contain an assortment of items that you can't, individually, choose – you see what turns up. This, if you don't like the contents, could result in waste. Other schemes deliver from a list, which may be available online. Your box will also need someone to be at home to take it in, or a safe (cool) place for it to be left. Boxes can be quite expensive – and the basic veg/fruit organic boxes have perhaps partially been made redundant by the wide range of organic produce available in normal shops. However, if the box contains truly local produce, that is a definite advantage (check whether or not this is the case).

For more information about finding box schemes, see Resources.

Farm shops and markets

Farmers' markets are becoming more widespread and frequent, and farm shops have long been a good source of all kinds of local produce. Again, not all the items for sale in some farm shops will be local, so if that is important to you, you need to check. Farma (see Chapter 2) has one of the most rigorous sets of criteria for its stallholders. The Resources section gives information on locating farm shops and markets. Be warned – buying at farmers' markets isn't the low-cost option you might imagine it to be.

A YouGov survey for the National Farmers Retail and Markets Association (Farma) showed that 30 per cent of the population would like to shop at a farmers' market or farm shop, but only 11 per cent do.

SUPERMARKET VERSUS FARMERS' MARKET:
how much will you pay?   *UK produce, approximate guide only*

	Typical supermarket	Typical farmers' market
Maincrop potatoes, kg	£1.30p	70p
Onions, kg	£1.20p	70p
Broccoli, head	80p	90p
Dessert apples, kg	£1.50p	£1.20p
Fresh broad beans, kg	£2.80p	£1.85p
Wholemeal loaf, large	£1.20p	£2.35p

Online ordering and other deliveries

Online grocery shopping is now worth in excess of £1.6 billion and this will double in five years, forecasters predict.

Because so many different types of trader are offering internet ordering and delivery, it is difficult to give hard facts about how good and how green these methods of shopping actually are. From local box-scheme sites to speciality online stores offering smoked salmon from Scotland, to the big supermarkets able to deliver a whole trolley load at a pre-booked time ... you can take your pick.

You can also order deliveries from some – usually local – grocers, butchers and so on by the old-fashioned method of telephone. Or in the case of milkmen, you can leave your order out with the empty bottles! Now there's a real taste of the past ... a taste which, according to the latest reports, our nationwide 9,500 milkmen and women are helping us to rediscover, partly by selling much more than just milk.

This shopping method certainly saves your own food miles, and your time – but it will only make an overall saving of UK miles if the retailer has an efficient delivery system going so that vans are not travelling empty too much of the time. While it should be more efficient for a store to deliver to several households in one vehicle, recent research found that the decrease in car carbon dioxide emissions was more than outweighed by the increase in emissions from lorries and vans in the same period.

'Virtual reality' shopping may also help reduce the amount you buy if you are a habitual impulse purchaser.

Green shopping tips

Do a big shop for non-perishables and items that will happily store in a dark cupboard for many weeks (such as cereals, rice, pasta, tea, jars, bottles and cans) once a month maximum. If you can, share the trip with a neighbour to make sure the car is full. Also:

- Make smaller frequent trips for fresh items to nearer/local shops.

- Make a list before you go shopping – this will help prevent impulse purchases and later waste in the kitchen.

- If possible, make a menu plan before you make the list – this will help you to order the correct amounts.

- However, if something on your list (e.g. strawberries) turns out to be an imported variety, be prepared to swap for a similar, British-produced fruit instead.

- Also be prepared to stray from the list if a particular product (e.g. a fish or vegetable) seems a good buy.

- Avoid buying a greater amount than you need. Go for loose vegetables, fruits, nuts, etc., if you can. Think of avoiding waste rather than getting 'great value for money'

– a 5kg bag of apples is not good value for you or the planet if most of them go rotten.

- Buy items with the furthest-away sell-by or use-by date that you can find. In a super-market, these will be right at the back of the shelf behind the oldest products, which the shelf-stackers will want to sell first. With stacked trays of vegetables, fruit and salads, they will be the ones in the bottom stack.

- Buy seasonal items in quantity if they will store (squashes, onions, root vegetables), freeze (raspberries, blackcurrants), make into sauces or soups (tomatoes, leeks) to freeze, can be bottled (many items) or turned into drinks, or can be divided with neighbours or friends.

- If you are not sure where an item has come from (i.e if the ambience of the shop, or general information, suggests that it is locally sourced but there is no factual labelling or information with the item), then ask until you are satisfied. A lot of retailers, it has to be said, do try to pass off goods as being greener, or more local, than they really are.

- Don't be afraid to make your own wishes and thoughts known to the manager of your local supermarket – the customer service area should have a book for complaints/suggestions.

- Try not to take young children food shopping – research shows they will usually persuade you to buy items you would prefer not to buy, especially brightly packaged items of junk food.

- At the checkout, try to view each item you've put in your trolley dispassionately. If you see anything you bought on impulse or don't really need, don't be afraid to put it back before it's gone through the till.

- When choosing an online box scheme or grocer, try to find those who are local to your own area.

Reading the food labels

Whilst for many years most food manufacturers and supermarkets have habitually labelled their foods for calorie content and other nutritional information, they have been – and often still are – less forthcoming about information on green issues: for example, how many food miles the product has travelled; whether or not it was air-freighted; how much greenhouse gas has been emitted to get it from farm to shop; packaging information; and, in the case of animal products, the conditions the animal was reared in.

While retailers are beginning to get the message that it is important to give us the information we want (or need, even if we never think about it), there's still a lot to be done.

FINDING OUT WHAT YOU WANT TO KNOW FROM THE LABELS

- The country of origin will give you a clue to food miles – but not always. Some animals, for example, will have been reared abroad, imported to be slaughtered and then, legally, described as UK produce (see box on page 139). Other items, such as prawns, will be caught in the UK and then sent abroad for processing before being returned here. It is unlikely that this will be printed on the bag of prawns in the freezer. Sometimes products are simply labelled as coming from the EU – and sometimes, even, the pack lists a choice of places where it may have originated, e.g. 'From the EU or Brazil'.

- The list of ingredients will give you a clue to how sustainably the item was produced – a long list of E numbers and other ingredients may indicate less green thought went into this particular item.

- There are various different symbols denoting certain standards of animal welfare and other issues. Here is a guide to

MADE IN BRITAIN?

There are several ways in which food that most of us would not describe as having been produced in this country can appear to be from the UK.

- The Trades Description Act says that 'goods are deemed to have been manufactured or produced in the country in which they last underwent a treatment or process resulting in substantial change'. So foreign meat which comes here to be cured or otherwise processed, or slaughtered, becomes British.

- Some local-sounding names, such as 'Wiltshire ham' or 'Lancashire hotpot' have never seen Wiltshire or Lancashire and may indeed come from abroad. Cheddar cheese can be made abroad.

- Cumberland sausages probably contain no meat from Cumberland and have not been made in Cumbria – and so on.

- You cannot even trust the word British in the product name – a label might describe a product as 'British peppered ham', for example, when the meat itself is not British although the peppering process has been carried out here.

- Some food manufacturers don't label country of origin anyway as it isn't a legal requirement on processed foods.

what they mean (organic labelling/certification has been discussed in Chapter 2 and Fairtrade, Rainforest and Marine Stewardship Council logos in Chapter 3). For more information, see the Resources section.

Red Tractor

Run by the Assured Food Standards (AFS), the Red Tractor symbol may be used on a variety of foods, including meat, dairy products, vegetables, fruit, flour and sugar. AFS represents and is owned by the food industry, from farmers to retailers, including the National Farmers' Union, the Ulster Farmers' Union, the Meat & Livestock Commission, Dairy UK and the British Retail Consortium. Observers include Defra and the Food & Drink Federation. Its aims are to raise the standards of hygiene, safety, animal welfare and the environment in British farming and food production, with independent inspections. The Union flag as part of the logo demonstrates that the food has been produced, processed and packed in the UK. Throughout the country 78,000 farmers and 350 processors use the logo.

However, the scheme has its detractors. It has been described as nothing more than 'a basic MOT' and animal-welfare standards under the scheme have been criticized by Compassion in World Farming. For example, the logo doesn't mean that chickens are free range, or that animals kept in barns have bedding, or are not kept in close confinement. In truth, the label can't be used as more than a very basic assurance on ethical or environmental criteria.

Farm Assured

Most 'farm-assured' schemes have been brought under the Red Tractor umbrella but a few still work separately, including Farm Assured Welsh Livestock, Northern Ireland Farm Quality Assurance, Genesis Quality Assurance and Quality Meat Scotland. The Red Tractor organization describes these as having 'separate but equivalent status'.

Union Flag symbol

Appears on a variety of produce to guarantee that it is British.

LEAF

This stands for Linking Environment and Farming. In order to achieve LEAF Marque status, farms have to demonstrate high standards of environmental stewardship and sustainable farming, both in the UK and abroad. The scheme supports both local producers and developing-world farmers. The standards are based on what LEAF regards as a commonsense approach, combining modern technology with basic principles of good farming practice. It covers areas such as soil management, crop nutrition, pesticide use, pollution control, waste management, water and energy efficiency and the protection of wildlife and landscape. However, it doesn't guarantee that food will be organic, non-GM, UK-produced or that animals have not been intensively reared.

Lion Quality

You will find the Lion symbol stamped on around 85 per cent of eggs in the UK, and on the egg boxes. It means that the eggs have been produced to high food-safety standards and includes compulsory vaccination against salmonella enteritidis of all young female chickens destined for Lion egg-producing flocks. It also covers improved traceability of eggs; a 'best-before' date stamped on the shell and pack; and on-site farm and packing station hygiene controls. However, it doesn't provide assurance of animal welfare or mean that the eggs are free range – most are factory-farmed.

Freedom Food

This is an RSPCA-backed animal-welfare scheme covering meat, poultry, eggs, fish and dairy products, which guarantees that farm animals are reared according to strictly monitored RSPCA standards. It covers each stage of the animal's life from birth to slaughter, and requires species-specific standards of food and welfare. Around 2,200 farms, producers, abattoirs and hauliers participate.

Free range

This can apply to meat, poultry and eggs and has a fairly wide range of interpretation. At best it means that the animals or poultry can roam and graze, but often this doesn't happen

— particularly in the case of poultry. The rules demand that chickens must have 'continuous daytime access to open-air runs' for at least half of their lives, but even though there may be access (e.g. holes in the walls of a huge barn), most of the chickens, it has been found, rarely use this facility. For more information on the meaning of free range and the differences between it and organic and conventional poultry farming (see page 61).

Vegetarian Society

To gain the Vegetarian Society logo (the seedling symbol), which appears on 2,000 products, the food has to be 100 per cent vegetarian with, for example, no gelatine, aspic, no meat or bone stock, no animal fats (except butter) and obviously, no meat, poultry or fish content, although milk and dairy products, and eggs, are allowed. Items must not have been produced in a place where cross-contamination with non-vegetarian products is possible. They must also be GM-free, not tested on animals, and eggs used must be free range.

Vegan

The Vegan Society logo – a sunflower – appears on thousands of products which avoid 'all forms of exploitation of animals for food, clothing or any other purpose'. Vegan foods are purely plant-based and free from all animal products, such as meat or animal milks, and other dairy products such as cheese, yogurt and cream, as well as eggs, honey and gelatine.

GM LABELLING

Since 2004, the EU labelling laws state that if a food contains or consists of genetically modified organisms, or contains ingredients produced from GMOs, this must be indicated on the label. For GM products sold 'loose', information must be displayed immediately next to the food to indicate that it is GM.

Products such as maize and soya flour, oils and glucose syrups have to be labelled as GM if they are from a GM source. But products produced with GM technology (cheese produced with GM enzymes, for example) do not have to be labelled. Products such as meat, milk and eggs from animals fed on GM animal feed also don't need labelling even though up to 30 per cent GM feed is allowed.

Any intentional use of GM ingredients at any level must be labelled. But there is no need to label small amounts of GM ingredients (below 0.9 per cent for approved GM varieties and 0.5 per cent for some other varieties) that are accidentally present in a food.

WORDS THAT MEAN NOTHING

On packaging you will often come across words like 'natural', 'wholesome', 'traditional' or names like 'nature's own' or 'farmhouse'. There are no laws covering words such as these or relating to how the food in a pack with such a label is produced, so they are best ignored. You will also often find photographs or illustrations that are misleading. For example, a drawing of a farmhouse on a pack of biscuits might make you think they have been made in a small, country kitchen, when in fact they come from a huge production line in a city factory. Again, these are best ignored.

AND A WORD ABOUT 'BEST BEFORE' AND 'USE BY'

Best-before dates are more about quality than safety – so when the date runs out, it doesn't mean that the food is dangerous, just that it may no longer be at its best. Use-by dates mean that the food should be eaten by that date. However, in my own experience, if you use common sense (e.g. if there is no sight or odour of deterioration) many use-by dates can be exceeded a little if the food has been stored correctly.

RECENT LABELLING SCAMS

There have in recent years been several large-scale cases (some involving major supermarkets) of items labelled as local, free-range, wild, corn-fed, etc., when they are not.

WHAT YOU MAY FIND ON LABELS IN FUTURE

In the years ahead it will become much more common for you to be able to find any or all of the following information on food labels, following greater commitment to openness both from retailers and the government:

- food miles
- life-cycle assessment – the environmental impact of that particular product
- whether the product has been air-freighted
- amount of greenhouse gases involved in growing and transporting
- packaging information (see page 143)

And sometimes products are labelled as coming from a particular region (e.g. Basmati on packets of rice) when they don't. You can't tell – but now testers can usually sort out the wheat from the chaff. The Food Standards Agency has devised a series of authenticity tests which can be used on meat, fish, fruit and vegetables to make sure you really are getting what it says on the label. They can discover, for example, whether or not a product is organic, how often an animal has been treated with antibiotics, whether it contains artificial fertilizers, and the country of origin. How, where, when and how often these tests will be used has yet to be decided.

Packaging

The average household spends about £500 a year on packaging. An analysis of a typical supermarket shopping basket carried out by the National Farmers' Union found that only 26 per cent of the cost is accounted for by food; the rest is packaging, processing, transport, store overheads, advertising and supermarket mark-up. How come?

The way our modern global food-supply system works means that much of our food is transported, as we've seen, over long distances. The further distances and longer time that food travels, the more packaging it may require to protect it, or so the theory goes. Certain packaging can help prevent moisture loss from fruit and vegetables, as well as helping prevent bruising and damage.

Packaging is also a means of displaying information – we can't read the food labels telling us what the food weighs, how much it costs and what is in it if there's no packaging to put it on. The following information is required by law: manufacturer's name and contact details, name of the product, description of the product, weight (some foods are exempt, for example bread), ingredients (listed in descending order of weight), cooking/heating instructions, storage instructions, best-before date.

And, of course, without packaging the manufacturers don't have anywhere to write their marketing blurb enticing us to buy.

Packaging also facilitates self-service. And our huge hunger for ready meals and convenience foods not only encourages but requires packaging.

Sometimes packaging can be used as a marketing tool. Over-large cardboard boxes can sometimes conceal contents which fill little more than half the pack, leading us to think we're getting more for our money than we really are. Easter eggs and biscuits are two typical examples of this.

But what's wrong with our huge packaging habit? How does it affect the environment?

Plastic packaging is oil based and all forms will have used fossil fuels during the manufacturing process. The packaging process is very energy intensive. Because a lot of packaging still cannot be recycled, the trucks used to take the resulting waste to landfill will also emit CO_2, while some packaging will also generate climate-changing methane emissions as it decomposes.

WHAT SUPERMARKETS AND MANUFACTURERS ARE TRYING TO DO ABOUT IT...

Although the supermarket line tends to be that packaging is often necessary to help protect the product and that removing it would cause more environmental damage through waste than it would save, in 2006 all the major supermarkets took a communal pledge to reduce packaging waste and all are on a drive to do so. Typically, they are:

- Discouraging plastic carrier bags. Typically, they are introducing recyclable bags that can be used many times, or giving incentives to customers to re-use their existing bags and new UK legislation is about to force supermarkets to start charging for every bag by 2009.

- Finding ways of reducing the amount and/or weight of packaging – for example by avoiding 'double packing' (e.g. plastic and then card over the top, or individual wrapping of several items contained in one box) and by making unavoidable containers (e.g. bottles, aluminium cans) thinner.

LOOSE FRUIT VERSUS PACKAGED

M&S carried out a series of life-cycle assessments as part of a packaging review. The work compared loose apples with four-packs of packaged fruit. They say that the two methods had very similar overall environmental impact due to higher levels of wastage in loose varieties. However, loose packaging created the least non-biodegradable waste.

- Using more compostable packaging.

- Reducing the size of bottles, jars and packs to save material, while retaining the same weight/volume of product inside.

- Reducing the size of labels and print to save paper.

- Selling milk in polythene bags, saving 75 per cent of packaging material.

- Using lightweight plastic bottles for wine instead of glass.

- Selling more items loose.

- In farm-to-store transport, using more re-usable packaging and storage systems.

- They are also, variously, organizing better label information about the packaging.

Other organizations are also doing their bit to help. For example, the Soil Association has new standards which now require that those packaging their certified organic produce 'take account of the environmental impact of their packaging'. For more information on packaging, see Resources.

...AND WHAT YOU CAN DO ABOUT IT

- Some supermarkets offer dumping facilities.

- Remove packaging at the checkout as a form of protest – an action endorsed by the Women's Institute *and* the government.

- Leave the worst types of packaging – and the foods they enclose – on the shelves (see table on page 146).

- Avoid items packed in two or three different layers of packaging – for example, a ready meal which may be in a foil tin, enclosed in a cellophane bag and then packed into a card box.

- Choose loose fruit and vegetables when possible. Some traders will let you put loose produce in your own re-used bags to save using new ones.

- Avoid individually wrapped small items (a classic example is individually wrapped dried fruits, which were recently being sold at ASDA; another is individually wrapped teabags).

- For items such as dried fruit and nuts, buy larger packs and divide them up yourself as necessary (e.g. for a child's lunch box, put a serving in an individual re-usable container).

- When you can find it, buy food and drink that you 'package' yourself by taking along your own container. For example, some local shops and market stalls will weigh or measure out items such as cereal, nuts, seeds, direct into your re-usable bag, box or dish, and others will let you fill your own bottle with, say, cider or apple juice.

- Take your own bags to the shop and never use plastic carriers. (If you do, re-use them.) If you are caught without anything to use, cardboard boxes may be better than the carrier bags.

- Store and recycle or re-use packaging.

PLASTIC HOUSEHOLD WASTE

- 11 per cent of the household waste in the UK is plastic, 40 per cent of it coming from plastic bottles.
- We use around 10–15 billion plastic carrier bags a year, most of which are made from petroleum.
- Plastic waste ends up in landfill where it can take centuries to break down, or as litter in the countryside and oceans.

TYPES OF PACKAGING: THE GOOD AND THE BAD

Name	Composition	Typical use	Recyclable	Re-usable	Biodegradable	Compostable
Tetrapak	plastic/foil/card	longlife drinks	not easily in UK	no	no	no
Standard plastic	petroleum†	all types of food and drink	yes	yes	no	no
Degradable plastic	petroleum/ plants	bags	yes	yes	no	no
Biodegradable plastic	plant based	bags	yes	yes	yes	yes
Polystyrene	petroleum	food trays	no	no	no	no
Polythene, PET, polyethylene	petroleum	milk containers, heavy-duty bags	yes	sometimes	no	no
Clingfilm	petroleum	wrapping fresh produce	yes	no	no	no
Bubble-wrap	petroleum	meat packing	yes	yes	no	no
Paper	wood pulp/ other plant fibres	labels, bags	yes	occasionally	yes	yes
Cardboard	paper	boxes, sleeves	yes	sometimes	yes	yes
Laminated card	vinyl-treated paper	boxes, display card	hard	no	no	no
Tinfoil	aluminium	containers, lids	yes	sometimes	yes	no
Aluminium	aluminium	cans	yes	no	no	no
Glass	sand	bottles, jars	yes	yes	no	no
Cornstarch	cornstarch	food trays, bags	yes	sometimes	yes	yes

Note: Some packages may be already made from recycled materials (e.g. rPET bottles are made from up to 50 per cent of recycled PET), which reduces energy and material costs.
*Tetrapak (see Resources) is trying to establish nationwide recycling depots by the end of 2008.
†The different types of plastic packaging and containers have slightly different formulations and content but all are based on petroleum/petrochemicals apart from biodegradable plastics.

So what *are* you putting in that trolley?

After all that – what do you end up putting in your trolley or basket? As a broad guideline, re-read the summary to Chapter 3, and take the Foods in Season (in the UK) list which may help you make choices.

For advice on particular foods, what to look out for and what to avoid, and for some brand names and suppliers, see the A–Z.

THE GOOD TROLLEY AND THE NOT-SO-GOOD TROLLEY

Here is a comparison of a good shopping trolley and a poor shopping trolley put together in autumn from the same basic shopping list of requirements for a couple.

Good	Not so good
Small organic chicken from the UK	Ready chicken meal, ingredients from several different countries
6 local organic eggs	Dozen standard eggs
Cornish line-caught fresh mackerel	Frozen North Atlantic cod
Hand-gathered wild mussels from Wales	Tiger prawns from the Far East
Fresh local seasonal tomatoes, sold loose	Pack of cherry tomatoes from Italy
New season's maincrop potatoes	New potatoes from Egypt
UK dark green cabbage, sold loose	Pack mangetout from Spain
Stoneground organic bread	Sliced pack bread
UK organic butter	Margarine
UK-produced cold-pressed rapeseed oil	Blended vegetable oil from more than one country
New season's fresh hazelnuts	Bag of salted peanuts, origin unspecified
Organic natural yogurt	Mass-market four-pack fruit yogurt
New season's UK apples	Nectarines from Australia
New season's UK pears	Grapes from South Africa

A FEW WORDS ABOUT COST

At first glance the good trolley on the previous page looks a lot more expensive than the less good trolley. But bear in mind:

- You are shopping for small portions of good food. Reducing the weight of what you buy – especially meat, fish, poultry and dairy produce not only saves money but also body fat and energy costs.

- Buying in season can save money – for example, the mussels, seasonal tomatoes, potatoes, cabbage, apples, pears and hazelnuts will be less expensive than the 'not so good' prawns, cod, cherry tomatoes, new potatoes, mangetout, salted peanuts and imported fruits.

- The money thus saved on portion sizes and seasonal foods can be offset on the more expensive cost of organic foods and top quality.

- Shopping for a green and cost-conscious (which is *not* the same as cheap) trolley may take a bit more time at first, but soon it becomes second nature to pick out the good choices and leave the others behind.

FACTBOX
Only one in every 200 carrier bags is re-used, yet most take over 1,000 years to decompose in a landfill site.

How do we get our shopping home?

Food's journey does not end once the food reaches the store: it needs to be taken – or delivered – to your home. All the signs are that we are now travelling further to shop. The *Wise Moves* report calculates that of the average 893 miles an individual travels for shopping each year, over a third (349 miles) are for food. This costs Britain up to £3.5 billion a year in traffic emissions, noise, accidents and congestion, according to calculations carried out for the government. In total, according to the Food Ethics Council, as a nation we drive almost 9 billion miles a year to shop for food.

- Local home deliveries should reduce energy used to get the food to your home. The van has, say, fifty deliveries to drop off in the area, so he is making one longish local journey. But if all those fifty people drove to the shop separately, then obviously the energy use would be much higher. However, if the van were empty but for your delivery, or were travelling up and down the length of the country to deliver just a few items, then the equation is less clear and indeed it seems as if the home-delivery carbon footprint may be larger than if you travelled to a supermarket to get the goods.

- Ordering food from your milkman may be a good option. A fifth of the items that Dairy Crest now sells off its milk floats are foods, such as juices, bread, eggs, butter and veg boxes. The milkman is coming round anyway (in some areas) and electric floats are environmentally better than vans. And if you happen to buy your milk from the milkman as well, the glass bottles can be washed and re-used around 100 times.

- Walking to the shops has its drawbacks. It is nearly impossible to do a big family shop on foot, as you would need to have many hands and be built like a weightlifter to get the stuff home. So you need to go every day. Walking or cycling should make your body healthier and more efficient.

- If walking or cycling isn't an option, public transport is a good idea for smaller shops. However, if we all decide to do that, the public transport system will be over-crowded — especially with all the shopping on board. So we need to spread the load: go out of rush hour.

- Driving to the shops can be very high in energy use — but it isn't necessarily so. It depends on the car used and its energy consumption; the amount of shopping you do per trip (going every day 5 miles each way to purchase a couple of items versus a bootload once a week — you can see which is better). Common sense is needed.

Changes in how we shop would affect not only retailers but also local economies and communities. While local shopping gives communities a boost, online buys and home delivery may do the opposite. Congestion and road-use charges could persuade ever more of us to shop out of town, contributing to urban decline and city-centre food deserts.

WHAT TO DO

Don't always rely on internet ordering. Patronize local shops, otherwise they may disappear. Try to combine car shopping trips with something else (e.g. collecting children, going to the dentist). But use home delivery if local shops offer that service and deliver to other people in your area.

Conclusion

Where we shop and how we shop are vital choices in our attempts to lead a more environmentally friendly lifestyle. It seems clear that while major changes may never be possible across the board, there are plenty of small things we can do on a regular basis to help.

WHAT TO DO

- Vary your choices of where to shop and if you use supermarkets try to do large, occasional shops, buying more regularly from smaller outlets.

- Limit the amount that you purchase to what you really need and will use; this saves both resources and waste.

- Avoid packaging whenever you can.

- Learn to read the information on labels and be wary of vague claims.

- Try to find more carbon-friendly ways of getting to the shops if possible.

- Think about buying in bulk to save or share when things are in season.

5 The Green Kitchen

The food that you buy is, at least in part, governed by others – the producers, growers, processors, shopkeepers.

But what happens to food once it's in your home is completely up to you. Each one of us can make small changes here, which can, individually and as a population, add up to a major difference in our environmental impact

Twenty-five per cent of the UK's carbon dioxide emissions are created in our homes, of which around a third is accounted for in the kitchen. In addition to this, how we store, prepare, cook, eat, clear up and dispose of our food also has an impact, positive or negative, upon other environmental factors such as water usage and waste.

Back at the start of this book we saw the Green family of the 1950s and what they ate; but it's also worth having a look at what their kitchen behaviour was likely to have been. They would probably have stored most of their food in a cool larder, or certainly in the coolest and darkest part of the kitchen or an outer store room. There was little in the way of kitchen gadgets – a grater, a hand whisk, a cleaver and a couple of sharp knives would have been about it (in those days we even had men called knife-grinders coming round on their bikes to sharpen our kitchen tools for us!). Food would have been cooked on a gas or electric stove, which may or may not have had a grill; there would have been a hob kettle, a sink (often containing a small bowl for the washing-up), a waste bin for compost. Everything was simple and basic – and, like the food choices they made, in many ways it is similar to what the modern green kitchen is trying to achieve.

FACTBOX

- UK households use £1.5 billion worth of electricity every year on cooling and freezing food and drinks.
- An energy-efficient fridge-freezer uses only around a third of the energy to do the same job as a ten-year-old appliance – that's a saving of up to £45 a year.
- Buying an energy-efficient fridge-freezer to replace your inefficient model could cut carbon dioxide emissions produced indirectly by your home by up to 190kg a year.

Energy Saving Trust

Storing food

The tendency nowadays is to stick everything in the fridge or fridges – but if you are lucky enough to have a cool area of the house you can store much of your food there. In the past many houses were built so that their kitchen/larder area was on the cooler, north side of the home. Today few homes have a larder, but there may be cool spots in the house – perhaps a north-facing conservatory, or the cupboard under the stairs, or an unheated spare room or downstairs loo or garage.

These types of places are ideal for storing fruit, vegetables and salads, especially if you can create some dark – large boxes would be ideal. Obviously you want to make sure your storage area is not easy to get at for the local mice, rats or foxes. Other items which are best stored in cool, dark conditions but don't necessarily need a fridge are oils, nuts, seeds, herbs and spices, as well as any items in glass containers (e.g. bottled fruits and vegetables, pickles and jams).

If you can free up fridge space in this way, you may be able to get away with using a smaller fridge, which would save energy. Items that do need to go in the fridge include meat, fish, poultry and dairy products. Eggs can be kept either at cool room temperature or in the fridge.

Food bought in bulk – or from your own garden – may need to be prepared and frozen. A chest freezer is best for bulk storage, but do try to make sure it is always as near full as you can and that you rotate items so that you're not using precious energy in keeping it working overtime to store foods which have been in there for years (and will probably end up being thrown away). Making a list and crossing off foods as you use them is a good way to keep tabs.

The ethics of discarding old, energy-guzzling fridges and freezers is tricky – but if you can downsize, buy the most energy-efficient one you can (A+ or A++) and try to find a large family nearby who can put your older, larger model to good use (see Resources for how to find a new owner). If your old machine gives up the ghost altogether, then the company that delivers your new one may take the old one to be disposed of locally; or you can ask the council.

Items in packets, cans and tubes, as well as dried grains can be stored in a room-temperature cupboard; try to keep a system where the newest ones go to the back and the oldest are at the front so you use them up first.

COVERING AND WRAPPING FOOD

- Clingfilm and food bags are made of plastic and are not usually biodegradable so keep their use to a minimum. A better bet are lidded dishes which can be used for many years.
- Instead of covering items with clingfilm, put them in a dish and cover them with a saucer; or you can buy lids.
- Unbleached greaseproof paper is a good idea for wrapping or covering and can be used in place of foil or clingfilm for all kinds of food.

See Resources section for where to buy.

FRIDGE AND FREEZER TIPS

- Defrost regularly any fridges and freezers that need manual defrosting, as when they are iced up they use more energy (and contain less space for food).
- Don't keep fridge or freezer doors open for long periods.
- Avoid positioning fridges or freezers near to the cooker or a radiator.
- Check the temperature of your fridge – while it wants to be at around 5°C, there is no need to keep it too cold. Your freezer should be between −18°C and −22°C.

Food preparation

- Leave skins and outer leaves on vegetables and fruit if possible, as discarding them may remove the part of the plant containing the highest levels of vitamin C and dietary fibre.

- Pre-washed organic fruit and vegetables don't need to be washed again. Dirty fruits, salads and vegetables, non-organic fruits, salads and vegetables that won't be peeled, and fruits, salads and vegetables labelled 'wash before use' need to be washed. Wash them in cool water and don't leave them to soak in the sink – this leaches vitamins B and C into the water.

- Don't prepare vegetables early and leave them soaking in a saucepan – again, the vitamins B and C will leach out. This is OK if you are going to use the cooking water as part of the meal.

- Remove foods such as joints, steaks, chicken breasts and fish from the fridge half an hour before cooking, so that they come to room temperature and will take less time to cook.

- Remove items from the freezer in plenty of time to defrost thoroughly so that you don't have to waste energy defrosting them in the microwave oven. For large joints this can take 36 hours in the fridge or up to 24 hours in a cool room.

- For safety, if defrosting meats, poultry and fish outside the fridge, make sure items are well covered so that flies, pets, etc. can't reach. This could be by using a large plate over a dish, with a dedicated defreezing box (from Lakeland) or with a mesh 'flynet', food-cover tent (available from most kitchen stores and online kitchen shops and often collapsible to save space).

Cooking methods

If you use electricity, consider switching to a supplier of renewable energy (see Resources) which may cost you a little more but is more environmentally friendly.

If you have to use gas, you can't do this (as gas comes from fossil fuels) but you can at least use a supplier who offers a green gas tariff – which usually means that some of what you pay for the gas is used to fund global-warming projects.

It is hard to lay down concrete rules about ways to reduce your total kitchen energy use because there are so many variables going on – space heat, hot water and cooking can all be sorted out in so many ways. At first glance it might seem as though an Aga-type system, which heats the kitchen, runs some radiators, provides hot water and is also a cooker and hob, would be the most energy efficient, but there may not be much in it if you have an efficient central-heating boiler system which also provides hot water, and a separate cooker/hob which is used only when you need it, in an efficient way. The reason that Aga kitchens are always so hot is that there is a lot of unused energy disappearing into the room – and often out of the window! Talking of which, if you are cooking and the kitchen gets hot, don't open the window – turn off the central heating, or whatever heating you have, instead.

Microwave ovens can also be an efficient way of heating small amounts of food in certain cases. If you live alone it will use much less energy to reheat a casserole, for example, in the microwave than in the oven. But if the comparison is between the microwave and heating the food in a suitable pan on the hob, then the difference may be small. Because of the huge variety of meal sizes and constituents, the differences in energy use of various microwaves, hotplates, ovens and so on, it isn't possible to make totally accurate comparisons – but the following tips will help you to save energy, whatever methods you use in your own kitchen.

FACTBOX
- **Fan ovens use around 20 per cent less energy than conventional ovens.**
- **Gas ovens are up to three times more efficient than electric ovens.**
- **Ceramic hobs are more efficient than conventional electric hobs.**

Energy Saving Trust

ENERGY-SAVING COOKING TIPS

- If you have a small amount of food to heat up (say, a single portion of baked beans or a bowl of soup), then heating it in the microwave may be preferable to any other method. Otherwise, use a small saucepan on a small hob.

- Using the hob will use less energy than using the oven. For example, a stew cooked on the hob is better in terms of energy than a casserole cooked in the oven. The efficiency of hobs depends more on the way they are used than on the type of fuel.

- Frying is better than grilling. The grill uses a great deal of energy, much of it wasted out into the room. Fry in a good pan (see Pots, pans ...) with a tiny amount of oil.

- Using the toaster is better than grilling.

- Boiling or steaming are usually just as quick, if not quicker, than using the microwave to cook vegetables from scratch for anything more than one person.

- Always keep lids on pans when you are cooking unless the recipe really requires that you don't.

- Steaming is a good option for many types of food, not just vegetables. Fish and chicken can be steamed with flavourings – indeed a whole meal can be cooked at once.

- If you are using the oven, try to use spare space inside for something else (e.g. if you are making bread, batch bake it and freeze the spare loaves, or if you are cooking a casserole in a low oven for many hours, make meringue and use the same heat, or dry out some tomatoes, or make crostini or croutons).

- In summer, make full use of cold no-cook meals to save energy.

- In general, the quicker a dish cooks, the less energy you use – but long, slow cooking has green credentials too, if you plan carefully, and even roasting can be OK with planning.

- What you don't want to do is choose meals/recipes/dishes that require several different cooking methods or sources of heat – for example, a pasta bake that requires pre-frying of the meat element, simmering of the finished meat sauce, a separate hob for making a white sauce, the oven for cooking – and perhaps even the grill to finish browning the top. See my suggestions on page 167 for swaps you could make for similar, greener meals.

FACTBOX
Always boil up only the amount of water you really need – a minimal amount for vegetable cooking, and just enough for that mug of tea. You can save up to £25 a year on your bill.

Pots, pans and accessories

Use the money you are going to save on gadgets (see Gadgets and utensils) to buy good-quality cooking pots and pans. If you are going to do more hob cooking, these will be invaluable.

- Heavy-based lidded pots will save hob-cooked casseroles from sticking on the base and will conduct low heats evenly and prevent overcooking.

- Heavy-based frying pans will allow you to fry, instead of grill, items such as bacon, sausages, steaks, tomatoes and fish using just a light smear of oil over the pan base. You can fry eggs this way too, turning halfway.

- Good-quality pans will retain a lot of heat, so get into the habit of turning the heat off before you have finished cooking – the foods will finish cooking in the residual heat. This works even better with electric hob solid plates or radiant rings, which retain heat themselves for some time. Examples of foods that cook well using this method are rice (if the pack says boil for 20 minutes, boil for 10, turn off, leave on the hob with the lid on and it will be done)

and all kinds of green vegetables – steam or boil for a couple of minutes, drain then leave, lidded, in the hot pan for a few more minutes on the hob.

- A tiered, lidded steamer pan is ideal for cooking various items in layers over boiling water on the same hob. You can also get divided pans so you can cook various vegetables separately but in the same pan. You can use an ordinary saucepan to steam foods if you buy a fold-up stainless steel steamer tray – put your shredded greens or whatever on the tray over whatever is cooking beneath, put the lid on top.

  You can also get bamboo Chinese steamers of different sizes.

Gadgets and utensils

It is a fact that half of the posh, so-called labour-saving electrical gadgets that we buy for our kitchens never get used – they just fill up the cupboards, and when you do use them, they burn a lot of electricity. But some of those that you do use may in fact be false friends. Take a processor – if you use it for slicing vegetables, by the time you have set it up, sliced the veggies, dismantled it, washed the necessary parts and re-assembled it, it would have been quicker and easier just to use a knife. So many small gadgets are a waste of time and energy.

Here's my list of all you really need, the first two being the only electric things I have always found completely necessary:

- **electric hand whisk**
- **electric blender**   if this comes with a grinder bowl, that could be useful for spices or coffee beans
- **meat cleaver** – many uses, including chopping herbs, onions and garlic, pressing garlic (much quicker and better than a garlic press) – as well as chopping chickens and so on
- **large and small scissors**
- **several sharp knives** of all sizes and varieties
- **knife sharpener**
- **plenty of stainless-steel spoons, ladles, spatulas** and so on
- **wooden long-handled and short-handled spoons and spatulas**
- **teapot or single-serve loose tea-holder, cafetière, kettle**

Kitchen waste

According to Wrap, the Waste and Resources Action Programme, every two hours the UK produces enough waste to fill the Royal Albert Hall, and kitchen waste accounts for at least 20 per cent of all waste. As we have seen, it has been estimated that one-third of our food ends up in the bin, with each adult wasting around £460 worth every year and 6.7 million tonnes of domestic food binned in total. This ends up in landfill, where it breaks down and produces greenhouse gases.

A lot of both the food and the packaging waste that we create is due, it has to be said, to our often cavalier attitude to it. Because in recent years food has been relatively inexpensive in relation to our earnings, as well as widely and instantly available, we don't cherish it and despise waste as our grandparents, and even our parents, would have done. And every time we chuck out items past their sell-by date, or with a layer of mould on the top after a few weeks at the back of the fridge, we're also usually chucking out packaging that we needn't have bought. So the first thing is to get the right mindset. Think of any food that comes into your kitchen as a precious commodity, and then you'll treat it as such. Once you have this mindset it is easier to change long-standing habits that create all the waste.

THE THREE RS
The mantra to help reduce kitchen waste is: **Reduce, Re-use, Recycle.**

Reduce
We've already discussed ways to reduce food and packaging waste in Chapter 4, such as buying your veg and fruit loose, and simply buying less food altogether (ideal if you are overweight). The next chapter will look at planning and cooking to reduce waste. Another must is to consider portion control in order to reduce the amount of food that is tipped in the bin after a meal. By all means, cook enough so that you have another complete meal for tomorrow or to freeze, but try to serve to people and yourself what you are fairly sure will get eaten.

To 'reduce' I would add try to buy what you

know you and your family like, and don't buy what you know you/they don't like, so that it doesn't languish in the cupboard for two weeks and then get thrown away. For example, there is no point at all in buying healthy beansprouts if you all dislike them. Also, plan your meals (see next section) or at the very least take a shopping list. And sort out your food-storage areas regularly, using up items that will need to be chucked out if they aren't eaten soon. I suggest checking the fridge twice a week, fresh fruit and veg kept outside the fridge twice a week, and larders and freezers every two months.

Re-use

If you can, use your local milkman for milk and other goods, and always return bottles for re-use.

You can re-use plastic shopping bags (if you aren't refusing them all) as binliners and, indeed, for further shopping until they reach the end of their life. You can then replace them with a few 'bags for life', sold by all major food shops and plenty of smaller ones too.

Items such as tinfoil can often be smoothed out and re-used.

Bottles from bought water can be re-used filled with tap water.

Jars can be washed and re-used for home-made preserves (if you don't want them, one of your neighbours may well be glad of them).

You can also offer items on swapping or give-away websites tailored for just this job (see Resources).

Recycle

'The current recycling of paper, glass, plastics, aluminium and steel in the UK saves 10–15 million tonnes of CO_2 equivalents per year,' says Wrap. 'This equates to taking 3.5 million cars off UK roads.'

Most local councils have their own recycling refuse-collection rules and these do vary from area to area. It is much easier to have separate bins, boxes or shelves for your different sorts of recyclable waste in or near the kitchen so that you sort them out as you go along, rather than trying to do it once a week or fortnight for the refuse collections or for your trip to the recycling centre. For smaller homes and single people you can buy bins which have internal divided compartments.

For people with a garden, a great idea is the hot Johanna compost-maker, in which you can put both uncooked and cooked plant waste *and*, unusually, animal waste such as meat, fish and bones (see Resources).

If you don't already have one, start a compost bin too. Even if you don't have a garden, you can collect plant waste for a neighbour who does (perhaps in return for a lettuce or two next year). If you all live in apartments, should there be a communal garden attached, contact the person responsible for its upkeep and offer to run a compost heap for it. There may also be compost-hungry garden-owners within striking distance of your flat who would collect.

You could buy and fit (quite expensive and bothersome) a sink waste-disposal unit, which minimizes your food waste and sends it into your sewage system where it will be treated and may eventually end up as a soil conditioner. While these are said to use only a small amount of water and minimal energy, it is simpler and less labour-intensive to produce your own compost for the earth. If you create only small amounts of plant waste, you can buy an indoor plant-composting bin that uses micro-organisms to create compost without odour (see wiggly-wigglers in the Resources section).

EACH YEAR:

- 4 billion longlife PET juice and milk cartons are thrown out.
- Each UK home throws out one 2-litre plastic milk or juice bottle or carton every day, with only one in ten of these being recycled – but more and more are being used to make clothing, such as school trousers and fleeces.
- 8 per cent of the world's total oil use is for plastics production.
- Plastics occupy around 25 per cent of UK landfill sites.
- Everyone in the UK throws away seven times their body weight in waste each year.

Cleaning up

A few tips for minimizing your use of water and energy in the kitchen clean-up process:

- If you can, collect a whole sink full of washing-up before you do it. Only greasy pans need very hot water; other items will come clean in a lower temperature.

- If you usually have a small amount of hand washing-up, buy a bowl to fit inside your sink so that you use much less water.

- If you have a dishwasher, use the lowest temperature cycle and, again, make sure the washer is full. A full load uses up less energy than doing it all by hand, research confirmed by the Energy Saving Trust shows.

- If you are buying a new dishwasher, check out www.waterwise.org.uk which will show you which machines use the least water and least energy.

- Use environmentally friendly cleaning stuff – washing-up liquid, surface cleaners and so on. You don't need a lot of different items; just two or three will do. Baking soda is handy to have under your sink, as it will do a lot of tough cleaning jobs.

- Use old material as wiping cloths rather than buying dishcloths or throwaway cloths. Don't buy packs of one-use wipes, and cut back on your use of paper kitchen rolls – most of the time a clean cloth (perhaps slightly damp) will do the same job just as well.

- Avoid aerosol oven and other cleaners – pastes are better. Also cut right back on putting bleach down sinks – while bleach may degrade into chloride, its manufacture is not environmentally sound and bleach-free options from companies such as Ecover are, in my view, a more ethical purchase.

- Don't leave the hot or cold water tap running unnecessarily.

- Used water can be re-used to water plants, even if it contains washing-up liquid.

Planning your meals

With so many concerns about green and ethical eating, it is sometimes easy to forget that, first and foremost, what we eat should be a pleasure.

Enjoyment of our food, and its preparation, is one of the great human comforts and passions. That's always been the way – from the times when humans hunted for their food and lived on no more than a dozen different items, through the centuries of discovering the delights of food from other countries, and then on to today's sophisticated world of fusion food, choice, plenty and overconsumption.

While today's trick may be to eat a little less, be more careful about what and when we choose to eat and where we choose to shop, our food should be as it always has been: the heart of life.

In this section we look at how to plan meals that are both green and nutritious, as well as delicious, easy to prepare and enjoyable.

A FEW THINGS TO CONSIDER

- The balance of tastes, flavours, nutrients and types of food over the course of your day/week and within your meal.

- What is in your cupboards/fridge/freezer that needs using.

- Energy-saving cooking method (see table below). Often you can cook the same or very similar ingredients in a different way and save a very high percentage of energy.

- Items cut or chopped small will cook more quickly than those left in large pieces, thus saving energy.

- Do you need to make extra (for freezing, to eat tomorrow, or to make other dishes)?

- What do you fancy?! Don't ignore your own preferences – that's what makes eating a pleasure.

The menus and recipes in Chapter 6 will help with ideas for what you might cook. You can also find hundreds of seasonal meal ideas online and in books and magazines – the Resources section gives some starting points.

MEAL-LINES

Housewives of past decades were adept at making several meals out of one 'starter meal'. For instance the Sunday roast-chicken leftovers

ENERGY-SAVING COOKING

Instead of this ...	... cook this:
High energy Roast chicken (1.5 hours), roast potatoes, hob-steamed vegetables, hob-made bread sauce.	**Lower energy** Roasting chicken cut into eight joints and arranged in a roasting pan with diced onion, sweet potato and tomato, cooked for 50 mins.
Baked salmon (25 mins) boiled new potatoes, stir-fried broccoli and peppers.	Poached salmon (8 mins) in base of steamer, with diced potatoes broccoli and beans also cooked in steamer.
Pork chop, grilled (15 mins).	Pork tenderloin, thinly sliced, dry-fried (4 mins).

would be used to make a chicken and vegetable stew the next day, and any other bits used for sandwiches. A roast topside of beef could then be minced and used for cottage pie with finely chopped vegetables. The carcass/bones of meat or fish would also be used for stock. This works well in the context of cutting down the amount of meat we eat, as the further down the line you go, the less meat there is and the more vegetables or carbohydrates. And it also takes full advantage of the cooking energy that has been used. Here are two samples of how a starter meal can become a meal-line:

Start: a roast hand or leg of pork.
Next: cooked pork sliced, marinated in teriyaki sauce, then stir-fried with vegetables and served with brown rice.

Next: all leftover pork minced, mixed with breadcrumbs, herbs, egg and seasonings and made into porkballs to serve with spaghetti and tomato sauce.

Start: a poached whole chicken with onions, carrots, celery, fennel and potatoes.
Next: cooked chicken slices added to squash, garlic, broccoli and shallots with spices and tomato sauce, served on rice.
Next: small pieces of chopped chicken added to chopped mushrooms, pine nuts, parsley and spring onions for a salad with leftover cold rice.

Your larder

A well-stocked larder is everyone's friend. A good selection of cans, jars and dried items can help you produce a green meal any time and can be a lifesaver if you didn't have the time or forethought to go shopping for fresh things today.

Here's my list of what your cupboard might contain. The meal plans and recipes call upon these items time and again. Where possible, buy British produce – and buy good quality.

- **Pulses, both dried and in cans.** While dried took less energy to produce, they take longer to cook, so both have their place. My cupboard contains cannellini, red kidney beans, green lentils, brown lentils, puy lentils, red lentils, flageolet, chickpeas, butterbeans, black eye beans, brown beans and mixed beans.

- **Dried grains** – a variety of pastas, couscous, brown and white rice, red rice, risotto rice, bulghar wheat, spelt, quinoa.

- **Cans of fish**, in water or oil or tomato sauce, including tuna, sardines, mackerel, rollmop herring (check labels and buy sustainably caught or farmed fish).

- **Couple of cans or jars of stand-by vegetables**, including peppers, sliced carrots, sweetcorn. Frozen versions are better, but these are adequate. I find cans of peas, beans and other vegetables not worth buying.

- **Cans of whole and chopped tomatoes**; tomato purée, sundried tomato paste.

- **Couple of cans of fruit in water** – prunes, apricots, pineapple are some of the best.

- **Dried fruits** – figs, apricots, prunes, sultanas, currants, raisins are the basics.

- **Nuts** – walnuts, hazelnuts, almonds are good basics.

- **Seeds** – pine nuts, sunflower seeds, pumpkin seeds are basics (if you buy or grow pumpkins or sunflowers you can dry and save your own).

- **Olive paste, basil and nut pesto** (locally made).

- **Variety of oils** – cooking olive oil, salad olive oil, lemon olive oil, groundnut oil, walnut oil, sesame oil and pumpkin seed oil are good basics.

- **Variety of vinegars** – red and white wine, balsamic, cider, white (also useful for cleaning!).

- **Flour** – a variety of bread flours, and some dried easy yeast.

- **Dried spices** – preferably whole as they keep better – including ginger, coriander, cumin, chilli.

- **A few dried herbs** – most don't keep well and lose aroma/flavour when dried, but oregano, rosemary, thyme and bay leaf are some of the best. Instead of buying expensive out-of-season herbs in bags or pots from the supermarket, it really is easy to grow them from seed in a pot on your windowsill most of the year round. Basil, mint, coriander are easy.

The L-word: leftovers

However carefully you plan, there will always be times when you have small amounts of 'this or that' left over, either raw or cooked. Here are some more ideas on what to do with them (many courtesy of my sister Ann, who lives alone and prides herself on her ability never to throw any food away).

CHEESE

- Odds and ends of hard cheese can be grated, put in a lidded container and frozen for use in sauces, gratins and with pasta and pizza. You can use the grated cheese from frozen.

- Blue cheese can be beaten into some thick yogurt or fromage frais with some paprika for a dip, or tossed into pasta.

MEAT

- End-of-pack bacon can be dry-fried and then crumbled or chopped and frozen. Use later for salad topping, to mix into scrambled egg or into casseroles.

- Unwanted fat trimmings can be hung out for the birds or fried up for them with leftover bread.

- All types of meat and poultry bones and giblets can be used to make stock.

- All types of meat and poultry can be minced or finely chopped and used in meat sauces, cottage/shepherd's pies, meatballs, burgers.

- Leftover chicken can be mixed with leeks and a white sauce and used in a pie or with mashed potato and vegetables.

FISH AND SEAFOOD

- Small amounts of prawns, crab or cooked salmon can be mixed with soft cheese and used as baked-potato filling or pasta sauce.

- Seafood, salmon and smoked salmon can all be stirred into scrambled eggs or used in quiches.

- Smoked mackerel or smoked trout can be beaten with any soft cheese or thick yogurt, lemon juice and seasoning for a quick pâté or sandwich filling.

- Prawns or shrimps can be added to cooked rice, with small cooked peas if you have any.

- White fish, salmon and crab can be mixed with mashed potato, beaten egg and seasonings of your choice for fishcakes or party-type fishballs.

BREAD AND BAKES

- Stale bread makes good crumbs, which can be frozen in a lidded container for gratin and casserole toppings.

- Leftover pieces of uncooked pastry can be rolled into cigars, topped with grated cheese and cooked into cheese straws.

- Stale plain cake makes a good trifle base, or simply drizzle it with fruit juice and serve with thick yogurt.

VEGETABLES AND PULSES

- A variety of cooked vegetables can be mixed with a cheese sauce and some pasta shapes or cooked potato, and baked for a quick supper – beans, peas, carrots, broccoli, courgettes and many more are ideal, and almost any combination is fine. Both steamed/boiled and roast vegetables work well. Small bits of cooked chicken can also be added if they are around.

- Similarly, cooked vegetables can be added to eggs to make a frittata.

- To use up uncooked greens, carrots and other vegetables which are looking a bit tired, simply simmer them in vegetable or chicken stock with some onion and garlic, and a can of chopped tomatoes (and/or some lentils) to make an easy soup, which you can freeze.

- Cooked or uncooked peppers, courgettes, tomatoes and other Mediterranean-type vegetables can be chopped small and stirred into couscous, bulghar wheat or rice for a salad, a risotto, or to serve warm.

- Leftover cooked pulses can be puréed for a mash to use with meat or fish, or stirred into stock and vegetables for a soup.

FRUIT

- Slightly over-ripe fruit can be picked over and turned into a smoothie or a fruit coulis.

- Fruit such as bruised apples, pears or plums can be chopped and peeled as necessary, simmered and spooned over cake, ice cream or yogurt for a breakfast or dessert.

- Very ripe bananas can be mashed and used to make banana/banana and walnut cake.

Feeding babies and children

In general, children over the age of one can eat what you eat, unless they have any particular allergies or medical needs. Between weaning (around six months) and one year, they can also eat most of what you eat, and research shows that the sooner after weaning you start them on a wide variety of foods, textures and flavours, the better and more easily they will take to them. All you need to do is remember to avoid salt in their foods and gradually to introduce them to more and bigger lumps in the months after weaning. Finger foods are a great idea.

The best thing you can do for your children is to instil in them a love of food, and an interest in it and how it is grown or reared. There are few things sadder than children who don't know how eggs are made or that a carrot comes from the ground rather than from a freezer or can. It always helps, if you have any land, if they can have a little patch to grow their own radishes, Greek cress and cut-and-come-again lettuce – all easy and quick to grow. See page 176 for more on growing your own.

Although it is always good that you can fall back on jars of organic babyfood now and then (such as Plum Baby or Hipp), or even buy an organic baby box of baby favourites from companies such as Abel & Cole (see Resources), it takes no time at all to make your own baby food from your own grown-up meals – you can freeze it in individual pots. Obviously not every meal you eat may be suitable for a very young child (perhaps avoid the hotter spices or richer dishes), but many will be.

Lunch boxes

Many of the lunches in the seasonal menus that follow can easily be converted into packed lunches for school, office or picnics.

If you are the person who regularly makes packed lunch for members of the family, here are some tips.

- To avoid boredom on the part of the person consuming the packed lunch, and to create nutritional variety, try not to put all the same things into the box more than once a week.

- Whilst it might be energy-wasteful to supply a different type of bread for every day of the week, you could perhaps use bread as your basis only two or three times a week, and on the other days supply a rice-, potato-, pasta- or couscous-based salad instead. Add small pieces of cheese, cooked meat, eggs, nuts, seeds or pulses, along with some chopped salad items or cooked vegetables, and you have a complete meal.

- Always include one or two pieces of fruit – firmer fruits will fare better, but with careful packing you can include almost any fruit.

- Instead of salty crisps, go for a small container with dried fruits, nuts and seeds in it.

- A slice of home-made cake is fine; otherwise a small bar of dark chocolate or a low-sugar muesli bar are good options for hungry lunch-boxers.

- Fill a bottle or flask with cold water to drink.

- Purchase an insulated lunch box which will keep the contents cool and avoid any risk of food poisoning. This is important not just in summer but also any time when the box will sit around in a centrally heated school or office for hours.

Parties

Party re-usable and/or disposable plates are the green option (see Picnics) and you can also make up your own green party bags for children or order them online (see Resources).

When catering for children's parties, don't forsake all your green ideals and provide a host of colourant- and additive-rich nuggets, burgers and sweets: stick with simple food with lots of fresh fruit, mini sandwiches, veggie sausages (home-made if you can find the time; otherwise see the Ready Meals section in the A–Z or buy organic ready-to-make burger/sausage mix). Small tomatoes, radishes or celery make ideal crudités for a hummus or butterbean and lemon dip. And it really doesn't take long to make a carrot cake and ice it with fromage frais beaten with some icing sugar and lemon juice – much more delicious than most of the commercial party cakes you'll buy.

Eating out of doors – picnics and barbecues

If you're packing a picnic, follow the lunch-box ideas. If it's a special picnic – Ascot! – you could make some mini Cornish pasties or similar (they can be vegetarian: just add some cooked lentils instead of the little pieces of beef or lamb) and take some firmish strawberries to eat with your fingers if in season, or any other juicy local fruit.

Find details for stockists of eco-friendly plates and cups, napkins and cutlery, etc., in the Resources section.

Around two-thirds of UK families now own a barbecue. Top-of-the-range portable beasts, which are, basically, posh outdoor oven/grill/rotisserie combos, are high users of energy – either gas or electricity. Gas is preferable to electricity as it produces approximately 40 per cent less carbon dioxide, and the best gas to choose is LPG. BP has a lightweight and therefore less energy-intensive cylinder which can be refilled.

This is better than the commercial easy-light barbecue bricks and commercial firelighters – a combination that emits more carbon dioxide than any other barbecue option. But opting for old-fashioned, local and sustainable woodland charcoal for your barbecue (lit with a long match and some paper and old-fashioned bellows) is the cleanest and greenest option of all (despite the fact that such charcoal still sends off emissions and potential cancer-causing particles).

However, very little local and sustainable charcoal is currently used on our British barbecues – most of it comes from tropical wood from countries such as Africa and South America, which contributes to deforestation and creates transport CO_2 emissions as well. For sources for eco-friendly barbecues and materials, see the Resources section.

Now just a word about patio heaters: don't! One lone patio heater emits up to 3.5kg of carbon dioxide in an average evening – that's more carbon dioxide a year than the average 4x4. If it is too cold to sit outside, then have your party or drinks inside, or wear a nice thick coat.

Growing your own

Your cooking and meals will almost always be more enjoyable if you can manage to grow a little produce of your own; you will also feel very virtuous.

While few of us may have the space, or indeed time, to have an allotment or large vegetable garden, it's quite easy to have a few things growing in a small border, in pots on a roof terrace or balcony, or on a sunny windowsill.

Try to grow only what you like, and if you aren't green fingered start off with those salads and vegetables that are easiest. These include rocket, cut-and-come-again lettuce, courgettes, radishes, new potatoes, spring onions and a variety of herbs, including rosemary, thyme, mint, chervil, sage. That's only a short starter list – depending on the weather and your luck or lack of it with caterpillars, slugs, snails, rabbits and so on, many, many vegetables are quite easy to grow.

If you have a flower garden, don't be afraid to sow or plant produce in between the plants. Many are very pretty and don't look at all out of place. Certain flowers will help protect the produce – for example, marigolds help ward off greenfly.

If you have a conservatory you could try chilli plants, pepper, basil or even cherry tomatoes in there – in decorative pots they look very attractive.

If your garden is large enough, consider planting some fruit trees – apples, pears, plums or damsons are all reasonably easy if you choose native varieties. You can buy dwarf varieties, or espaliers to train against your wall. Other fruits that are not hard are raspberry, blackcurrant or loganberry canes or gooseberry bushes. I've been harvesting copious quantities of soft fruit for years and have never netted or caged them – the birds eat some, I eat some. That's fine.

More and more people are choosing to live the 'good life', with chickens and ducks in their back gardens. Although I have never had them myself – apart from a couple of beautiful ducks who flew in from a neighbouring farm and stayed for two weeks before being reclaimed (sadly) – I have many neighbours and colleagues who do. It only takes a few hens to give you almost round-the-year fresh eggs.

Interestingly, you can keep more or less any livestock in your back garden – including pigs, sheep and goats if you are so inclined – without any law to stop you. If you are interested, see the Resources section.

A pocket vegetable patch and a few hens this year – next, perhaps a full blown smallholding? Many people do get the bug ...

Picking your own

How about a healthy walk in the fresh air – and coming home with some free food to eat as well? From the edible baby leaves of many 'weeds' in the spring through to the herbs of summer, and the berries and nuts of autumn, the great outdoors is a huge pick-your-own farm without the cost. If you don't pick it, much of it will go to waste.

Try to harvest food from unpolluted areas (not right beside a dual carriageway, for example).

There are several books on wild food (see Resources). While surely everyone knows what a blackberry or a hazelnut looks like, if you're going for the less well-known foods, and especially mushrooms, you do need to know what you're doing, so some 'prep' is essential. If you don't take the book with you, at the very least look it up once you get it home – and if you're not sure, don't eat!

Here are just a few ideas:

Early spring: nettles, dandelions and other small green leaves.
Late spring/early summer: wild garlic, elderflowers, wild fennel, sorrel.
Summer: samphire, wild strawberries.
Autumn: blackberries, whinberries, hazelnuts, sweet chestnuts.

Conclusion

Your kitchen is the (green) powerhouse of your ethical-food campaign. It should also be a source of great pleasure and enjoyment for you and all who enter it to experience the food that is served there.

The next chapter gives you ideas for seasonal menus and recipes to enjoy.

6 The Pleasure Factor:
Seasonal Menus and Recipes

These nutritionally balanced menus contain many of the recipes in the second part of the chapter. When planning your own menus, take into account what leftovers you have – these menus assume feeding a family of four, but if there are only two of you you could eat a soup two days in a row.

To the daily menus add plenty of liquids – water, herbal teas, for example.

And eat two pieces of fresh seasonal fruit a day and one green-leaf seasonal salad.

Four seasons' menus
Spring menu

Day 1

Breakfast
Yogurt
Bramley apple and cinnamon purée
Honey

Lunch
Watercress soup (p. 191)
Wholegrain bread

Supper
Spring chicken traybake (p. 196)
Chard

Day 2

Breakfast
Porridge with sunflower seeds
Spanish orange

Lunch
Lentil soup
Wholegrain bread

Supper
Asparagus frittata (p. 196)

Day 3

Breakfast
Muesli
Cherries

Lunch
Oatcakes
Hummus
Rocket salad

Supper
Whole pod broad beans and bacon
(p. 195)

Day 4

Breakfast
Spiced rhubarb fool (p. 199)
Chopped hazelnuts

Lunch
Open sandwich of goat's cheese on dark
rye bread with chutney

Supper
Trout in caper sauce served with
spinach, garlic and pine nuts
(p. 194)

Day 5

Breakfast
Porridge with sultanas
Spanish orange

Lunch
Broad bean and lemon purée used as a
    dip
Crudités – e.g. carrot, spring onions,
    radishes

Supper
Spiced lentil, carrot and cauliflower
    ragout with brown rice

Day 6

Breakfast
Boiled egg
Wholegrain bread
Honey

Lunch
Fresh asparagus with lemon butter
and a little hard grated cheese

Supper
Clam chowder (p. 191)

Day 7

Breakfast
Muesli
Apple
Cherries

Lunch
Grated beetroot, carrot and white cabbage salad
Canned mackerel fillet

Supper
Penne with goat's cheese, rocket and sundried tomatoes
    (p. 194)

Summer menu

Day 1

Breakfast
Fromage frais
Strawberries
Chopped nuts

Lunch
Panzanella salad (p. 205)

Supper
Fresh crab with chilli and spaghetti
(p. 201)

Day 2

Breakfast
Boiled egg
Wholegrain bread
Peach

Lunch
Courgette soup with mint pesto
(p. 200)
Bread

Supper
Rack of lamb with herb crust (p. 205)
Roast tomatoes
Couscous

Day 3

Breakfast
Natural yogurt
Poached blackcurrants with vanilla

Lunch
Corn on the cob with butter

Supper
Pan-cooked megrim
Tomato and olive salsa

Day 4

Breakfast
Tomatoes on wholegrain toast

Lunch
Mackerel pâté
Oatcakes
Mixed leaves

Supper
Stir-fried mixed vegetables with pine
nuts and seeds tossed in quinoa

Day 5

Breakfast
Muesli
Apple
Blueberries

Lunch
Pea and lettuce soup (p. 200)
Wholegrain bread

Supper
Chicken with garlic, aubergine and
    tomato (p. 204)
New potatoes

Day 6

Breakfast
Braised plums topped with oat flakes
    and seeds

Lunch
Rye crispbreads
Fresh tomatoes topped with wafers of
    mature cheese and drizzled with
    basil pesto

Supper
Sea bass with lemon, fennel and fresh
    mixed herbs (p. 203)
Stir-fried sprouting broccoli

Day 7

Breakfast
Yogurt
Raspberries
Granola

Lunch
Spanish avocado with vinaigrette
Fresh figs with fromage frais

Supper
Warm cannellini bean, tomato, garlic and onion salad
Crusty bread

Autumn menu

Day 1

Breakfast
Scrambled eggs and chopped tomato on
dark rye toast

Lunch
Pear, stilton and walnut salad (p. 216)
Crusty bread

Supper
Easy vegetable tagine (p. 214)
Brown rice

Day 2

Breakfast
Porridge topped with blackberries

Lunch
Spiced butternut squash soup (p. 209)
Dark rye bread

Supper
Mussels in beer (p. 209)
Fromage frais and autumn berry
compôte

Day 3

Breakfast
Yogurt and autumn berry compôte
(p. 217)

Lunch
Mushrooms on toast (p. 215)

Supper
Pheasant casserole (p. 211)
Mashed potato

Day 4

Breakfast
Muesli topped with apples

Lunch
Fresh figs, air-dried ham, wholegrain
bread

Supper
Pasta puttanesca (p. 215)
Leaf salad

Day 5

Breakfast
Toast, home-made mixed berry jam
Fromage frais

Lunch
Tomatoes on toast

Supper
Whole mackerel with a herb and
orange stuffing (p. 210)
Cucumber salad

Day 6

Breakfast
Porridge topped with blueberries

Lunch
Hazelnut pâté
Oatcakes

Supper
Lamb shanks with apricot (p. 212)
Kale

Day 7

Breakfast
Toast, honey, bacon

Lunch
Jerusalem artichoke and potato soup
Bread

Supper
Stir-fried peppers, tomato, basil and red
onion topped with a poached egg
Crusty bread

Winter menu

Day 1

Breakfast
Porridge
Sultanas
Chopped nuts

Lunch
Potato and leek soup
Wholegrain bread

Supper
Pumpkin risotto (p. 223)
Leafy greens

Day 2

Breakfast
Bramley apple compôte
Fromage frais
Honey

Lunch
Baked beans on wholegrain toast

Supper
Pork with apples and cider (p. 221)
Winter greens
Mashed potato

Day 3

Breakfast
Toast with honey
Yogurt

Lunch
Celeriac and blue cheese soup (p. 218)

Supper
Spiced dahl and vegetable curry
(p. 222)
Flatbread

Day 4

Breakfast
Porridge topped with chopped dried
apricots and sunflower seeds

Lunch
Pasta salad with rocket, sundried
tomatoes, spring onions and pine nuts

Supper
Steamed sea bream with ginger (p. 219)
Steamed kale
Rice

Day 5

Breakfast
Boiled eggs
Toast

Lunch
All Saints' lentil and rice salad (p. 224)

Supper
Rabbit and prune casserole (p. 222)
Winter cabbage

Day 6

Breakfast
Compôte of mixed dried fruit
Yogurt

Lunch
Sandwich of goat's cheese, chutney and
coleslaw

Supper
Mixed root vegetable and borlotti bean
casserole
Brown rice

Day 7

Breakfast
Muesli
Chopped pear
Hazelnuts

Lunch
Rice salad with chopped celery, nuts,
seeds and apricot

Supper
Grilled sardines with gremolata (p. 218)
Crusty bread
Apple

Seasonal recipes

The recipes in this section are included primarily because they're all dishes I enjoy. They also follow the guidelines for green eating, as explained elsewhere in this book. They make best use of seasonal foods and most of the ingredients can be sourced in the UK. I've included some meat and dairy produce but have limited the quantities. Happily this philosophy not only fits in with green eating but also with healthy eating guidelines!

   Most of the recipes aren't too energy-consuming in the cooking – if the oven is used I give suggestions on how best to make full use of the heat and where appropriate I give further green tips and variations. Lastly I have kept an eye on the number of ingredients – especially bottles and jars of this and that which have come from all around the world to reach our store cupboards.

- All recipes serve four unless otherwise stated
- Try to purchase food items that have been produced using sustainable methods – organically, for example.
- Try to buy fruit, vegetables and other ingredients from local sources when you can.
- In most of the recipes that use olive oil, you can use good-quality British rapeseed oil instead (cold-pressed for salad dishes).

SPRING

WATERCRESS SOUP

2 maincrop potatoes
2 bunches watercress (about 175g in total)
25g butter
1 litre vegetable stock
salt and black pepper

1 Peel and chop the potatoes. Trim the largest stalks from the watercress and pick over, removing any yellowing leaves.

2 Heat the butter in a large saucepan until melted, then add the potatoes, stir well, and add the stock and seasoning. Bring to simmer and cook, covered, for 20 minutes or until the potatoes are tender. Allow to cool a little and then stir in most of the watercress.

3 Tip into an electric blender and blend until smooth. Check seasoning. Re-heat to serve hot, or chill to serve cold, garnished with the remaining watercress leaves.

TIPS
- For a more substantial soup you can add a chopped leek with the potatoes.
- You can stir in a little single cream before serving, if you like.
- You can grow landcress in the vegetable patch – it is very, very similar to watercress, quick to grow, and no trouble at all.
- British watercress (which is mostly grown in Hampshire and Dorset) is in season in the shops from April until October.

CLAM CHOWDER

1.5kg fresh clams
1 glass dry white wine
500ml skimmed milk
500ml fish stock
250g maincrop cooked potato chunks
1 large onion
1 tbsp olive oil
3 rashers back bacon, cut into strips
50g butter
1 heaped tbsp plain flour
fresh chopped parsley

1 Prepare the clams (see Tip overleaf); put them in a large lidded pan with the wine and over a high heat shake them for half a minute, then start removing those that have opened, using a slotted spoon, to a dish. Put the lid back on, shake for another few seconds, and continue until all the clams have opened. If there are some that don't open, discard them. Reserve the clam cooking liquid by pouring it through a fine sieve into a large jug. Add the milk and fish stock to the jug.

2 Let the clams cool down a bit. Meanwhile dice the potato into 1cm cubes, and peel and finely chop the onion. Heat the olive oil in a large pan and sauté the bacon over a medium-high heat until beginning to turn golden, then remove from the pan to a dish, using a slotted spoon. Turn the heat down, and add the onion and potato and cook over a medium heat, stirring, until softened but not brown. Add some seasoning.

3 When the clams are cool, shell most of them and reserve about one-eighth in their shells; now tip any juices from the clams into the liquid in the jug, once again passing it through the sieve.

4 Add the butter to the pan and melt, then stir in the flour and cook for a minute, turning the heat up a little. Gradually add the fish/milk liquid, stirring all the time with a large wooden spoon (it helps if you have pre-heated the liquid in the microwave, but if not just add it more slowly), until the mixture thickens somewhat.

5 Return the clams and the bacon to the pan, stir well, and simmer gently for 2–3 minutes. Garnish with plenty of parsley.

TIPS

- Add 2 tsps smoked paprika instead of the bacon if you like.

- Try a mixture, if you can get them, of carpet-shell (palourde) and almond (amande) clams.

- Buy wild clams only up until the end of April.

- Buy clams caught by sustainable means (not dredged).

- To prepare the clams, soak them in cold water for 20 minutes, then drain them and rinse them thoroughly under cold water, discarding any with broken shells. If you find any that are open, give them a sharp tap – if they don't close, you must discard them.

RED MULLET WITH OLIVE SALSA

4–8 red mullet fillets, depending on size
2–3 tbsps olive oil
2 large garlic cloves, very finely chopped
1 mild/medium-large fresh red chilli, seeded and finely chopped
8 sundried tomatoes in oil, skinned, seeded and chopped, plus 1 tbsp of the oil
good handful fresh flat-leaf parsley, finely chopped
8 large stoned black olives, finely chopped
freshly ground black pepper and a little salt

1 Brush a large heavy-based frying pan with half the olive oil and pan-fry the mullet fillets, skin-side down first, over high heat. After 2 minutes, turn the heat down to medium and fry the other side for a further 2 minutes.

2 Meanwhile, make a salsa by combining all the remaining ingredients in a small bowl (taste before adding extra salt). When the fish is cooked, serve each portion garnished with the salsa (there will only be a little each – it is quite potent).

TIPS

- Serve these with a purée of seasoned white beans (e.g. cannellini) into which you've stirred 1–2 tsps fresh finely chopped rosemary leaves. You can mash them with a fork and heat in the microwave.

- Samphire would also be nice if you want a green vegetable, but it doesn't come into season until late spring.

- When fresh tomatoes are in season later in the year, add a couple of ripe de-seeded chopped tomatoes to the salsa; it goes with most types of fish fillets, including sea bass.

- If you're not keen on raw garlic, you could either add the chopped garlic to the pan after the fish is cooked, stirring it over the remains of the head for a minute to soften before adding to the salsa, or you could add a little garlic-infused olive oil instead, or simply use a little chopped raw red or other mild onion.

TROUT IN CAPER SAUCE

4 brown trout fillets
1 tbsp olive oil
60g unsalted butter
2 tbsps capers in brine, drained and washed
2 tbsps chopped fresh chervil or dill
juice of a lemon
black pepper

1 Heat the oil in a large heavy-based frying pan and add the fillets, skin-side down. Fry over a medium-high heat for 3 minutes; turn and cook for a further 2 minutes on medium heat. Transfer the trout to warmed serving plates.

2 Add the butter to the hot pan, allow to melt and add the remaining ingredients. Stir for a minute until the butter is beginning to turn light brown, then spoon over the trout and serve.

TIPS

- Try serving with purple sprouting broccoli or spinach.

- You can also use whole cleaned trout on the bone, in which case cook for 5 minutes on the first side and 4 minutes on the second.

PENNE WITH GOAT'S CHEESE, ROCKET AND SUNDRIED TOMATOES

300g penne (dry weight)
175g (or thereabouts) jar soft sundried tomatoes in oil
200g soft goat's cheese log/s
4 good handfuls small rocket leaves
salt, black pepper

1 Cook the penne in plenty of lightly salted boiling water for 10 minutes or until just tender; drain.

2 Meanwhile, drain the tomatoes, reserving their oil, and roughly chop them. Roughly chop the goat's cheese.

3 When the pasta is ready, tip it into a serving dish and stir in the oil, tomatoes, rocket and goat's cheese. Season with black pepper.

TIPS

- This amount makes four smallish main courses/lunches or six good starters.

- Sundried tomato jars vary a little in weight but it doesn't matter – just add as many as you like and if there are some left over you can use them in various other ways.

- By late April and May garden rocket should be ready to pick. You can also grow it in pots in an unheated greenhouse and it will be ready mid-April.

- Leave out the pasta and you have a good, easy salad for lunch with some crusty bread.

WHOLE POD BROAD BEANS AND BACON

Eating the whole pod of the bean — which is much like a mangetout but tastier — is much less wasteful than shelling and throwing the pod away, and it saves time on the shelling! But if you can't get small whole pods, then use the shelled beans and make sure to compost the waste.

500g broad bean pods
good handful parsley
small handful chives or garlic chives
100g unsmoked lean back bacon, chopped
3 tbsps olive oil
very good handful mint
juice of half a lemon
black pepper

1 Steam or boil the broad beans until tender when pricked with a sharp knife — about 15 minutes; drain.

2 Meanwhile, chop the herbs, and when the beans are nearly ready, heat a third of the olive oil in a large frying pan and cook the bacon over a medium-high heat until it begins to crisp.

3 Add the cooked beans to the pan with the rest of the olive oil, the herbs, lemon juice and pepper. Stir well, reduce heat to low and cook, stirring occasionally, for a few minutes. Serve immediately.

TIPS

- If you have a vegetable patch, sow the broad beans in the autumn for the earliest pods.
- This dish is a great light supper with some wholegrain bread.
- You could add some cooked new potato chunks to the frying pan to brown a little when you cook the bacon.
- If the pods have any fur on the insides, then you are too late to eat them whole.
- If using shelled broad beans, they need cooking for only a few minutes.
- Try a similar dish with runner beans in summer.
- Any leftovers can be served cold as a lunch salad next day.

SPRING CHICKEN TRAYBAKE

350g spring carrots, scrubbed
1 small celeriac root, peeled and sliced
1 small swede, peeled and sliced
2 tbsps olive oil
1 large leek, cut into thick rounds
sprigs fresh thyme and rosemary
1 medium roasting chicken, cut into 10 (see Tip)
100ml chicken stock
2 tsps Dijon mustard
salt and black pepper

1 Heat the oven to 190°C. Toss the carrot, celeriac and swede in a large roasting pan with the olive oil and some seasoning and bake for 10 minutes.

2 Remove the pan from the oven, add the leek and herbs and toss again before tucking the chicken pieces amongst the vegetables. Return to the oven and cook for a further 15 minutes, then pour in the chicken stock and cook for another 25 minutes or until the chicken is golden and cooked through and the vegetables well coloured and tender.

3 Serve the chicken and vegetables on to individual dishes with a slotted spoon, and then mix the mustard into the gravy in the pan before spooning the juices over the plates.

TIP
- Use a meat cleaver to halve the chicken, then cut each breast and leg into two and remove and trim the wings.

ASPARAGUS FRITTATA

500g asparagus (see Tip)
6–8 large eggs (depending on how hungry you are)
salt and black pepper
handful fresh chopped mint
100g crumbled feta or firm goat's cheese (optional)
1½ tbsps olive oil

1 Break or chop off any woody asparagus stems and put in the compost bucket. Cut the remaining asparagus into 4cm pieces, keeping the tips separate. Steam for 2–7 minutes, depending on thickness (see Tip), adding the delicate tips for the last 1–3 minutes of cooking. Once cooked, refresh the asparagus under cold water, draining thoroughly.

2 Beat the eggs in a bowl with a dash of water and some salt and pepper. Stir in the mint and the cheese.

3 Heat a 24cm non-stick frying pan with the olive oil over medium-high heat and add the egg mixture. Turn the heat down to low and sprinkle the asparagus evenly around the egg mixture. Cook for around 10–12 minutes or until the frittata is nearly set. At this point you need to brown the top: you can either turn the heat up and flip the omelette over, using two large spatulas, and cook for around 30 seconds before turning out (original side up) on to a plate to slice; or you can carefully use a cook's blowtorch to brown the top (a sprinkling of grated cheese will help this process); or the classic but more energy-consuming method is to put the pan under a grill for a minute to brown. Serve hot or cut into wedges and serve cold.

TIPS

- This recipe is a great way of using sprue – the thin asparagus which is often the first to come through and will continue to come through along with the fatter spears. Sprue needs only a couple of minutes' cooking, while thick, fat spears will need around 8 minutes.

- If you have any cooked potatoes to hand, these make a good addition to the frittata (sliced). You can also add cooked bacon or ham.

- A good alternative to the asparagus is thin spears of sprouting broccoli – often abundant at this time of year. Cook them in a similar way. Small tender broad beans are also good.

SPINACH WITH GARLIC AND PINE NUTS

1kg spinach leaves
3 tbsps olive oil
100g pine nuts
2–4 cloves garlic, peeled and chopped
salt and black pepper

1 Pick over the spinach leaves (at this time of year they should be small and tender), rinse in water and toss thoroughly in a colander to remove as much of the water as you can.

2 Heat the oil in a very large pan and add the pine nuts, stir for a minute over medium-high heat until lightly coloured and remove with a slotted spoon to a dish. Add the garlic, stir for a minute until softened and again remove with a slotted spoon to the dish with the nuts.

3 Now add the spinach leaves to the pan, stirring constantly with a long-handled wooden spoon, until they have wilted. Add the nuts, garlic and plenty of seasoning to the pan and stir well before serving.

TIPS

- You can use green beans instead of spinach when they come into season.
- You can use flaked almonds or even walnut pieces instead of the pine nuts (walnut pieces won't need pre-cooking in the oil).
- This goes well with chicken and fish dishes.

SPICED RHUBARB FOOL

Very early rhubarb (Feb/March) is forced but you will harvest early sticks in the garden from around April. If you're going to buy rhubarb crowns to plant, get an early variety and a late one to prolong the season.

500g fresh rhubarb
juice and zest of an orange
150g white sugar
level tsp ground cinnamon
small piece fresh ginger, peeled and finely grated or chopped
500ml thick natural yogurt

1 Trim the leaves and the base off the rhubarb stalks and chop into short chunks. Mix together the orange juice, zest, sugar, cinnamon and ginger. Add the rhubarb to the orange mixture and stir well.

2 In a heavy-based lidded pan, poach the rhubarb very gently for 15 minutes or until it is soft but still has some shape.

3 Allow to cool and stir into the yogurt in swirls.

TIPS

- If the rhubarb makes a lot of juice, strain some of it off before adding to the yogurt. You can save the juice and use it as part of a smoothie or spooned over breakfast yogurt or cereals.
- This is also good stirred into custard or natural fromage frais instead of yogurt.
- If the oven is on, you can tip the rhubarb mix into a baking dish, cover and bake at around 180°C for 20 minutes instead of poaching.

ELDERFLOWER CORDIAL

20–30 elderflower heads
2 lemons
750g sugar
1.5 litres water
4 tsps citric acid

1 Rinse flower heads throroughly in cold water. Slice lemons, put in pan with flowers, citric acid and most of the sugar.

2 Boil the water and pour over the flowers in the pan. Stir to dissolve sugar. Cover with muslin cloth. Stir 2–3 times a day and skim off any scum that forms.

3 After 2 days, strain through muslin into bottles and use within 2 weeks, or keep some out and freeze the rest in ice-cube trays. To serve, dilute with water to taste (about 1:5).

TIPS

- Pick the flowers when they are in good condition, on a sunny day in May
- Try to avoid flowers at the roadside and take just a few flowers from each tree. Elder flowers are borne on elder trees or bushes and are found in mixed hedging all over the country.

SUMMER

COURGETTE SOUP WITH MINT PESTO

1kg medium-sized courgettes
2 tbsps olive oil
4 large cloves garlic, peeled and chopped
1 litre vegetable stock
juice of half a lemon
salt and black pepper

For the pesto:
2 good handfuls fresh mint leaves (see Tip)
50g chopped mixed nuts (or almonds or pine nuts)
75ml olive oil (about 5 tbsps)
salt and black pepper

1 Top and tail the courgettes and slice into 0.5cm rounds. Heat a large frying pan with 1 tbsp of the olive oil and, over medium-high heat, fry the courgettes (you will need to do this in two batches, adding the remaining 1 tbsp olive oil with the second batch), turning each slice over after about 4 minutes – if the underside is pale golden, it is ready to turn – and cooking for a further 4 or so minutes until all the courgettes are soft and golden.

2 Push the second batch of courgettes to the sides of the pan and add the garlic to the centre, stir-fry for a minute or two, then tip all the courgettes and garlic into an electric blender (if your blender is small, do this in two halves).

3 Add the stock, which can be cold or warm but not boiling hot, and blend to smooth, then tip the lot into a large pan over a medium heat to warm through, adding the lemon juice for the last minute or so. Add plenty of black pepper and some salt to taste. If serving cold, allow to cool then serve drizzled with the mint pesto.

4 To make the pesto, pick the mint over and remove any hard stems. Put into a blender with the nuts and half the 75ml olive oil, and blend, adding the rest of the oil in two batches and blending a little more. Add a little seasoning to taste.

TIPS

- Common mint (spearmint) is best in this pesto but you can also use apple mint.

- The soup is also nice served warm.

- Later in the year, you can use lemon basil instead of the mint.

- If you have a glut of new mint, pick it young and tender and make a lot of this pesto, or a mint sauce (mix chopped mint with a classic vinaigrette) and freeze in ice-cube trays.

PEA AND LETTUCE SOUP

500g fresh small peas (see Tip)
6 medium spring onions *or* 1 small mild onion
1 butterhead lettuce *or* 400g green lollo rossa-
   type leaves
25g butter
1 litre vegetable stock
1 tsp caster sugar
1 large clove garlic
salt and black pepper

1 Shell the peas; trim and slice the spring onions or peel and finely chop the onion. Pick over the lettuce and discard any browned outer leaves; roughly chop.

2 Heat the butter in a large saucepan over medium heat and soften the spring onions for 3 minutes, or the onion for 5 minutes. Add the stock, peas, lettuce, sugar, garlic, salt and pepper and bring to the boil. Simmer for 5 minutes then allow to cool slightly and put through a blender until smooth.

3 The soup can be served either hot or cold.

TIPS

- You can use frozen peas if you like and follow the same method.
- You can garnish the soup with some chopped fresh mint or basil, and if you have any cream or thick yogurt you can add a dollop of that.

FRESH CRAB WITH CHILLIES AND SPAGHETTI

300g spaghetti or spaghettini (dry weight)
2 cloves garlic
2 large fresh medium-hot chillies
2–4 spring onions depending on size
4 tbsps olive oil
juice of 2 limes
salt and black pepper
4 fresh dressed crabs (see Tip)
good handful flat-leaf parsley

1 Cook the spaghetti in a large pan of lightly salted boiling water until just tender – about 10 minutes.

2 While the spaghetti is cooking, peel and finely chop the garlic and de-seed and finely chop the chilli. Chop the onion, then heat the oil in a frying pan and, over a medium heat, stir-fry the garlic, chilli and onion for a couple of minutes to release the flavours into the oil; don't let the garlic brown. Add the lime juice and seasoning and then stir in the crab flesh just to warm through.

3 When the spaghetti is cooked, drain it and tip into a warm serving bowl. Stir in the crab chilli mixture and garnish with the parsley before serving.

TIP

- The brown flesh of the crab is very strong so you may prefer to use only half of this. The remaining brown flesh can be mixed with natural fromage frais and a little lime or lemon juice and black pepper to make a good sandwich filling or toast topping.

SEA BASS WITH LEMONS, FENNEL AND MIXED FRESH HERBS

1 small fennel bulb
2 lemons
2 sprigs rosemary
handful thyme sprigs
handful parsley
handful fennel leaves
1–1 ½ tbsps olive oil
4 medium sea bass fillets
25g butter
1 small glass dry white wine (about 75ml)
salt and black pepper

1 Cut the base and frondy top off the fennel (saving some of the leaves for the dish), then chop it fairly small. Put it in a dish with a tablespoon of water in the microwave on high for 2 minutes to soften.

2 Meanwhile, top and tail one of the lemons and cut the body into four rounds. Juice the other lemon. Remove the leaves from the rosemary and thyme sprigs and finely chop the rosemary leaves, parsley and fennel leaves.

3 Heat half the oil in a large non-stick frying pan (spreading it round with a brush to make sure it coats the entire base of the pan, but you don't want more than a thin layer otherwise you will create a lot of smoke) and, over high heat, fry the seasoned bass fillets, skin-side down, for 2–3 minutes (see Tip) with the lemon slices.

4 Turn the fillets and lemon over, turn the heat down to medium and fry the other side for 1–2 minutes. Remove the fish and lemon from the pan on to a warm dish and keep warm.

5 Add the butter and a dash of olive oil, and let it melt on medium heat, then add the chopped fennel bulb and stir for a minute or two. Add the wine, herbs, some seasoning and most of the lemon juice, bring to simmer and stir for several minutes until the fennel is tender. Serve the bass fillets (skin-side up if you want) on the fennel mix, garnished with the cooked lemon slices.

TIP

- Sea bass will cook quickly – so although you want to brown and crisp the skin you don't want to overcook the flesh. The exact cooking time depends on the heat and size of the pan and the thickness of the fillets, so you need to watch this carefully.

CHICKEN WITH GARLIC, AUBERGINE AND TOMATO

2 red onions
1 aubergine
4–5 medium tomatoes
20 large cloves new season's fresh garlic, unpeeled
2 tbsps olive oil
4 chicken legs, each cut into 2 pieces, *or* 1 whole chicken, cut into portions
1 handful chopped fresh mixed summer herbs of choice (see Tip)
salt and black pepper
200ml fresh tomato sauce (see recipe, page 206)
a little chicken stock or water

1 Peel and cut the onions into quarters; top and tail the aubergine and cut it into thickish rounds, halving any very large ones. Quarter the tomatoes. Then, in a large heavy roasting pan, toss the vegetables and garlic in the olive oil and arrange them and the herbs evenly in the pan base. Arrange the chicken pieces on top and season everything with a little salt and plenty of pepper.

2 Cook at 200°C for 15 minutes, then mix together the tomato sauce with a little stock or water to thin it down and drizzle it over the pan contents (there won't be a huge amount, so don't try to cover everything). Turn the heat down to 180°C and cook for a further 30–40 minutes or until the chicken is cooked through and the vegetables soft. As necessary towards the end of cooking, pour a little water or chicken stock around the edges of the pan and vegetables, avoiding the golden tops of the chicken – you want to create some tomatoey juices to spoon over the meal.

TIPS

- I know this is the second chicken traybake in this recipe collection, but it is such an easy and economical way to make a 'roast' and you can vary the ingredients for each of the seasons.
- Nice with couscous or pasta, or you could put small new potatoes on skewers and bake them in the oven while the chicken cooks to save energy. If you have a large enough pan you could add parboiled potato slices to the rest of the vegetables.
- The garlic cloves should be soft and nutty inside – just pick them up in your fingers and suck out the tasty centres. Old garlic doesn't roast this way very well: it tends to just dry out.
- It is good if the herb mix includes oregano; thyme and finely chopped rosemary also go well.

RACK OF LAMB WITH HERB CRUST

100g breadcrumbs
small handful fresh thyme sprigs
2 sprigs fresh rosemary
handful fresh apple or spearmint
handful fresh parsley
3 tbsps olive oil
2 racks of British lamb, most of the fat removed

1 Remove the thyme leaves and rosemary leaves from their stalks. Chop all the herbs, mix them together in a bowl and combine with the breadcrumbs thoroughly.

2 Pour in the oil and mix well, then press the crumb mix into the fat sides of the racks. (Stand the racks propped up against each other in a small roasting tin to make this easier.) Cook at 190°C for 25 minutes or until the crumb is golden and the lamb still pink inside. Divide each rack into two sets of cutlets to serve.

TIP
● You could use the oven heat to roast some tomatoes to go with this.

PANZANELLA SALAD

200g – four large slices – stale-ish farmhouse-type bread
2 tbsps olive oil
500g ripe tasty tomatoes
15cm piece cucumber
1 large red pepper
2 cloves garlic
bunch basil
8 black stoned olives
approx. 6 tbsps classic vinaigrette (see recipe, see page 207)

1 Brush the bread slices with the olive oil and dry them out in a warm oven (when you are using the oven for something else) until somewhat crisp, or toast them lightly.

2 Roughly chop the tomatoes into a serving dish, then chop and add the cucumber and the de-seeded pepper. Finely chop the garlic, tear any large basil leaves and roughly chop the olives, then add all of them to the dish.

3 Toss everything in the dressing, then tear the bread into bite-sized pieces and add that to the dish. Serve immediately.

TIP
● For a more substantial salad you could add some pieces of goat's cheese or even some quartered hardboiled egg, though neither of these is traditional to this Italian salad.

TOMATO SAUCE

1kg fresh, ripe tasty tomatoes (see Tip)
1 large mild onion
2 cloves garlic
4 tbsps olive oil
1 tbsp tomato purée
pinch brown sugar
a little salt and some black pepper

1 Make a cross in the stalk end of each tomato skin. Put them into boiling water for 2 minutes, drain and peel off the skins. Quarter the tomatoes and scoop out the seeds. If there are any green bits near the stalk end, remove them as they won't cook down and will spoil the sauce.

2 Peel and finely chop the onion and garlic. In a large pan, heat the oil and over a medium heat sauté the onion, stirring frequently, until it is soft and transparent – about 8 minutes. Add the garlic and cook for another minute or two, then tip in the tomatoes, tomato purée and sugar, stir well and bring to the simmer.

3 Simmer gently for around 30 minutes, stirring from time to time until you have a rich sauce. Season to taste.

TIPS

- If you can get fresh plum tomatoes, these are very good to use. They are also quite easy to grow in an unheated greenhouse – I choose the variety called Agro. Beefsteak tomatoes are also good.
- If the tomatoes aren't as tasty as they could be, you can add some sundried tomato paste to beef up the flavour.
- If you have a glut of tomatoes or they are cheap in the market, make plenty of this sauce and freeze it.
- Out of season, you can use two 400g cans tomatoes instead, which does make the recipe quicker to prepare.
- You can add various items to this sauce, depending on what you want to use it for: mixed herbs for a meat sauce; chopped fresh chillies, which might be good in a curry, and so on.
- You can purée the sauce and add ground almonds for the last 10 seconds of blending for a sauce that goes well with fish.

NEW POTATO SALAD

600g new potatoes
good large handful apple *or* spearmint leaves
good large handful parsley
6–8 spring onions *or* 2 shallots
100ml classic vinaigrette dressing (see Tip)

1 Clean the potatoes and cut any larger ones. Cook in boiling lightly salted water for 20 minutes or until tender, drain and bash lightly with a masher to break up roughly. Tip into a serving bowl.

2 While the potatoes are cooking, finely chop the mint, parsley and onions. When they are in the serving bowl and still nice and warm, tip all the herbs in and mix to combine, then pour in the dressing and mix that in thoroughly too.

3 Cover and leave to cool to room temperature before serving.

TIPS
- For a simple vinaigrette, mix together 00ml olive oil with 10ml red wine vinegar and 10ml balsamic vinegar, a little salt and black pepper, a level teaspoonful of caster sugar and a teaspoonful of Dijon mustard. Shake all together in a clean screw-top jar. Taste and add a little more vinegar or seasoning as necessary.
- This salad goes well with cold or hot lamb.

STRAWBERRIES IN WINE

600g strawberries (see Tip)
third of a bottle sweet white wine (see Tip)

1 Hull and halve or quarter the strawberries and arrange them in four serving glasses.

2 Pour the wine evenly over the berries, cover the glasses and chill for about an hour. Serve.

TIPS
- Although most of the commercial strawberries in the UK now are Elsanto, you can find other, tastier, varieties in local markets. They are also surprisingly easy to grow on the patio in tubs.
- The better the quality of wine, the nicer this dessert will be.

TIPS

- You can use other orange-fleshed squash or pumpkin in this recipe. One of my favourites, and one of the easiest to grow in the UK, is Crown Prince.

- You can use green herbs to garnish the soup, or swirl in some thick yogurt or sour cream.

AUTUMN

SPICED BUTTERNUT SQUASH SOUP

2 medium onions
2 medium cloves garlic
2 tsps coriander seeds
1½ tsps cumin seeds
¼ tsp ground nutmeg
small knob fresh ginger
2 tbsps olive oil
1 medium to large butternut squash – about 1kg
1 litre hot chicken or vegetable stock
sea salt and freshly ground black pepper

1 Peel and finely chop the onions and garlic, then grind the coriander and cumin seeds and peel and grate the ginger.

2 Heat the oil in a large saucepan, add the onion and, over a medium heat, cook, stirring occasionally, for about 10 minutes or until the onions are soft and transparent. Meanwhile, peel the squash, de-seed it, and chop into small pieces.

3 When the onions are soft, add the prepared spices, the nutmeg and the garlic to the pan, stir well and cook for a couple of minutes to release the aromas, then stir in the squash, with some salt and plenty of black pepper, and stir for another minute.

4 Pour the stock into the pan, stir, bring to a simmer and cook for about 15 minutes or until the squash is soft. Allow to cool a little then blend in an electric blender and reheat. Check seasoning and serve.

MUSSELS IN BEER

1kg mussels in their shells
2 tbsps olive oil
2–3 shallots, peeled and very finely chopped
2 cloves garlic, peeled and well crushed
275ml bottle pale ale
good handful finely chopped parsley

1 Clean and de-beard the mussels as necessary, discarding any that are broken or open.

2 Heat the olive oil in a saucepan large enough to take the mussels easily and sauté the shallots and garlic over medium-high heat, stirring frequently, for a few minutes until soft.

3 Add the mussels and the beer, combine well and bring to simmer. Put the lid on and leave to cook, shaking the pan now and then, until all the mussels have opened – up to 5 minutes. (Discard any that remain closed.)

4 Serve the mussels in bowls with some of the juices poured over and the parsley sprinkled on top.

TIPS

- Serve with crusty bread if liked.
- Add some finely chopped fresh chilli to the shallots and garlic for a bit more of a bite.
- This dish makes a good quick supper for four, or could be a starter for six.

WHOLE MACKEREL WITH HERB AND ORANGE STUFFING

good handful fresh dill leaves (see Tip)
4 medium to large spring onions, trimmed
1 orange
80g breadcrumbs
2 tbsps rapeseed oil (use British)
salt and black pepper
4 small mackerel, gutted and cleaned
1 tbsp olive oil
few dill springs to garnish, if liked

1 Chop the dill leaves and the trimmed spring onions finely. Remove 2 tsps zest from the orange using a zester or a fine grater, being careful not to take the white pith as well.

2 Mix together the dill, onions, zest, breadcrumbs, rapeseed oil, seasoning and 2 tbsps orange juice in a bowl.

3 Make a couple of slashes on each side of the mackerels (to help them cook through more evenly), then fill the insides of the fish with the stuffing. Brush the oil over the base of a very large frying pan (or you may have to use two), add the mackerel and, over medium-high heat, cook for 6 minutes a side or until cooked through and golden. Garnish with dill if liked.

TIPS

- If you have the oven on you could put the stuffed mackerels, drizzled with oil, in the oven for about 25 minutes instead, at around 190°C.
- If you are having to use two pans to cook the mackerel, it may take no more energy to cook them under a medium-high grill instead, for a similar length of time.
- If you can't find any fresh dill, you could use fennel instead, or even crushed dill or fennel seeds.

PHEASANT CASSEROLE

2 oven-ready pheasants
12 shallots
1 head celery
750ml vegetable stock (see Tip)
25g butter, soft
1 tbsp plain flour
25ml cream
Salt and black pepper
chopped fresh parsley

1 Cut each pheasant in half and remove as much of the skin as you can (but if you don't it doesn't matter too much). You can also trim off the backbone if you like. Peel the shallots, trim the celery and cut it into four wedges.

2 Put the pheasant, vegetables and stock into a large saucepan and bring to simmer; put the lid on and simmer gently for about 45 minutes or until the pheasant joints and vegetables are cooked through (test with a sharp knife). Remove the meat and vegetables from the pan using a slotted spoon, and keep warm (see Tip).

3 Bring the stock to a fast boil and reduce down to 300ml (about half) – you will have

to do this without the lid on. Meanwhile, beat together the butter and flour in a small bowl until you have a paste.

4 When the stock is reduced, add the paste, stir well to melt and simmer with the lid on for 10 minutes, then stir in the cream, taste and add a little salt if necessary and some black pepper. Serve the sauce with the pheasant and vegetables, garnished with chopped parsley.

TIPS

- If you have no means of keeping the pheasant and vegetables warm while you make the sauce, put them back into the saucepan for the last 2–3 minutes of cooking time to heat through.
- Try making your own stock – it's very easy. Simply put the celery trimmings, a large chopped carrot, a chopped onion, a bay leaf, a bouquet garni and some peppercorns in a pot with a litre of water and simmer for half an hour; strain.
- You can use guinea fowl or chicken instead of the pheasant.
- This is nice served with mashed potato and a green vegetable.

LAMB SHANKS WITH APRICOT

2 medium onions *or* 12 shallots
4cm piece cinnamon stick
2 tsps cumin seeds
2 tsps coriander seeds
½ tsp ground chilli
1 tsp saffron threads (see Tip)
2 tbsps olive oil
4 small lamb shanks
400ml lamb or chicken stock (see Tip)
juice of half an orange
2 tsps runny honey
 salt and black pepper
12 halves soft, dried apricots, each cut into two
(see Tip)

1 Peel and cut the onions each into six wedges, or peel the shallots. Grind all the spices.

2 Heat half the oil in a large flameproof casserole or large heavy-based saucepan with a good tight-fitting lid. Brown the shanks all over, over a high heat, then remove them from the pan. If the pan base has a lot of burnt bits, wipe it over with a cloth.

3 Heat the remaining oil in the pan and sauté the onions or shallots over a medium heat, stirring from time to time, until they are soft and just turning golden. Add all the spices and stir for a minute, then return the lamb to the pan with enough of the stock so that the shanks are about two-thirds covered; add the orange juice and honey. Add a little salt and some black pepper. Bring to a simmer, turn the heat down to very low, put the lid on and cook for an hour. Add the apricots, stirring them well into the liquid. At the same time, if necessary add a little more stock.

4 Put the lid back on and cook for a further half hour, or until the lamb is melting off the bone and you have a rich sauce. Check the seasoning and serve with rice, couscous or bread and some green leaves.

TIPS
- You can use turmeric instead of the saffron.
- It's easy to make lamb or chicken stock, following the principle on page 211 for vegetable stock, but adding the meat trimmings/bones to the pan. Cook for an extra 15 minutes.
- You could use fresh figs for the recipe instead of apricots – six halved figs would be about right. Brown Turkey figs will crop well in the UK if you grow the tree on a south-facing wall.

EASY VEGETABLE TAGINE

1 large onion
2 cloves garlic
1 heaped tsp cumin seeds
2cm piece cinnamon stick (see Tip)
2 tbsps olive oil
2 medium courgettes
3 plum tomatoes
1 level tbsp harissa paste
400g can chick peas, drained, *or* 250g chickpeas, cooked weight
250g runner beans or green beans, sliced
2 tbsps sultanas
1 tbsp tomato paste
juice of a lemon
225ml vegetable stock
1 level tbsp plain flour

1 Peel and chop the onion and garlic and grind the spices. Heat the oil in a large flameproof casserole or heavy-bottomed saucepan and add the onion. Sauté over a medium heat, stirring frequently, for 8–10 minutes or until soft and just turning golden. Meanwhile, top and tail the courgettes and slice them, and chop the tomatoes.

2 When the onion is soft, add the garlic and spices and stir for a minute, then add the harissa paste and stir again. Tip in the remaining ingredients apart from the flour and 3 tablespoons of the stock, stir well, bring to a simmer, put the lid on and simmer on low for 30–40 minutes, or until everything is tender.

3 Mix together the stock and flour and add to the pan, stirring in well. Simmer for a further 10 minutes and check seasoning before serving.

TIPS

- This really is a movable feast – you can alter the vegetables to suit yourself. At this time of year, you might include squash, pumpkin and/or aubergine.
- You can also add various bits and bobs – such as preserved lemons, black stoned olives, fresh coriander leaf (at the end of cooking) and so on.
- The dish will also cook in the oven if you happen to have it on for anything else.
- Grinding small amounts of spices in an electric grinder is not always that successful – using a pestle and mortar is a good idea. You can use ready-ground cinnamon if you prefer.
- Serve with couscous, rice, pasta or bread.

PASTA PUTTANESCA

350g spaghetti (dry weight)
2 tbsps olive oil
1 medium onion
2 cloves garlic
2 fresh mild red chillies
16 black stoned olives
2 heaped tbsps rinsed and drained capers
level tsp smoked paprika
400g can chopped tomatoes

1 Put a large pan of lightly salted water on to boil. When it boils, add the pasta and return to the boil. Meanwhile, peel and chop the onion, heat the oil in a frying pan and sauté until soft and transparent – about 8 minutes – stirring from time to time. Peel and chop the garlic, de-seed and finely chop the chillies, and roughly chop the olives.

2 Stir the garlic, chillies, olives, capers and paprika into the frying pan and stir for a minute or two, then tip in the tomatoes and bring to simmer.

3 When the pasta is cooked after about 10 minutes, drain, tip into a warm serving bowl and lightly stir in the sauce.

TIPS
- You can garnish with fresh basil leaves or parsley if you like.

- If you happen to have a can of anchovies at the back of your cupboard, then put those in as well (puttanesca traditionally uses them); if not, the capers will give the required tartness on their own. Don't buy anchovies specially, as the MCS says Bay of Biscay anchovy stocks are at an all-time low and Portuguese anchovy stocks are possibly overfished, so they have put anchovies on their 'Avoid' list.

MUSHROOMS ON TOAST

450g field mushrooms (see Tip)
4 cloves garlic
good handful thyme sprigs
3 tbsps olive oil
1 level tsp paprika
1 tbsp soy sauce
2 tbsps sour cream (optional)
4 large slices bread of choice
25g butter

1 Slice the mushrooms, removing any stalks that are tough or damaged (you can use these for meat stock). Peel and finely chop the garlic and remove the thyme leaves from the stalks.

2 Heat the oil in a large non-stick frying pan or wok and stir-fry the mushrooms for a few minutes until tender but not mushy. Add the garlic, thyme, and paprika and stir for a minute, then add the soy sauce and sour cream, if using.

3 Toast the bread, butter the slices and top with the mushroom mixture.

TIPS
- You can use a combination of different types of fresh mushrooms – you may find wild mushrooms for sale at your local market.

- You could use Worcester sauce instead of the soy sauce if you have any in your cupboard, but it does contain anchovies (see above) so I'm not that inclined to use it in my kitchen at the moment.

PEAR, STILTON AND WALNUT SALAD

1 crisp lettuce head or similar amount of crisp
salad leaves (see Tip)
60g walnut pieces
100g ripe Stilton cheese (see Tip)
2–3 Comice *or* other ripe pears
Dressing:
4 tbsps walnut oil
1 tbsp white wine vinegar
1 heaped tsp wholegrain mustard
1 level tsp caster sugar
salt and black pepper

1 Mix all the dressing ingredients together in
a screw-top jar, taste and adjust seasoning as
necessary.

2 Wash the salad briefly and pat dry; arrange
in a serving bowl. Scatter in the walnut pieces.
Crumble the cheese and scatter in. Peel, core
and cut the pears into 8 slices each and add to
the salad. Drizzle the dressing over and serve.

TIPS

- Make sure the cheese and the pears are at
  room temperature for the best flavour.

- Don't peel the pears too early or they will go
  brown.

- You can use other cheeses. Traditionally this
  salad is made with the creamier Roquefort,
  but I prefer to use British cheeses if possible.

- Try to get new season's walnuts and shell
  them yourself.

- Slightly bitter salad leaves go well in here –
  curly endive or Belgian chicory, for example.
  You could also throw in some rocket if you
  like. Whatever you choose, don't go for very
  soft, limp leaves.

AUTUMN BERRY COMPÔTE

20g butter
2 tbsps caster sugar
vanilla pod
200g blackberries
200g autumn raspberries
100g blueberries

1 Heat the butter in a non-stick frying pan over a medium heat and add the sugar with the vanilla pod, stirring until the sugar is melted.

2 Add all the fruits to the pan, stir gently and heat through until they are beginning to cook, then take immediately off the heat and spoon into serving dishes.

TIPS
- You can vary the fruit proportions according to what you have/can buy. The last crop of British raspberries is harvested in September. You can buy late varieties to grow in your own garden – they are very easy.
- Serve with thick natural yogurt or fromage frais, or use to top a sponge dessert.

APPLE AND QUINCE NUT CRUMBLE

2 quinces
500g cooking apples
75g caster sugar
50g butter
75g brown sugar
50g porridge oats
50g plain flour
50g chopped de-skinned hazelnuts

1 Peel and core the quinces and cut into very small pieces. Put a little water in a pan, cover with a lid and simmer for 10 minutes to soften – quinces are very hard.

2 Peel and core the apples, cut into chunks and arrange in a suitably sized pie or baking dish (a soufflé dish is ideal). Tip in the quinces and stir them together with the apples and the caster sugar.

3 Make the topping: melt the butter in a saucepan and then stir in the brown sugar and allow to dissolve, then stir in the oats, flour and nuts. Spoon the topping over the apple mix and cook in an oven, when you are using it for something else, for 25 minutes or until the topping is golden and the fruit cooked. Serve warm or cold.

TIPS
- You can use blackberries or raspberries instead of the quince, in which case don't pre-cook them.
- Quince gives a fabulous, scented, unique flavour – it really is a superb, under-used fruit. The trees are lovely – big floppy leaves and very pretty flowers in spring.

WINTER

CELERIAC AND BLUE CHEESE SOUP

1 celeriac, about 800g
1 large onion
1½ tbsps rapeseed oil (use British)
500ml vegetable stock
500ml milk
bay leaf
salt and black pepper
125g any British blue cheese (see Tip)

1 Peel the celeriac and cut it into small cubes, then peel and finely chop the onion. Heat the oil in a large lidded saucepan, tip in the vegetables and stir them around over a medium-high heat for a couple of minutes.

2 Add the stock, milk, bay leaf and some seasoning and bring to a simmer; turn the heat down, put the lid on and simmer for 30 minutes or until the vegetables are tender.
Stir in the cheese and allow to cool slightly.

3 Blend the soup in an electric blender until smooth; reheat and check seasoning to serve.

TIPS
- You can make the same soup using winter celery if you like. You will need one large head and you want to strip the tough membranes from the outer stalks.
- You can use all stock and no milk if you like, but the result will be a little less creamy.
- I used Dovedale mild blue cheese but you could use Stilton. Otherwise you could use a French blue cheese such as St-Agur.

SARDINES WITH GREMOLATA

12–16 fresh sardines, cleaned and prepared
1 heaped tbsp rinsed and drained capers
2 large handfuls flat-leaf parsley, roughly
  chopped
zest of a lemon
8 green stoned olives
3–4 tbsps olive oil
salt (see Tip) and freshly ground black pepper
1 large lemon, cut into 4 wedges

1 Pat the sardines dry and make 2–3 slashes in the flesh on each side.

2 Make the gremolata: put the capers, parsley, lemon zest, olives and 2 tbsps olive oil, a little salt and plenty of pepper in a mortar, then pound into a paste with the pestle. Add another tbsp of olive oil once you have the paste done, if it seems to need it, and stir that in thoroughly. (For a rougher gremolata you could simply finely chop the capers, parsley, lemon zest and olives together, then mix with the oil and seasoning.)

3 Spread the gremolata in the sardine slashes and cook for 3–4 minutes a side in a large hot frying pan brushed with olive oil (see Tip). Serve with bread and lemon wedges.

TIPS
- If you have some sea salt flakes use those. As the olives and capers are salty, don't add more than a level tsp, at least until you've checked the taste of the gremolata.
- If you have to use two pans to cook the sardines, you might as well use the grill

instead which will use only a little more energy. If you do, have the grill on high. Alternatively, if you have anything else you can cook in the oven, you could bake the sardines on a roasting tray for 15–20 minutes or until golden and 'spitting'.

- Serve with bread.

STEAMED SEA BREAM WITH GINGER

4 large spring onions
1 knob fresh ginger, about 4cm by 2cm
1 tsp caster sugar
2 tbsps dry sherry
2 tbsps soy sauce
2 tbsps sesame oil
1 tbsp fish sauce (Nam pla/nuoc nam); available in most supermarkets, but if you cannot find it, omit it
4 sea bream fillets

1 Finely chop the spring onions and peel and finely chop the ginger. In a bowl, combine all the ingredients except the fish.

2 Lay the bream fillets in a shallow dish which will fit in your steamer and pour the sauce over the top. Put the dish into the steamer tray and put the lid on. Steam the fish for about 5 minutes or until cooked through, and serve with the sauce.

TIPS
- You can use other fish in season, such as sea bass.
- You can vary the ingredients to suit yourself – you could use lemon juice instead of the sherry, and you could add some finely chopped fresh mild chilli.

CUMBERLAND SAUSAGE AND BEAN CASSEROLE

2 large onions
4 cloves garlic
2 tbsps rapeseed oil (use British)
8 Cumberland sausages
400g can cannellini beans (see Tip)
1 heaped tsp smoked paprika
400g can chopped tomatoes
1 bay leaf
dash of red wine *or* vegetable or chicken stock
a little salt and plenty of black pepper

1 Peel and finely chop the onions and garlic and heat the oil in a large flameproof casserole, then add the onions and sauté over a medium heat until soft and transparent. Add the garlic and stir for a minute, then remove all the onion from the pan using a slotted spoon and add the sausages.

2 Turn up the heat and brown the sausages, turning to colour them all over. When they are browned, add all the remaining ingredients, stir well, bring to simmer, put the lid on and cook for 30 minutes. Check the seasoning, remove the bay leaf and serve.

TIPS

- You can use other beans in the casserole, such as butterbeans or borlotti, or a mixture. Whatever you choose, softer beans are best as they help to thicken the sauce.
- You can use other varieties of sausage, but make sure they are very good quality with a high meat percentage and nicely seasoned.
- If you have the oven on, you can cook this in the oven instead, at around 170°C for 30–40 minutes. Or in an Aga you could cook it very low for several hours.

PORK WITH APPLES AND CIDER

2 large onions
2lb pork (see Tip)
a few sage leaves
1 tbsp rapeseed oil (use British)
300ml dry cider
2 tsps concentrated chicken stock (see Tip)
salt and black pepper
3 dessert apples (see Tip)
2 tbsps sour or other cream
good handful fresh parsley

1 Peel and chop the onions, cut the pork into large pieces and chop the sage leaves. Heat the oil in a large heavy-based lidded frying pan or flameproof casserole and sauté the onion over medium heat, stirring frequently, until soft and transparent. Remove with a slotted spoon and add the pork to the pan. Turn up the heat and brown it on all sides, then return the onions to the pan with the sage leaves, cider, stock concentrate and seasoning; bring to a simmer.

2 Meanwhile, core the apples and cut each into 8 wedges, then add them to the pan, pushing them down well. When the casserole has come to simmer, put the lid on and turn the heat down low. Cook for 1–1½ hours, depending upon the type of pork you have used, or until everything is tender and cooked through.

3 Remove the pork and apples from the pan with a slotted spoon and keep warm; turn the heat up and reduce the sauce down about a third. Stir in the cream, check seasoning and serve the pork and apples with the sauce, garnished with the parsley.

TIPS

- You can use shoulder or loin of pork, or even pork tenderloin fillets. Shoulder contains more fat and the result should be meltingly tender, but if you're watching your weight the loin or tenderloin might be a better alternative, in which case take care not to overcook.
- Try to use British apples such as Cox or Granny Smith – tart eaters are better than very sweet apples.
- You can buy chicken stock concentrate in small bottles, or you can make your own by reducing home-made chicken stock right down.
- You can serve the dish without adding any cream, but it does give it a nice finish.

RABBIT AND PRUNE CASSEROLE

1 large rabbit
2 medium onions
100g stoned ready-to-eat prunes
1½ tbsps rapeseed oil (use British)
1 bay leaf
level tsp grated nutmeg
300ml chicken stock
salt and black pepper
1 small cooking apple
25g butter, softened
1 rounded tbsp plain flour

1 Joint the rabbit and remove the ribs as they contain little meat. Peel and chop the onions and halve the prunes. Heat the oil in a large heavy-based lidded saucepan or flameproof casserole and sauté the onion until soft and transparent. Add the rabbit, prunes, bay leaf, nutmeg, stock and seasoning, bring to a simmer and cook for 15 minutes.

2 Meanwhile, peel and core the apple and chop into fairly large pieces, then add to the casserole. Continue cooking for another 30 minutes or until the rabbit is tender.

3 Make a paste of the butter and flour. Push the rabbit to one side of the pan and add the paste, stirring it in to melt. Bring back to simmer, stirring, until the sauce thickens. (Or if you find it easier, remove the rabbit with a slotted spoon while you thicken the sauce and then return it to the pan.)

4 Check seasoning, remove bay leaf and serve.

TIPS

- Trust me, prunes really do go very well with rabbit and this simple casserole is delicious.

- If you like you can omit the cooking apple and add a dash of cider vinegar or dry cider to the pan instead.

- Serve with mashed potato and green vegetables.

SPICY DAHL AND VEGETABLES

1 large onion
2 cloves garlic
small knob fresh ginger
1 tbsp rapeseed oil (use British)
1 level tsp turmeric
2 tsps garam masala
a mug (about 250g) of red lentils (dry weight)
1 cauliflower
125g frozen peas, thawed
a little salt

1 Peel and finely chop the onion, garlic and ginger. Heat the oil in a large heavy-based lidded frying pan and sauté the onion over a medium heat, stirring frequently, until soft and turning golden.

2 Add the garlic, ginger, turmeric and garam masala and stir well for a minute, then add the lentils and stir again, cooking for a minute or two.

3 Now add about 300ml hot water and bring to the boil. Turn down the heat a little, put the lid on and simmer for 25 minutes. Check and add a little more water if things are looking dry, as the lentils will absorb much of the liquid.

4 Meanwhile, divide the cauliflower into smallish florets and steam, microwave or boil the cauliflower and peas until just tender and add them to the lentils in the frying pan for the last 5 minutes of cooking. Add a little salt to taste.

TIPS

- You can vary the vegetables according to what you have.
- The dhal is good served with brown rice or some crusty bread.
- You can use split yellow peas instead of the red lentils.

PUMPKIN RISOTTO

50g pine nuts
2½ tbsps olive oil
600g Crown Prince or other orange-fleshed pumpkin (weight including skin and seeds)
1 small onion
1–2 garlic cloves, finely chopped
small handful sage leaves
850ml vegetable or chicken stock
150ml dry white wine
300g Arborio rice
30g butter
50g Parmesan cheese
salt and black pepper

1 Heat a large heavy-based lidded frying pan brushed with a little of the olive oil and toast the pine nuts over high heat until golden, taking care they don't burn once they start adding colour. Remove with a slotted spoon to a dish and reserve.

2 Peel and seed the pumpkin (save the seeds) and cut the flesh into smallish bite-sized pieces. Heat 1 tbsp of the olive oil in a large, lidded frying pan, season the pumpkin well and sauté it over medium heat, stirring from time to time, for 6–8 minutes or until it has cooked through and taken on a bit of colour. Remove with the slotted spoon. Peel and finely chop the onion, garlic and sage, and add the onion to the pan with the remaining oil. Sauté it over a medium heat, stirring frequently, until it is soft and transparent and just tinged with gold.

3 Meanwhile, put the stock and wine in a large microwaveable jug and heat in the microwave until nearly boiling; remove from the microwave carefully. When the onion is soft, add the garlic and rice and stir for a minute. Now start adding the hot stock mixture to the rice, a soup ladleful at a time, and bring each to the simmer. Wait each time until the liquid is absorbed before adding more. Repeat until there is only about 100ml stock remaining, at which point taste a few grains of rice to see if they are cooked (but still with a bit of bite). If not, add more stock.

4 Add the pumpkin, pine nuts, sage, butter and cheese and stir through for a minute or two until the pumpkin is warm and the butter and cheese melted, before serving.

TIPS
- You can use an extra-mature hard British cheese such as farmhouse Cheddar instead of the Parmesan.
- The pumpkin seeds can be washed, dried out and the kernels eaten, or you can sow them next spring.

ALL SAINTS' LENTIL AND RICE SALAD

This recipe is based on a version served almost daily at the café in All Saints' Church in Hereford, owned by great chef Bill Sewell. I think it is truly delicious.

150g Puy lentils
enough brown rice to come to the 300ml mark in a measuring jug
1 medium butternut squash *or* 2 large carrots *or* 1 small swede
300g cauliflower, divided into small florets
50g soft sundried tomatoes, cut into very small dice
100g rocket or any crisp winter leaf
handful fresh mint leaves if available (see Tip)

For the dressing:
¼ tsp Tabasco
50ml soy sauce
50ml balsamic vinegar
25ml sesame oil
40ml rapeseed oil (use British)
a small blob stem ginger with a bit of syrup
1 level tbsp sesame seeds

1 Cook the lentils in a saucepan in plenty of unsalted water – this will take about 25 minutes.

2 In a separate pan, simmer the rice with 500ml boiling lightly salted water with the lid on until cooked – about 30 minutes and allow to cool.

3 Meanwhile, once the lentils and rice are on, peel, de-seed as necessary and chop into 1.5cm pieces the orange vegetable of your choice and steam them over the lentils until tender but not overcooked (this will take about 8 minutes); add the broccoli (see Tip) or cauliflower for the last 2–3 minutes. Refresh all the vegetables in cold water.

4 Whizz together all the dressing ingredients in an electric blender. When the lentils are cooked, drain them well and stir the dressing into the lentils while they are still warm. Now, in a large serving bowl, mix all the cooked and raw vegetables, leaves and mint into the dressed lentils and stir in the cooked cooled rice.

TIPS

- In summer, use broccoli instead of cauliflower and fresh tomatoes instead of sundried.

- You can have mint leaves all year round if you keep a pot on your windowsill. Otherwise, you can chop mint leaves and freeze them – or, failing that, you can stir some mint sauce into the dressing.

PEARS IN WHITE WINE

4 medium to large firm British pears
juice of a lemon
350ml medium-dry white wine
100g caster sugar
1 whole cinnamon stick
1 piece stem ginger in syrup, very finely chopped

1 Peel the pears, leaving the stalks intact, then sprinkle them with lemon juice so that they don't discolour. Put them on their sides in a lidded saucepan (choose a pan in which the pears will sit on the base with little space to spare) and add the wine, sugar and cinnamon stick.

2 Bring up to simmering point, cover the pan and simmer very slowly for about one hour, turning now and again so that the pears cook evenly in the wine.

3 When the pears are cooked, transfer to a bowl to cool, leaving the poaching liquid in the pan. Remove the cinnamon stick.

4 Bring the pan liquid up to boiling point and boil to reduce by half or until you have a syrup thick enough to coat the pears.

5 Take the pan off the heat and stir in the chopped stem ginger.

6 Leave to cool, then spoon the sauce over the pears, cover and chill to serve.

TIPS

- You can use red wine instead, in which case omit the ginger and lemon juice.

- You can poach quinces in a similar way but they will take longer to cook.

7 Eating Out, Travel and Leisure

In less than twenty years, says Tara Garnett in her authoritative *Wise Moves* report, we will be spending more on eating out or on takeways than we do on food for home consumption.

Already, according to Defra, young adults – people under thirty – spend 42 per cent of their food budget on eating out. Food eaten outside the home should be a pleasure; too often our increasingly mobile lives make it a necessity; and too often it is a disappointment. And, with much less opportunity to monitor what we're eating, or, indeed to find ethical meals wherever we happen to be, eating out is a minefield for the ethically conscious consumer. The fact is that, while some in the catering industry are making belated moves towards more environmentally friendly offerings, very few have caught up with the ethical movement at all.

A glance at most menus will tell you that many of the ingredients come from far afield, while the price lists of fast-food joints reveal that the animals reared to produce the food cannot have been kindly farmed. Look further, behind the scenes to the kitchens, and you'll find energy wastage, packaging wastage, food wastage on a grand scale.

But – and it's a big but – we've still got to eat when we go out and about. No one is going to tell you, least of all me, that you should stay indoors to be green and never have a restaurant meal or a café snack again.

So, from the grabbed coffee on the way to work, to the full gourmet dining experience, this chapter attempts to point you in the direction of the better options for all kinds of meal, drink and snack occasions. Let's start with the minimum – a drink ...

Coffee and sandwich to go, anyone?

TAKEAWAY DRINKS

As we've already seen, only a little of the coffee that we drink is fairly traded, but if you are a regular consumer you should try to seek it out when you can. Most of the coffee-house chains offer a Fairtrade option. If there is no sign up where you buy your coffee, ask. Black coffee or the soy alternative saves consuming yet more dairy produce, and normal filter coffee uses up less energy than do expresso, Americano or cappuccino.

Takeaway coffee is usually sold in paper cups lined with plastic. Generally these are not recyclable, but Pret A Manger is an exception. Other companies, such as Starbucks, use some recycled waste in their cups and, indeed, Starbucks will fill your own mug with their coffee at a discount if you take it along. Do a similar thing with water dispensers at your workplace: don't use the supplied disposable plastic cups – use a glass or cup of your own. Hard-walled polystyrene cups can be collected in bags for recycling once your workplace has enough (see Resources).

Another alternative is to make a flask of coffee before you leave home. Less expensive by far. And take your own spoon so you don't waste those wooden or plastic swizzlers.

Drink tap water at work. The cooler wastes energy in keeping water cool (take your own flask of water if you are worried about room temperature), though it is no worse than a bottle of water from a vending machine.

TAKEAWAY SANDWICHES – ARE ANY OF THEM GREEN?

The chain coffee houses vary tremendously in their green credentials. While most offer Fairtrade coffee, not many offer a range of green choices such as organic bread or fillings, free-range eggs, vegan or vegetarian options and biodegradable packaging. A few offer one or two of these options; others have none. An initial look at their selling may lead you to think the options for sale are all healthy – and there are attempts to reduce salt and to provide some low-fat sandwiches and muffins– but many items are still very high in fat and calories. Some cakes and muffins contain more calories and fat than several of the items for sale at the nearest chain burger bar.

Some sandwich and salad bars and supermarket sandwiches major more on 'healthy eating' than greenness, or simply on fast, cheap food, and as such you will find little information on the origins or sustainability of their ingredients. For example, common are:

- Salad items and fruits available all year round which have been imported and/or hothouse grown – tomatoes, lettuce, peppers, cucumbers – and little or no attempt to provide seasonal sandwich fillings or salads.

- Fillings such as 'tuna' and 'salmon' of unspecified origin or type.

- 'Ham' and 'turkey' made using re-formed meat – a cheap and unnecessary process.

- A high emphasis on meat and cheese/processed cheese and few vegan filling options.

- Origin of eggs unspecified – probably battery.

- Dressings and mayos with long ingredients lists.

- Nothing Fairtrade or organic for sale.

As there are so many independent sandwich shops – some using sandwiches and baguettes bought in from large sandwich-making companies, who are, it must be said, more concerned with their own sustainability than that of the food; and some making their own from goodness-knows-what ingredients – it is hard to offer any tips on which of these to frequent, except to say keep a very, very open eye, and ask questions. If you don't get the right answers – or just a baffled look – buy elsewhere, or make your own.

At least the supermarket sandwiches – and the larger chain sandwiches – give ingredients lists and nutritional information on their packaging, which is a start, whereas with these small shops who make up your sandwich from trays of ingredients laid out in front of you, it's impossible to deduce much at all.

If you live in London, you can buy Fresh! organic sandwiches from some Sainsbury's, Tesco and Budgens, and from some Boots nationwide. Fresh! have good standards of ethical sourcing and production.

A QUICK LOOK AT THE MAJOR PLAYERS
Starbucks

Buys an increasing amount of Fairtrade coffee and is involved in a 'Conservation Coffee Programme' which encourages 'the production of coffee using traditonal cultivation methods that protect biodiversity ...' Sells organic shade-grown coffee, as well as herbal and speciality 'Tazo' teas; attempts to reduce waste and recycle. All eggs are free range, salad and sandwich packaging biodegradable and compostable. However, as Starbucks continues to open thousands of new shops each year worldwide (currently there are around 15,000) it becomes harder to find independents.

Costa Coffee

Offers a Fairtrade coffee option and has set up its Costa Foundation to help the communities from where it sources its coffee, for example building schools. However, there is no information about its food ingredient sources.

Pret A Manger

Probably the most environmentally friendly lunchtime sandwich takeaway chain of them all. The company isn't a franchise and has a long list of green credentials in the way it sources, prepares and packages its natural, additive-free food, and in its use of 100 per cent green energy and its waste policy. Its take on compostable packaging is interesting: see box below.

Pret avoids air-freighted food and tries to source as much UK-produced and seasonal food as possible. All its food is at least free range 'or equivalent' and it tries to buy only organic, ethically traded, locally sourced, sustainable food and insists on high standards of animal welfare. Its wild salmon and tuna follow MSC guidelines. While one could say that phrases such as 'trying to' and 'where possible' are not the same as saying 'we do' – nevertheless, Pret does seem to be trying hard.

Subway

Now bigger than KFC, Burger King and Pizza Hut in terms of number of shops, the US-owned sandwich franchise has a subtitle 'Eat Fresh' and prides itself on low-fat sandwiches 'made fresh in front of you' – 'a better alternative to greasy fast food', it says. This at least saves on plastic packaging, as your 'sub' is presented in a paper bag. While several of the comments above about sandwich bars apply to Subway (for example, they tell me that none of their products are organic, Fairtrade or Freedom Food, and only their 'egg omelette' eggs are free range) they say their tuna must be caught by 'Dolphin-safe' methods and that they are currently 'exploring' their options regarding organic and Fairtrade foods.

A COMPOSTING PROBLEM

Pret A Manger announced recently that it would no longer be using biodegradable packaging made from PLA (cornstarch) on the grounds that the UK cannot provide adequate composting sites and collection services. Most PLA packaging ends up in landfill and never properly degrades, whereas at least plastic containers can be readily recycled.

The fact is that, while more and more companies are producing sandwiches in biodegradable, compostable packaging, as long as we continue to dump our sandwich box in the nearest bin that isn't going to help. If you buy compostable – take it home and compost it. At the moment, much fast-food packaging simply ends up in landfill where it won't get the air or moisture it needs to compost down.

Fast-food chains and takeaway meals

From American burger bars, fried chicken shops and British fish and chips, to takeaway Chinese, Indian, Thai and Japanese – in the Western world, and particularly in the UK, we seem to have an ongoing love affair with the takeaway.

Perhaps it is a way of providing an affordable and instant taste of 'world cuisine' which is non-threatening, familiar and marginally exotic at the same time ...

It would seem hard to reconcile most of these places, though, with ethical principles: more than most catering establishments, they are based on maximum profit for consumers who literally want a quick and filling food fix, which can mean that green considerations in ingredients production, sourcing, transport and so on may be minimal.

BURGER, PLEASE?

Jilly Greed of the National Beef Association says, 'Seventy per cent of the beef served in the hospitality sector is imported, with limited traceability and no proper audit trail giving country of origin, animal welfare and food-safety assurances.'

Many of our beef imports come from the Americas. In the USA, for example, cows are fattened up in crowded lots containing around 100,000 cattle, then slaughtered in giant production-line factories and immediately cut up to be packed and processed. Automated meat-recovery systems remove every last scrap of edible material off the carcass and huge grinders turn this into hamburgers. Thus the beef in your fast-food chain or other takeaway meal will probably come from not one, but many different animals.

McDonald's

This franchise, which serves 2.5 million customers a day in the UK, is doing its best to be seen to 'go green' after years of being castigated by the media and campaigners for its lack of ethical credentials. The vans which service its 1,000 British outlets are converting to run on used McDonald's cooking oil, all its coffee is sustainably grown Rainforest Alliance, its eggs free range; it also sells semi-skimmed organic milk. Its fish is MSC-approved hoki, and chicken, pork and beef are farm assured. It says a 'significant proportion' of its ingredients are locally sourced, and there is now more choice of vegetables and fruit on the menu. On the downside, the hoki comes from New Zealand, and many of McDonald's ingredients, such as sauces, processed cheeses, and breads contain sometimes long lists of additives. Its vegetarian patty, fries and some other foods contain trans fats. Its yogurt and mint sauce contain an amazing twenty-six ingredients, with just 5 per cent yogurt and 0.1 per cent mint. Its packaging and polyethylene cups contribute to landfill and roam the streets on the wind of every major town and city.

And, of course, it sells lots and lots of beef, which, as we saw in Chapter 3, requires more land and energy in its production than any other source of protein. Whilst McDonald's sources all its beef from the UK or Ireland for its British restaurants, other burger chains may not do so (see box left).

Burger King

Still the 'home of the Whopper' a beef (and processed cheese if you want it) feast burger with up to 6oz of beef inside. Despite an initial response from Burger King's public relations company, Cow PR, promising they would look into my enquiries (about the company's environmental policy and a few specific questions), and despite several further emails and phone calls over a period of months, I received no information at all. BK was the only company I approached who elected to remain silent.

So, while I can tell you that its chicken strips contain thirty ingredients and additives, and antibiotic growth promoter, says the company; it also says that 'rearing conditions are strictly regulated to ensure animal welfare' and that there is 'complete traceability from farm to restaurant' with independently audited farm checks on the suppliers. However, Greenpeace takes issue with KFC because it has found links between the company's suppliers and soya feed from deforested areas of the Amazon. KFC tells me that it is 'currently working with both the Carbon Trust and AEA to develop a Carbon Policy for 2008, from which we will be defining actions to be taken through training, design and technology'.

Pizza Hut

Part of the Yum! group, with 700 UK outlets and 150 franchises. Its business brochure proudly declares that in 2006 Pizza Hut bought over 8,500 tonnes of cheese – enough to cover the surface of four football pitches – and enough Pepsi to fill nine Olympic-size swimming pools. Pizza outlets are facing big price hikes because of the world shortage of wheat and increase in prices of cheese, particularly mozzarella. Pizza Hut themselves have told me that, on the plus side, all their beef and pork is UK-sourced, as is most of their chicken (some comes from Brazil and Thailand); they use British vegetables in season, otherwise from Europe; they use 'dolphin-safe' skipjack tuna; they sell Fairtrade coffee. But they don't use organic products and their eggs are not free range. They say they are now trialling and developing 'a new waste policy for implementation in 2008.'

that its Ocean Catch fish patty is made with Alaskan pollack – an approved fish on the MCS list – I cannot tell you what Burger King has done in the last few years to minimize its environmental impact; I cannot tell you its policy on sourcing ingredients; I cannot tell you whether its eggs are free range ... in fact, I cannot tell you much at all about the greenness of Burger King. But their PR's lack of response may tell its own story.

KFC

Is part of Yum!, which also owns Pizza Hut and Starbucks. After several years of bad press and campaigns exposing a shocking lack of animal welfare at supply farms, things for the KFC chickens seem to be looking up somewhat. The chickens used by KFC (which used to be called Kentucky Fried Chicken and has 700 UK outlets, of which 60 per cent are franchises) are now mostly British-reared without

Fish and chip shops

The staples of the British fish and chip shop – wild-caught Atlantic cod, plaice from waters around the British Isles, and some haddock – are all on the MCS's 'Avoid' list and thus 'chippies' are seeking other fish for their menus. Some offer rock salmon which rates a 5 from MCS – the worst! Coley, pollack and megrim are alternative white fish, but individual shops vary in what they offer – some may serve farmed cod in future – so you can only go along and see what they have from the MCS 'Green-light' (see page 106). The chips will usually be from UK-sourced potatoes, and the mushy peas are a green food in both ways. Compared with many other fast foods, if you choose the right fish, a fish and chip meal is fairly unprocessed and quick to cook – and doesn't get too bad a rating. Let's hope that more fish and chip shops take their lead in the future from Geale's of Notting Hill, and Tom's Place in Chelsea, who offer only sustainable fish.

Indian

Indian takeaway food can be a good choice for the green consumer. There is always a wide choice of vegetarian options as a large percentage of people on the Indian continent don't eat meat. Lentils and other pulses figure highly – a vegetable curry with a side order of dhal would be ideal. As the Indian takeaway sector is so large and so variable it is very hard to make any overall conclusions about sources, production, policies and so on, but I can safely say that much of the content of the meals will be imported because of the nature of the cuisine. You may be more assured of good-quality ingredients if you take away from a restaurant rather than somewhere which is just a takeaway outlet. And there are a few organic Indian outlets to choose from.

Chinese

Similarly, try to go for Chinese and Thai food that is sold from an established restaurant. Chinese food also has its plus points in that there tends to be less emphasis on meat and more on rice, noodles and vegetables. Dairy produce isn't used. However, you may find endangered fish on the menus (see page 107) and as it will be hard to establish the provenance of the prawns in the dishes, they're probably best avoided.

Japanese

YO! Sushi is the leader here. The company tells me it is committed to using only seafood from well-managed and sustainable fisheries and that it works closely with the MSC and Freedom Food (RSPCA). None of its tuna is from endangered species and is sourced only from vessels using approved, dolphin-safe fishing methods. The Yellowfin tuna that YO! Sushi uses is predominantly sourced in the Maldives and Sri Lanka, according to its website; its salmon is Scottish non-organic farmed salmon.

There are various other sushi outlets in the UK offering fish whose provenance is not easily discovered, but Pret A Manger also do sushi – for their green credentials, see above.

Cafés, pubs, restaurants – seeking out green options

While the good news is that there are increasing numbers of cafés and restaurants that let us know all about the food we are ordering – where and how it was reared/produced/caught, whether or not it is local, or even whether it is UK-produced or imported – 90 per cent still don't provide this information.

It's not easy to seek out the minority who do. If you're travelling around you need food when you need food and the nearest organic social-conscience café may be 50 miles away.

The Country Land and Business Association campaign, Ask If It's Local, which encourages consumers to question food origin when eating out, is a good beginning to raise public awareness, feels Jilly Greed of the National Beef Association. But, she says, there is still insufficient menu transparency to guide the consumer or to prevent imported foods masquerading as British, regional or local.

And it is a sad fact that not all environmentally aware caterers with the best of ingredients employ chefs who will, necessarily, put fabulous food on your plate.

However, until the situation improves, we do the best we can in patronizing the places which do make a green effort and there are a few organizations or people around to help pin these down.

If you live in the London area, the Ethical Eats initiative from the London Food Network will head you in the right direction. Several organizations will help you find organic and vegetarian cafés and restaurants across the country. But be aware that not all of these establishments will source their produce from the UK, or comply with most of the environmental issues that you might want.

Tip: Wherever you go – ask for tap water rather than bottled water.

EATING OUT, TRAVEL AND LEISURE

Travelling

PLANES AND TRAINS

If you're travelling by plane, some airlines, including Swiss Air and Lufthansa, provide organic meals on request, but generally there is little if any ethical consideration in airline food, or indeed in train catering. If you're not travelling too far, I suggest you take your own, or buy from Pret or similar before you board.

GREEN DAYS OUT AND WHERE TO EAT

Everyone loves a day out and there are all kinds of places you can go to have a green time as well as a great one, and, usually, be offered wholesome, often organic, food. Or take a picnic – often tables or picnic areas are provided. Here are a few ideas:

- Visit an organic farm. One of the most well-publicized in the UK is Daylesford Organic in Gloucestershire, which has a bakery and creamery as well as a farm shop and well-reviewed organic café, but the Soil Association (see Resources) lists more than 100 all over the country. Great for the kids, as there are usually farm trails and plenty to see.

- Farm shops and pick your own. Combine a day out with picking or buying your own local, and often organic, food. Many farm shops and pick-your-own establishments have cafés attached.

- Environmental projects/exhibitions. There's the Eden Project in Cornwall, the Centre for Alternative Technology in Mid-Wales, and the Living Rainforest project in Berkshire. Or try Nature's World in Middlesbrough, which has a variety of trails, including an eco-trail; organic and wildlife gardening; a 'future world' exhibition; and a computerized recycling game.

- Walks, cycle rides, nature trails. Every area has a Ramblers' local group who often organize walks with good food stops. Bewilderwood in Wroxham, Norfolk, is an environmentally friendly adventure forest with boating, cycle hire and organic food. The RSPB has nationwide bird reserves open to the public and several of these have food on offer, or try the Wildlife Trusts or Wildfowl and Wetlands Trust.

- Gardens open to the public. Garden Organic lists several organic gardens to visit on its website. The National Trust has many gardens and houses with cafés/ tearooms serving local or organic food.

If you have time to turn your day out into a short break, there are a growing number of organic and vegetarian B and Bs – or try camping. Cool Camping lists sites where you can eat organic and/or local, or cook a green one-pot meal on a campstove (see Books section in Resources).

All places mentioned by name, and where to find listings of, for instance, pick-your-own establishments, can be found in the Resources section.

HOLIDAYS, HOTELS AND EATING ABROAD

There is a small selection of eco-friendly hotels in this country and abroad, but the numbers are increasing year on year. Listings sites appear in Resources.

While holidaying or travelling abroad, you will probably find greener meals and greener accommodation by selecting small, local, perhaps family-run, establishments. When seeking a meal abroad, always try the local food – you may have travelled and burnt a lot of carbon, but the food doesn't have to! And often the local food is delicious, exciting and well worth trying. (Sometimes it isn't, but that's another story.) It is also likely to be much less expensive than bland hotel or chain food.

It's a good idea to purchase a guide to the country/city you're visiting or go online and find out details of the local cuisine in their language and yours, and the best local restaurants (although often the most authentic local restaurants don't have a website). If you don't speak the language it can be hard to order otherwise.

Lastly, the Slow Food Movement has lists of excellent restaurants following their creed for food that is 'good, clean and fair' in every respect, in various countries.

There may be a case for choosing bottled water while you travel abroad, as you don't want to contract a stomach bug. You could, however, use water-purifying tablets. At the very least, try to buy a local brand of water.

Conclusion

While it is not easy to eat 'green' while out and about, it is becoming easier. And the more that we all ask for – even demand – environmentally sound principles from our catering and hotel industries, the more likely we are to get them.

8 Your Green Foods A-Z

While I have given national and online stockists for many of the items included here, always try to buy locally if you can. When buying online, check that the supplier doesn't live at the other end of the country. In the Shop section of Resources you will find online companies who can put you in touch with local producers.

Apples

OVERVIEW: Apples originated in the Middle East around 4,000 years ago but have been grown in the UK since the eleventh Century. Henry VIII started the first Kent apple orchards in the early sixteenth century. Today only 30–35 per cent of apples sold in the UK are grown here. The British season is August to October. Commercially, controlled atmosphere is used to prolong storage times for up to a year (see page 88).

SELECTION AND STORAGE TIPS:
Choose British apples, which should be labelled as such. Choose the less common varieties when you see them, as this will help to keep them in our orchards. Granny Smith, by the way, are not British but Australian. Any 'old' English variety is worth seeking out for flavour. Dessert: UK Cox (many Coxes are imported and lacking flavour), Worcester Pearmain, Egremont Russett, Laxton's Superb; Dessert/cooking: James Grieve; Cooking: Bramley, Blenheim Orange; Cider: Kingston Black, Dabinett. If you buy apples in the autumn from the southern hemisphere, they will have been stored for around six months. Apples should be stored at home in cool, dark conditions.

BUY: Farmers' markets and WI shops are good places to look for unusual apple varieties. Try www.farmfreshexpress.co.uk if you live in the south-east.
   More information on varieties: www.orangepippin.com; www.allaboutapples.com

   Grow your own: Try Lord Lambourne, Jupiter, Elstar, Fiesta; or Annie Elizabeth and Bramleys for cooking. Buy trees: www.brogdale.org (home of the national fruit collection, Faversham, Kent); www.appletrees.org.uk
   Make cider/juice: www.vigopresses.co.uk has a free ebook and equipment.

Bread and flour

OVERVIEW: 90 per cent of the bread bought in supermarkets and sandwiches is made using the 1960s-invented, fast, high-energy Chorleywood process, and so it is far removed from the traditional bread of old. The large bread factories add improvers and other chemicals to help the bread keep, and the bread often contains surprisingly high levels of salt, fat and sugar. Thankfully, there are still plenty of artisan bread-makers and flour producers to be found across the UK

   Not all bread labelled 'organic' is traditionally made – it can be made using the Chorleywood process. If you aren't sure of the history of the loaf, ask. In general, stoneground/slow-rolled bread flour and traditional baking methods produce a loaf which is heavy and with a much denser texture.

BUY BREAD: Organic bread is widely available nationwide, but for traditionally made loaves buy online from www.graigfarm.co.uk, an ethically run organic company in Wales with a wide range of breads. Metfield breads, sold mainly around London, are all organic: www. metfieldbakery.com. Abel & Cole sell organic breads local to your area via their website www.abel-cole.co.uk. Hundreds of local delis and farmers' markets (see Resources) sell locally made good-quality breads – see what your area has to offer.

BUY FLOUR: Making your own bread will save you about 45 per cent on a bought loaf, but most bread flour for sale here is imported as the British weather doesn't allow us to grow 'hard' wheat, which has the high protein and gluten content necessary for a well-risen loaf. Try a variety of traditionally milled flours and tips from www.wessexmill.co.uk (stockists nationwide or buy online) and www.dovesfarm. co.uk for a variety of UK-grown grains including spelt (old wheat-type grain), which makes an excellent loaf (no online buying at present). Doves Farm also tell me that ordinary plain British flour will make a delicious loaf if you don't mind the 'low rise'.

Breakfast cereals

OVERVIEW: The majority of today's most popular big-brand family cereals are likely to have gone through intensive factory production; and often contain a long list of ingredients, many of which will have been shipped or flown in from around the world. Here's an example of a typical list of ingredients: wholegrain wheat flour (29%), rice flour, sugar, vegetable oil, dextrose, maize starch, glucose syrup, maltodextrin, salt, emulsifier: soya lecithin, trisodium phosphate, colours: caramel and annatto, antioxidant: tocopherols, vitamins and minerals: vitamin C, niacin, pantothenic acid, vitamin B6, riboflavin (B2), thiamin (B1), folic acid, vitamin B12, calcium, iron.

And the 'healthier' cereals, such as muesli, may be no better in this respect, although are less likely to contain many additives. Granolas are an oven-toasted muesli type and so more energy has been used in their production. Traditional cereals such as porridge oats, breakfast biscuits and Shredded Wheat are a greener choice in that they contain nothing other than wheat, so, although processed, they are simple. Check labels for country source of main ingredient. Cereals can be very high in sugar, salt and additives – read the nutrition panel.

MAKE YOUR OWN: If you enjoy muesli, make your own with British-grown oat/barley/

wheat flakes bought locally, and add hazelnuts, walnuts, sunflower and pumpkin seeds. Store this base in an airtight container and add fresh chopped seasonal fruit when you serve. Much of our dried fruit is not grown in this country.

BUY: Oat-based muesli: www.wessexmill.co.uk. Doves Farm organic cornflakes and wheat biscuits from several supermarkets – see site for stockists. Jordan's do organic porridge oats, muesli and fruit-n-fibre packed in compostable bags and recyclable card: www.jordans-cereals.co.uk Pertwood Organics produce some very nice cereals www.pertwood.co.uk. Rude Health mueslis, porridge oats and other cereals are all organic and environmentally friendly (Sainsbury's and local health-food shops). www.alara.co.uk sell an organic, Fairtrade and sustainable range of mueslis, although the food miles involved in their compilation are sometimes massive.

Cakes, bakes and bars

OVERVIEW: One supermarket mint-crisp cake bar contains twenty-eight different ingredients and two different lots of wrapping. It is one of hundreds of different varieties of commercial cake sold by the billion every year – and it doesn't even taste that good.

BUY: You can buy good-quality cakes with ingredients that will provide real nutrition, and without E numbers, if you hunt a bit. The local deli, farmers' market or WI shop will have good cakes for sale and if you want organic, you can buy at www.theorganiccakecompany.co.uk (also sold in some shops in the south-east). The Village Bakery from Cumbria www.village-bakery.com sells organic cakes cooked using renewable energy and with recyclable packaging (online and some supermarkets). Eat Natural bars are good quality, simple nut and fruit bars available in health-food stores and supermarkets.

Cheese

OVERVIEW: The dairy industry rates high on the list of foods that are wasteful of resources – and just over 10kg of milk are needed to make 1kg of cheese. In the UK only around 65 per cent of the cheese we consume is of British origin, even though around 700 varieties are made here. If you are going to eat cheese, eat small amounts and try to buy local and seasonal cheeses. Two of my favourites are Cornish Yarg, semi-hard and tangy, wrapped in nettles, and Hereford Hop, similar to an excellent rich, creamy Cheddar, wrapped in hops (organic version available from www.malverncheesewrights.co.uk), while Dovedale is one of the best of the soft and creamy English blues. Most of the best-known 'British' cheeses, such as Cheddar, Cheshire and

Lancashire, don't have to be produced in those areas. Only a few cheeses (e.g. Stilton, Buxton Blue) have a protected designation of origin status, meaning they can't be produced outside a certain region – for more see www. cheeseboard.co.uk. However, in practice the smaller local cheeses are unlikely to be produced far outside 'their' area.

Goat's and ewe's milk cheeses are more environmentally friendly than cow's milk cheese, as these animals have a smaller carbon footprint. Cheeses made using organic and/or unpasteurized milk are quite widely available – www.cheeseboard.co.uk has a short list of varieties.

CHOOSING/STORING: Avoid processed cheeses and those commercial varieties that have added ingredients, such as fruit. Firm cheese is best wrapped in greaseproof paper. When buying soft cheese see if your local shop will sell it to you in your own container. Store hard cheeses and English Brie-type cheeses in a cool room rather than the fridge, or at least remove them from the fridge for an hour or two before serving.

MAKE YOUR OWN: You can make your own cottage and curd soft cheeses quite easily at home. www.cheesemaking.co.uk has everything you might need.

BUY: www.nealsyardcreamery.co.uk sells delicious soft and fresh cow's and goat's cheeses and runs partially on windmill and solar power. www.nealsyarddairy.co.uk sells a wide variety of artisan cheeses. www. specialistcheesemakers.co.uk has a great deal of local cheese information and lists of cheese-makers with contact details. www. cheddargorgecheeseco.co.uk sells the only Cheddar cheese made in Cheddar.

Chicken and Poultry

OVERVIEW: While our intake of organic chickens is increasing steadily – in 2006 we ate 12.4 million organic birds – 90 per cent of the chickens that we eat in the UK are from intensive farms, mostly in this country, although some are imported. In 2007, ASDA began selling factory-farmed chickens at only £2 each – and we bought them in droves, a fact of which we shouldn't be particularly proud.

Good-quality, responsibly farmed chickens are relatively expensive but by eating a little less, and appreciating it more, we don't need to spend a great deal more money.

A third of the Christmas turkeys we buy come from abroad – maybe as far away as South America. Many British-reared and imported turkeys are intensively farmed in similar fashion to table chickens.

A word here about goose liver pâté – foie gras. If you care about animal welfare, don't buy it. The geese are force-fed until their livers have swollen up to twelve times their normal size before they are slaughtered. Few UK stores now sell the stuff, but you may find it on restaurant menus.

CHOOSING: Organic chickens raised in small flocks with the freedom to forage on traditional land — woods and fields — are the gold standard. Free-range chickens may be kept in sheds and simply have the availability of the outdoors which they may not, or hardly ever, use. Corn-fed chickens may or may not be organic. When buying, at least look for a Freedom Food label or a Red Tractor (see pages 39–40).

You can find speciality chickens — older breeds with different flavours. These may taste more 'gamey'.

BUY: www.sheepdrove.com are exemplary in this respect, with a full breakdown of the lives of their flocks on their website. They also sell turkeys, goose and duck. www.sjorganics.co.uk (01267 253570) is a small farm with high animal-welfare standards in West Wales, producing 'Welsh gold' chickens, guinea fowl, Muscovy duck, geese and turkey on 20 acres, and all birds are killed and plucked on their own farm. For traditional turkey try www.kelly-turkeys.com (01245 223581) or seldomseenfarm.co.uk (01162 596742). For free-range geese try www.goodmansgeese.co.uk (01299 896272) or www.manorfarmgame.co.uk (01494 774975).

Chocolate

OVERVIEW: Our liking for mass-produced chocolate and confectionery in the Western world is undoubtedly one reason why we have such a collective obesity problem, as these items are consumed for pleasure rather than need, and they are high in fat, sugar and calories. Their manufacture is energy-intensive and also accounts for many food miles. The growing and harvesting of the cocoa bean, while providing work in developing countries, is also linked with poor working conditions and pay. Non-organic cocoa-bean production involves high pesticide use and ill-health for the workers. Most chocolate, even the best-quality bars, contains soya lecithin — soya cultivation is responsible for much destruction of the Amazonian rainforest. However, if you are going to buy chocolate, buy fairly traded organic. When choosing chocolate for Easter, avoid eggs — they are usually very high on packaging and low on actual chocolate. Or give real eggs — Clarence Court www.clarencecourt.co.uk do a hand-selected speciality pack of unusual eggs; from some Waitrose, ASDA and Sainsbury's.

BUY: Several organic brands are available, including Green and Black (only some of their chocolate — Maya Gold — actually *is* Fairtrade; they also do a Maya Gold Fairtrade and organic cocoa); Co-op Fairtrade (various types); Swiss Organica, various types, some also vegan; Traidcraft Organic Swiss; Andre Deberdt. Buy from www.alotofchocolate.co.uk (0845 094

6498) or www.chocolateorganic.co.uk (0117 973 3624); or find several of these brands in your local shops. Also try www.montezumas. co.uk (0845 450 6306) – while their chocolate isn't Fairtrade (see page 82) it is 'fairly traded'. www.CHOCaid.com donates from each organic, fairly traded purchase to help world hunger.

Coffee

OVERVIEW: Coffee was the first Fairtrade produce to reach the UK back in the 1990s and yet Fairtrade coffee still accounts for only around 1 per cent of all the coffee sold. While the supermarkets fall over each other to promote their Fairtrade coffee credentials, one does wonder why *all* of the commodities sold cannot be fairly traded: it should be a given, not a rarity. In the meantime, shunning coffee isn't the answer – for many smaller coffee-producing countries, the bean is the main source of their total income.

BUY: The family-run Roast and Post Coffee Company www.realcoffee.co.uk (01454 417147) has a wide selection of Fairtrade and organic coffees which they roast and send to you either whole or ground, as you prefer. The Fairtrade Foundation recommends www. alotofcoffee.co.uk (0845 094 6498), or try www.unionroasted.com (0207 474 8990). Kenco sells single-country instant coffee from Brazil, Costa Rica or Colombia, all of which is

certified by the Rainforest Alliance. Cafédirect coffee is all fairly traded.

Citrus Fruit

OVERVIEW: Oranges don't grow in this country and traditionally many of our imported oranges have come from Spain, but now we import around 60 per cent of our total from outside the EU – from, for example, South America – so our greed for oranges creates a heavy carbon footprint. Although a few organic and/or fairly traded oranges arrive in the UK, most are not – and more pesticides and insecticides are used on oranges than on any other crop. It is a similar story with lemons, grapefruit and limes. If you buy non-organic, don't use the peel in recipes.

BUY: Since 2003, fairly traded oranges have been on sale in the UK and are usually available in all the main supermarkets. Organic citrus fruits from Landridge can be bought online at www.ethicalfoods.co.uk

Eggs

OVERVIEW: According to 2006 figures from the British Egg Information Service, we bought 44 per cent free range, organic or barn eggs and 56 per cent cage (battery) eggs.

Local, rare-breed eggs are often available at farmers' markets and in local delis, while one or two of the supermarkets are also now stocking locally produced eggs, or at least those from within 100 miles or so. If not, they are at least beginning to stock one or two rare or old-breed eggs – for example, Waitrose stocks Columbian Blacktail, Burford Brown and Old Cotswold Legbar, and all its eggs are free range or organic and British. Organic eggs will probably contain more of the healthy omega-3 fats than non-organic because of the organic hens' foraging diet.

TIPS: Happily, producers of battery eggs can no longer put 'farm fresh' on the boxes – they have to say 'from caged birds'. Be aware that even 'free-range' eggs don't guarantee good living conditions for the hens, so look for organic eggs. For more background on UK egg production, see page 61, and for label explanation see page 140.

BUY: For obvious reasons you will find few producers or suppliers who will mail you your eggs (one exception being www.castlefarmeggs.co.uk who sell eggs from hand-reared old breeds). If you live in a rural or semi-rural district you should be able to find people who keep chickens and, at certain times of year, will have a surplus for sale or for swap.

Fish and shellfish

OVERVIEW: For a detailed appraisal of the kinds of fish that you should eat, see pages 104–9.

TIPS: One of the better wild white fish as a replacement for cod and plaice is megrim – sometimes known as Cornish sole – or try line-caught Cornish sea bass or pollack. Avoid any brightly coloured smoked fish (e.g. yellow smoked haddock, bright pink salmon) which will have been fed dye-containing feed to alter the natural colour, or dyed during processing. Even kippers and smoked mackerel may have been dyed. Choose organically farmed or sustainable wild fish, neither of which will have been artificially coloured. Remember, if the fishmonger doesn't tell you where the fish came from, ask – and try to avoid wild or farmed fish imported from other continents. For freshness, look for clear, bright eyes, pink/red gills, shiny skin, sea-fresh smell and, if you can press the flesh, it should immediately spring back. Any strong fishy smell means it is past its best.

BUY: Most of the supermarkets are now committed to supplying sustainable fish and avoiding at-risk fish, either already or in the near future. The store fish counters should display clearly where the fish was caught – and often you will find the method of catching displayed as well. Many local fishmongers are

quickly catching on to the importance of this, so patronize a stall which does comply. Even the mass-market fish manufacturers are getting the message: Birds Eye fish fingers now come in a MSC-certified Alaskan pollack variety.

Online you can buy sustainable fish at www. graigfarm.co.uk (Wales-based) or www.abel-cole.co.uk The Fish Society (www. thefishsociety.co.uk – 0800 27934374) has excellent environmental credentials and donates 10 per cent of its profits to marine conservation organizations. At www.lochfyne.com (01499 600470) you can buy Scottish sustainable/organic seafood, including farmed sea trout and halibut, and smoked fish. For traditionally smoked and organic salmon and trout try www.hebrideansmokehouse.com (01876 580209).

Fruit

OVERVIEW: Much of the fruit that we eat is imported. Even our traditional British fruits such as apples, pears and plums often come from all over the world. Try to buy most of your fruit in season and from a local area. When you buy imported fruit, try to buy only fruit which is important to you and which isn't grown in the UK – oranges and bananas, for example, may be on your list. In this case, you can get organic and Fairtrade versions of both and that's what you should go for. Be aware that non-organic fruits are some of the most heavily sprayed (with insecticides and fungicides) foods that we eat.

TIPS: To tide you over the winter months, either freeze or bottle some fruits – fruit cooked or puréed first and bagged will save freezer space and usually freezes better. You can dry fruit yourself in a low oven, but the drying process loses most of the vitamin C of the fresh fruit. Avoid buying out-of-season fruit like berries in winter – research shows that less expensive fruits such as oranges and red-skinned apples contain as much goodness. Try to purchase loose fruits to save on packaging.

BUY: All the supermarkets stock at least some Fairtrade and organic fruit, and most are making efforts to stock more local fruits in season. Local farmers' markets will have a range of produce for most of the year. www.farma.org.uk and www.farmersmarkets.net www.lfm.org.uk

Game

OVERVIEW: Game is, in theory, any animal or bird harvested 'from the wild'. Sales of game meat in the UK are rising rapidly – pheasant, venison and grouse have seen a nearly 50 per cent rise in the past three years. Wild duck, partridge, hare and wild boar are also popular, and the category could also include rabbit and pigeon, woodcock and quail.

While game was traditionally hunted in the 'wild', the boundaries between what is actually truly wild and what is not are now muddy. Farmed game, according to the 1993 MAFF regulations, is 'wild land mammals which are reared and slaughtered in captivity', but 'captivity' doesn't include 'wild land mammals living within an enclosed territory under conditions of freedom similar to those enjoyed by wild game'. So venison, for example, which has been enclosed in parkland and fed and watered by an estate gamekeeper, is allowed to be called wild. But the trade association is called the British Deer Farmers' Association. And all over the internet you will find traders selling items such as 'farmed wild boar'.

Very little of the pheasant and partridge sold in shops today is truly wild. Most pheasant, for example, is reared using bought-in eggs (often from France). The chicks are kept in enclosed pens where their feathers may be clipped, their beaks 'bitted' (to stop them pecking each other), and they are monitored for signs of disease, fed on pellets then corn, and then turned into 'release' pens. Although they may finally be let out to roam nearby for a few weeks, they may still be fed to keep them in the vicinity, where eventually most will be shot down by wealthy 'guns' standing in rows while dogs beat the birds from their cover. The surplus dead pheasants not taken home may even be buried, rather than eaten or sold on.

Whichever way you look at it, this is intensive farming rather than gamekeeping. According to Animal Aid, every year in Britain around 35 million pheasants and millions more partridges are mass-produced.

Pheasant meat today is a high-fat, high-cholesterol product, just as farmed salmon is much higher in fat than wild salmon. Venison remains a low-fat, low cholesterol choice. If you can find grouse, this will be properly wild.

BUY: From November to February you can find proper wild venison in season, at a price – the rest of the year it will be frozen or farmed, or imported farmed from New Zealand. Wild tends to be stronger than farmed and cannot be organic as it isn't farmed. www.country-cuts.co.uk and www.kielderorganicmeats.co.uk and www.eynons.co.uk and www.eversfieldorganic.co.uk sell wild venison, as do many local country game merchants and markets. You can buy organic farmed venison from Healthy Venison by phone (01446 781900), and organic pheasant and venison from www.graigfarm.co.uk. www.lcgame.co.uk sell truly wild ducks, boars, venison and rabbits, and naturally reared pheasant. For a wide selection of wild game and home-made game pies, try www.manorfarmgame.co.uk (01494 774975).

Herbs

OVERVIEW: There is no doubt that fresh herbs are superior to most dried varieties – drying can remove much or most of the aroma and flavour of the herb. While sun-drying is a low-energy way to preserve herbs, freeze- or oven-drying will of course use energy. As most herb plants are quite small, and most are also easy to grow, I would always recommend that you have a few pots on your windowsill or in your conservatory – mint, basil, coriander, thyme and marjoram are a few good starter ideas. You can buy the seedlings in supermarket pots and try potting them up into containers with 3–5 seedlings in each; they won't always thrive, but sometimes they do.

BUY: For chemical-free plants, try www.theherbfarm.co.uk For bunched seasonal herbs try your local farmers' market or most of the supermarkets. If you live in the London area, www.organicdelivery.co.uk sells a good range of fresh British-grown herbs. Waitrose sells various organic growing herb pots which are specially produced to be kept in the kitchen for months, or even planted outside.

Honey

OVERVIEW: Sadly, the honey bee population of the British Isles, North America and other parts of the world has been decimated by, some estimate, up to 90 per cent in recent years by Colony Collapse Disorder, and nobody is completely sure what has caused this, although global warming, pesticides and GM crops have been named as possible culprits; and the modern practice of 'factory farming' honey bees, which gives us much of our low-cost commercial honey, may also be to blame in that it may encourage parasites and disease. Thus honey from British bees kept in traditional hives is in ever more short supply. Much of our honey is, in fact, imported from countries as far afield as Australia, New Zealand and China.

Some people say that *all* honey is unethical as it is gained by stealing the bees' natural food and replacing it with an unnatural diet, and vegans don't eat it. Organic British honey doesn't really exist, as the organic standards require a 4-mile 'essentially organic' radius zone around the apiary, which is nearly impossible to find in this country. Thus if you find organic honey it is almost always imported and I feel that good local British honey is probably preferable. While the dark manuka and other honeys of New Zealand have gained much coverage for their health-giving properties in recent years, most natural 'raw' unpasteurized dark honeys will have similar properties, including all the enzymes and live pollens which pasteurizing (heating to 65°C for 8 hours) mostly destroys.

BUY: The British Beekeepers' Association (www.bbka.org.uk) lists local area member groups and their contact details – these should be able to point you in the direction of 'real' honey for sale in your area. Or try www. beedata.com which has an online list of small local producers and their contact details. www. graigfarm.co.uk (01597 851655) sells several local honeys from the hills near its Welsh base. If buying imported honey, choose a fairly traded one, e.g. Equal Exchange organic honey from the smaller co-operatives such as Nicaragua or Mexico (www.goodnessdirect.co. uk). Or try a vegan honey substitute, organic agave nectar, available from VeganEssentials.com

Ice cream and desserts

OVERVIEW: Like much mass-market chocolate, by their nature ice creams and creamy, sugary desserts are 'wants' rather than 'needs', and their dairy content, their need to be frozen at home and transported in chillers, and, often, their intensive manufacturing process, means that they rate quite highly as producers of carbon emissions. They may also add to obesity and provide calories that we don't really need. Best kept for an occasional dessert.

BUY: If you are going to purchase creamy desserts, go for organic and local where possible. For instance, www.september-organic. co.uk (01544 312910) sell organic ice cream based on local and seasonal flavours, such as blackberries, elderflowers and apples, from their Jersey herd in Wales and the Midlands. Waitrose sell own-label organic Fairtrade coffee and chocolate ice cream and several other brands. Try goat's cheese cheesecake from Windrush Valley goat dairy farm (01451 844828).

Juice, smoothies and soft drinks

OVERVIEW:

Juice: We drink 14 litres of orange juice each a year in the UK, mostly from thousands of miles away. With 48 per cent of the market, Brazil is the biggest exporter of orange juice in the world, followed by the USA. One study has estimated that twenty-two glasses of processing water and 1,000 glasses of irrigation water are needed to produce just one glass of Brazilian orange juice. Add to that the transport, processing and packaging energy and you have a very non-green drink. Most of the juice that we drink here (of all varieties) is squeezed in the country of origin. Then it is either evaporated to concentrate it and reconstituted here before packaging (and in the case of long-life juices, pasteurized at high temperature), or lightly pasteurized and frozen, or sterile-packaged to be exported. Short-life chilled juices may be made from concentrate or frozen juice, and lightly pasteurized. A small amount of our juice is freshly squeezed from fresh fruit imported whole into the country, unpasteurized, and needs to be drunk within 48 hours or so. Non-organic fruit will have been sprayed with chemicals. British-grown and squeezed juice is mostly apple or pear.

Juice drinks: These contain a range of ingredients of which fruit is likely to form a small percentage. Artificial sweeteners, sugar, colourants and flavourings are likely. The word 'drink' may appear in small lettering. Cranberry 'juice' is almost always in 'drink' form rather than natural juice.

Smoothies: Like the juices, most smoothies will contain imported fruit and some also contain dairy produce such as yogurt. Innocent, the market leader, uses cornstarch bottles which will compost in eight weeks and has other good green credentials; a small compensation for their (non-air-freighted) fruit imports.

Soft drinks: Mass-market squashes and cordials are ready for dilution and most contain a high percentage of sugar or artificial sweetener, as well as E numbers including colourants. Best avoided. Local or smaller producer brands are more likely to contain quality ingredients and no strange additives. Elderflower cordial will contain imported lemons, though, and almost all contain sugar.

BUY:

There are hundreds of local brands of freshly pressed juice available across the country in delis and farm shops for much of the year. Companies with national distribution are increasing in number. Suffolk-based www.jameswhite.co.uk (01473 890202) makes a great range of quality fruit and vegetable juices and drinks and does home delivery. www.belvoirfruitfarms.co.uk of Lincolnshire (01476 870286) does a range of elderflower, lemon and other presses, including organic.

MAKE YOUR OWN:

There's a range of home juicing kits, from pretty wooden apple presses (should you have your own trees or a local supply), www.vigopresses.co.uk (01404 892101), to worktop juicers from any kitchen store.

Meat

OVERVIEW: For a detailed discussion on the pros and cons of meat-eating, see page 99. In general, most of us enjoy meat, but we should be concentrating on eating smaller portions, a bit less frequently, and on choosing the most environmentally friendly, compassionately farmed meat that we can find. This usually means organic, produced in this country. As a bonus, this almost always tastes better than mass-produced meat. For example, the pig-farming industry tends to use just three breeds. Buying your pork from small specialist producers will allow you to taste the breeds of old – such as Tamworth and Gloucester Old Spot.

Lamb lovers should consider Welsh lamb, which is a protected name – the lambs usually live in the hills for much of the year, and are thus free range and often as good as organic. As a special treat try salt marsh lamb.

It's worth mentioning veal here. This meat, which is from young calves, has long been shunned by the British public as cruel. The calves are borne by dairy cows and, as the milk industry wants their food – the mother's milk – the male calves are removed from their mothers after birth. They are usually shipped to Europe, kept confined in veal pens, fed an unnatural diet to keep the flesh pale, and killed for veal at about six months old. Even if we don't buy veal, if we drink cow's milk then we have to think about what happens to these male calves. Without a veal trade they would probably be shot after birth. Neither option is good. Now some British dairies are producing what they call rose veal – veal from male calves reared to organic or near-organic standards with pink, natural meat. The reasoning is that the calves have as good and as long a life as organic lamb or pork. If our dairy industry is to continue, this sounds to me like a good compromise.

BUY: www.helenbrowningorganics.co.uk (01793 790460) sells all kinds of organic meats, including rose veal from her farm in Wiltshire, either online or at a few outlets including some Co-ops and Sainsburys. www.eversfieldorganic.co.uk (0845 603 8004) and www.wellhungmeat.com (0845 230 3131) do good meat boxes online and you can get biodynamically reared meat from www.heritageprime.co.uk (01308 482 688); Gloucester Old Spot and many other breeds from www.northfieldfarm.com (01664 474271); and Welsh lamb from www.welshlambdirect.co.uk (01654 767101).

Milk

OVERVIEW: The dairy industry, as we've seen, is quite energy-intensive up to farm-gate point, and beyond that is responsible for a hefty amount of food miles around the country. Packaging of milk has become an issue now that much of the milk we consume is bought in non-biodegradable plastic containers. Milk rounds are making a return to popular-

ity and with them the glass bottle, which can be recycled many times. Producers are also looking at new packaging that is kinder to the environment, such as pouches. Long-life milk in tetrapaks saves on energy as it can be stored at room temperature until it is opened. You could buy in bulk and perhaps save transport energy too if you only visit the shops frequently because of the need for milk. However, the extra heat treatment for the UHT milk uses more energy than ordinary pasteurization and the packs themselves are hard to recycle. Organic milk is widely available. All mass-market milk today is pasteurized, but you may get raw milk at local farms.

Mushrooms

OVERVIEW: Most of the mushrooms for sale in the UK have been produced at mushroom farms. Due to an increase in demand for wild mushrooms of different varieties, such as ceps and boletus, these are being farmed too – probably a good development, as too many potential pickers could damage the wild mushroom's natural environment and there are reports that some species have been wiped out in some areas of the country.

Dried mushrooms are a good store-cupboard idea as they take little space and will keep for months without refrigeration. Soaked in warm water, they are fine for almost all mushroom recipes. Keep the soaking water and add to stock or gravy.

Mycoprotein (Quorn): A meat substitute made from fermented fungus, mixed with albumen and factory processed to look like meat. It is often used in a similar way to tofu (see page 261). Mycoprotein is available in basic forms (sliced, diced) or as part of ready meals for vegetarians in major supermarkets and elsewhere.

BUY: Brigitte Tee has been selling authentic New Forest wild mushooms for years, www.wildmushrooms.co.uk (01590 673354) but you can buy an excellent selection of all types of mushroom, some of which are farmed, at www.smithymushrooms.co.uk (01704 840982).

Pick your own: see page 178.

Nuts and seeds

OVERVIEW: Nuts are, in fact, seeds – apart from peanuts, also known as groundnuts, which are legumes. Rich in unsaturated fats and protein, vitamins and minerals, they are an important part of a diet which relies less on meat and dairy produce. While many of the nuts and seeds that we eat in the UK are imported from all round the world, several varieties are indigenous. Hazel- or cobnuts, walnuts and sweet chestnuts are the ones you are most likely to find which have been grown in this country, while pumpkin and sunflower seeds may also be British.

Pesticides are widely used in the production of nuts – some of these are particularly toxic to honey bees. After harvesting, they are fumigated with methyl bromide which can cause health problems for workers and is known to have a particularly bad effect on the ozone layer, according to *National Geographic*. Organic nuts are available and it sounds like sense to seek these out when you can.

Once shelled, nuts lose flavour and their polyunsaturated fats may degrade, especially if chopped. Smoking, toasting and keeping in warm, light conditions will also have an adverse effect on the nuts and seeds.

BUY: Northern-hemisphere nuts are generally ready to pick in the autumn. If you buy fresh nuts in the shell from September to November they will be at their best. www.graigfarm.co.uk (01597 851655) sells organic, fairly traded nuts.

Oils

OVERVIEW: Most of the oils that we buy are imported or come from imported produce – olive oil being the obvious example. But there are UK-produced alternatives. Hemp-seed oil is a good basic cooking oil, thanks to its high smoke point, optimal ratio of essential fatty acids, and the fact that it can be readily produced in Britain. But perhaps the British oil likely to do best in the mass market in future is rapeseed oil. While much of the rapeseed oil in the supermarkets is highly refined, a number of British producers are going for cold-pressed, top-quality oil which tastes very nice and can be used instead of olive or groundnut oil in most recipes and for salads.

If choosing non-British oil, go for European seed, fruit and nut oils, such as olive oil, almond, walnut, sunflower. Nut oils should only ever be purchased in small bottles because they oxidize (turn rancid) quickly. Pumpkin seed oil, which is stronger in flavour and colour, has a slightly longer life. Argan oil is the authentic choice for Moroccan-Berber dishes and has a mildly nutty flavour.

I would tend to avoid all mass-produced imported oils when you can. Soya oil is widely available and has good keeping qualities, but soya production is responsible for deforestation and other environmental problems. Perhaps the worst oil to buy is the ubiquitous 'vegetable oil', sometimes called 'blended vegetable oil' (a blend of rapeseed, safflower, soya and/or unspecified others) – the cheapest oil on the shelf but, because of its variety of ingredients and its production methods (see Tips below), likely to have the largest carbon footprint of them all.

All types of non-organic oil crops will usually have been intensively sprayed with pesticides, many of which are fat-soluble. Choosing organic will minimize your exposure to these.

TIPS: Oil-extraction methods, in a 'nutshell' are:
Cold pressed: Once associated primarily with olive oil, this method does also apply to many other oils and indicates that no form of heating or refining was used during extraction. In general, it signifies quality. A small proportion of cold-pressed oils are pressed using traditional methods, but expeller pressing is usual. Cold-pressed oils (particularly first-pressing oils – often there is a second or even a third extraction process) are highest in health-giving nutrients and plant chemicals such as anti-oxidants, as well as in flavour and colour.
Expeller pressed: This is a chemical-free mechanical process – the oil is forced out under pressure, which, particularly when used on hard seeds or nuts, can generate heat due to friction. But for cold pressing, the expeller pressing is done under controlled temperatures, typically below 50°C.
Solvent extraction: Many mass-market vegetable-oil manufacturers use chemical solvents such as hexane, along with heat as high as 250°C, and harsh refining, bleaching or deodorizing methods. This removes colour, nutrients and flavour, and increases shelf life and smoke point.

Used cooking oils: Although there are collections nationwide for used cooking oil from restaurants, there is no similar service for domestic oil. However, this may change: visit www.reuze.co.uk/vegoil for more information.

BUY: British Hillfarm cold-pressed rapeseed oil from Waitrose or www.hillfarmoils.com (01986 798660). Cold-pressed rapeseed oil Oleifera from the Scottish–English borders at Sainsbury's or online – all the rape is local and the producers have a good green outlook – www.borderfields.co.uk (01890 885 010). www.graigfarms.co.uk offer a variety of organic cold-pressed oils, including rapeseed oil, but these mostly come from a French supplier. Various organic oils from www.oliveoilstore.co.uk including in large 3-litre cans, which save on glass (pour into old cleaned bottles or jars and divide amongst friends or neighbours).

Pasta

OVERVIEW: Most of the pasta that you buy in the major shops is made with durum wheat, often from Italy, Syria or Canada. But because wheat is used for biofuel and because of adverse weather in recent years, there is a world shortage – even Italy imports around 40 per cent of its wheat for pasta. Other wheats can be used to make pasta, but these give a softer finish and are less satisfying. However, I have been assured by Clare Marriage at Doves Farm in Berkshire, who grow spelt flour, that this flour would make a good alternative to durum if you make your own pasta. You could mix it two-thirds to one-third with ordinary plain British wheat flour. However, British demand for spelt is now so high that Doves are having to import some of their grain. Wessex Mill (see Bread) tell me that their strong bread flour will also make good pasta.

Dried pasta, which accounts for most UK sales, is dried in large dryers circulating hot, moist air, which takes around 6 hours. This uses energy but, on the other hand, dried pasta is energy-free to store and there is little waste.

Organic pasta is widely available and, as non-organic wheat crops are routinely sprayed with pesticides and herbicides, this might be a sensible option.

TIPS: Dried pasta, stored in an airtight and insect-proof container in a dry place, will keep for at least two years. Refining and bleaching of the flour used in white pasta destroys 65 per cent of the vitamins and nearly 90 per cent of the minerals, so buy wholewheat most of the time – this retains all the vitamins and minerals and is high in fibre, so you're wasting neither refining energy nor nutrients. Couscous is not a grain but a form of pasta.

BUY: Organic and wholewheat pastas are widely available in most supermarkets, health-food stores and delis. Organic spelt and other flours can be bought from www.dovesfarm.co.uk.

Preserves and spreads

OVERVIEW: Making your own preserves, jams, chutneys and so on is a green way to use up gluts of fruit and vegetables in your garden or at the market. You can also usually get away with adding much less sugar than is in those you may find in the supermarket.

BUY: However, if you can't make your own, there are several good brands widely available with several Fairtrade and organic sorts to choose from. Duchy Originals do superb organic Somerset-made soft-set jams and marmalade containing up to 60 per cent fruit (some commercial brands contain as little as 35 per cent fruit and 45 per cent is the norm) – from Waitrose, Tesco or www.ocado.com Both Tesco and Morrisons do a Fairtrade organic Seville orange marmalade.

Pulses

OVERVIEW: Peas, beans and lentils are known as pulses, and have been used as food for thousands of years. The lentil was probably one of the first plants to be grown by humans. Pulses provide an important source of protein and iron for vegetarians and are a vital, high-fibre, low-cost food throughout the world. Many whole pulses (e.g. aduki, chickpeas, whole lentils, marrowfat peas, mung beans) can be sprouted at home quite easily to add vitamin C to their profile (there is no vitamin C in dried pulses, but it is present in the fresh beansprout). Some of my favourite pulses are chickpeas, brown and green lentils, borlotti beans, cannellini beans and black-eye beans. While most pulses bought in the UK will have travelled far to reach us, they still have a lower carbon footprint than most of our other sources of protein.

COOKING: One advantage of dried pulses is that they will store very well for long periods if kept in a dry, airtight container away from the light. However, it is best to eat them as fresh as possible. Pulses toughen on storage and older ones will take longer to cook. Most dried pulses need soaking for 4–12 hours before they can be cooked; notable exceptions are all lentils and split peas, which cook through from dry in less than an hour.

Always discard the soaking water, rinse and cook in fresh water without any salt, which toughens the skins and makes for longer cooking. Kidney beans especially, which contain a toxin called lectin that causes stomach upsets, need adequate soaking and cooking to destroy the toxin (10 minutes' very fast boiling followed by an hour or two of simmering or until tender). Soya beans contain trypsin inhibitor which can prevent proper digestion; to destroy this they need one hour's fast boiling before simmering until tender – often 3–4 hours.

Pressure cooking: The temperatures achieved in pressure cooking are adequate to destroy both lectin and trypsin inhibitor. Pressure cooking also considerably reduces cooking times – kidney beans 10–20 minutes, soya beans 1 hour – and therefore energy use. If you eat a lot of beans, a pressure cooker may be a good investment.

Fresh pulses: These can be cooked like any other vegetable – steamed or boiled for a few minutes. Pod runner beans in your garden for a simple form of kidney bean. Fresh frozen soya beans can be bought at supermarkets and cooked like peas.

Soya beans: These are found in much of our food and, because of their association with agribusiness and deforestation, I would serve them only occasionally and choose other pulses instead for much of the time. Soya crops throughout the world may be genetically modified, but buying organic beans means they will be virtually GM-free. The beans can be ground into flour, fermented, or can undergo several other processing methods to form a variety of foods. Soya is used as a vegetarian substitute for meat and dairy protein as it is high in good-quality protein.

Soya flour: Made from ground soya beans, this is a useful gluten-free flour as a substitute for wheat flour in breads, cakes and so on.

Textured vegetable protein (TVP): This is soya flour that has been factory processed and dried. TVP has a sponge-like texture and is available either cut into small chunks, or ground into granules resembling minced beef – it can be flavoured to resemble meat.

Soya beancurd: Also known as tofu, this is made from coagulated soya milk. Tofu is sometimes known as soya cheese, and is sold as blocks packaged in water. It can be bought as silken tofu (soft and creamy in texture), or as a denser, firmer version (the firmer kind may also be purchased smoked, marinated, or, in Chinese groceries, fermented to give a strong, cheese-like flavour). Plain silken or firm tofu is the least energy-intensive of all the forms of soya apart from the basic bean.

Tempeh: Fermented soya bean paste with a chewy texture and strong flavour; it can be used as a meat substitute.

Miso: A fermented condiment made from soya beans, rice or barley, salt and water.

Soya milk: Made by boiling soya flour in water, then straining.

BUY: Most pulses prefer warm climates and are grown throughout the world – Africa, Asia and the Americas – therefore they represent a lot of food miles. Cans or dried? Beans dried before being shipped weigh less so use up less energy to transport, and save on packaging, but most need long cooking times. Canned beans are pre-cooked. I always keep a selection of both. Either way, they have less environmental impact than most meat products. Stock a variety, as they all have their own flavours, textures and uses – in soups, pâtés, dips, burgers, salads, as a side vegetable or dhal, and in stews. Baked beans in tomato sauce are usually the white haricot bean. Organic pulses are widely available in supermarkets, health-food shops and online, e.g. www. ethicalsuperstore.com. Alpro soya products, the manufacturer guarantees, are all GM-free.

Ready Meals

OVERVIEW: As we saw in Chapter 3, most ready meals are very high in strange additives, may be sourced from all over the world, can contain meats, etc. produced in less than ideal conditions and deciphering the packs is not always easy.

However, there are several companies who are now producing quite good ready meals – some organic, some chilled, some frozen, but all trying to make decent-quality meals you can actually eat and enjoy, often from locally sourced produce and with environmentally sound principles.

BUY: One of my own favourites for good frozen meals is Cook www.cookfood.net (0870 8707338) – they also do a children's range, side dishes and party dishes, and take a keen interest in nutrition. In foil pouches comes the locally sourced and well-reviewed www. lookwhatwefound.co.uk range, which can be kept at room temperature before opening (sold in some supermarkets or online). The Patchwork Traditional Food Company make a small range of lovely meals using local and traditional British produce www.patchwork-pate.co.uk; while www.mannaorganic.co.uk make all-organic ready frozen meals for delivery nationwide or in some shops around the Devon area.

Rice and grains

OVERVIEW: Grains are the major staple food throughout the world and although the wheat grain provides most of the Western world's carbohydrate, other grains are more important elsewhere. From the long-grain and fragrant rices of Asia to the rye and buckwheat of Eastern Europe, the corn of Mexico and the barley of North Africa, we can't manage without grains. While there are concerns that grain production (also now used for biofuels, of course) is responsible for deforestation and decrease in biodiversity, and encourages GM and monoculture, the fact is that grain uses far fewer of our resouces to feed us than does, say, meat or dairy (see page 34 for a further look at this topic).

To help protect diversity it may be a good idea, though, to choose a variety of different grains rather than relying on just one or two – say, pasta and rice, as we do in this country. To reduce food miles, the best choices are oats, barley and rye, all of which can be grown in the British Isles and northern Europe. Pot barley is a good addition to soups and casseroles. Other choices include spelt, quinoa (which is higher in protein that most grains), amaranth and red rice from the Camargue. Cornmeal is good for polenta and can also be used for pasta, as can millet, which is a more nutritious grain than rice and wheat and needs much less water to grow.

If buying grains, choose wholegrain most of the time, rather than refined or 'white' grains. Wholegrains have gone through little processing, thus saving energy, and also contain more nutrients.

BUY: You will usually find a good stock of different grains at your health-food shop. www. naturallygoodfood.co.uk online shop has a good variety, including organic and Fairtrade grains.

Spices

OVERVIEW: Many spices originate in continents such as Asia, Africa and the Americas, and so will have travelled many food miles to reach us. However, most are light in weight and are used in such small amounts that they don't make a great contribution to our carbon footprint, while making so much difference to our enjoyment of food. They also dry well and the ready-ground versions can be stored in recyclable glass jars or in cardboard drums. However, it is better and greener to buy the whole dried spice and grind it yourself when you need to; the spice will keep its aroma and flavour for longer then, so you don't throw away all those packs with just a spoonful or two used. Fresh spices, when you can get them, are even better.

We can grow some spices in the UK – I have grown all kinds of chillies successfully for years, as well as coriander seed, dill and even lemongrass, in an unheated greenhouse. Garlic, which I classify with the vegetables, is also reasonably easy to grow in a warm summer.

Dried ground spices and dried herbs are one of the few foods in the UK which may be irradiated before reaching the supermarket shelves – another reason to buy them whole, or fresh. The Food Standards Agency says that irradiation is used because, in spices that are dried in the sun, irradiation kills bacteria without changing their flavours or aromas. Only a small percentage is irradiated and the spice should by law be labelled as such.

BUY: www.getspice.com sells a range of organic spices and plenty of others, and for organic ethical spices try www.ethicalfoods.co.uk.

Sugar

OVERVIEW: Sugar invariably gets a very bad press in Britain, mainly from a nutritional point of view – empty calories, and all that – and sugar figures in many of the high-calorie snacks and drinks that encourage us to eat more than we need. The Department of Health does, however, 'allow' us to get up to 10 per cent of our daily calories in the form of sugar before we need to feel guilty, and so, given that a little is OK, that leaves the environmental and carbon footprint issues.

You may be surprised to hear – as I was – that around half of all the sugar that we eat in the UK is grown here, mostly in East Anglia and the West Midlands, in the form of sugar beet. British Sugar (BS), which basically runs the UK sugar-farming and production industry and owns Silver Spoon, Billington's and other companies, lays out a cogent argument for the environmental friendliness of their beet.

Compared with most of our other staple crops, sugar beet is quite green. In brief, the industry has reduced the amount of pesticides, herbicides and organophosphates it uses by around two-thirds overall since 1982; and reduced nitrogen fertilizer application by a third since 1970. Nitrogen soil residues and leaching are low; soil erosion has been reduced significantly by planting cover crops and improved soil management; field margins are left to grow naturally; and sugar beet rarely needs irrigating as the roots go 2 metres deep. BS also collect all the soil that arrives at their factories on the beet roots and recycle it as topsoil; similarly they recycle stones for things like road building. And the pulp left over after the sugar is extracted is used for a variety of purposes such as animal feed. For a detailed look at the British sugar industry's environmental impact, go to www.britishsugar.co.uk.

The downside is that from sugar beet to white granules takes a not inconsiderable amount of processing energy. How is beet sugar made? Raw sugar crystals are obtained by 'brewing' sliced beet with hot water, refining and purifying (with the use of lime and carbon dioxide) and vacuum-crystallizing the resultant juice to make the ubiquitous refined white crystals. Any brown sugar from beet will have been coloured using cane molasses – beet doesn't produce molasses suitable for eating.

The rest of our sugar, mostly in the form of sugar cane, is imported from countries such as Mauritius, Barbados and Jamaica. Sugar from cane can be refined in a similar way to beet, but can also yield less-refined sugars in varying shades of brown and degrees of unrefinedness;

it may also be processed to form golden syrup or treacle. (While this less-refined sugar may look and taste better than white, it contains virtually no more nutrients.) I think, however, that the word 'unrefined' on any sugar label is a misnomer as all sugar fit for the table or cooking has gone through some processing.

The sugar-cane industry across the world can't boast the same environmental credentials as sugar beet, that is for sure. Cane needs lavish irrigation; cane plantations show massive soil erosion; chemical spraying is common; and standards and pay for plantation workers are often poor. However, Tate & Lyle, one of the world's largest sugar cane companies, is planning to make all its retail sugar packs in the UK Fairtrade by the end of 2009. And, as with several other of the world's cash crops, natural bio-rich environments have been, and continue to be, lost. Lastly, of course, cane sugar weighs heavy and comes a long way to reach the UK. On the plus side, Billington's tell me that once the juice is removed from the canes, they are used to fuel the mills and supply the local grid.

Nevertheless – my advice? Use sugar sparingly.

BUY: To support a British industry which employs 23,000 workers, buy a little refined white Silver Spoon (all UK-grown) sugar for basics; buy a little Fairtrade sugar (e.g. Billington's Fairtrade) and some organic (e.g. Billington's or Silver Spoon imported organic range). www.bynature.co.uk sells organic and fairly traded Steenberg cane sugars.

Tea

OVERVIEW: After water, tea is the most commonly drunk beverage in the world and grows in more than thirty countries. China, India, Sri Lanka and Africa are some of the best known. Our most popular British teas are usually a blend from different tea estates and many different countries. Blends can incorporate thirty or more individual teas, which may not make the most carbon-footprint sense. Single-estate – or even single-country – teas will reduce the energy used in tea production. It will also help if you buy loose leaf instead of bags.

Millions of people live and work on tea estates around the world. Pesticides are widely used on plantations, where workers often apply them without proper protective masks or clothing, or they may drink from pesticide-tainted streams. According to *National Geographic,* tests of China-grown green teas, touted for their health-boosting properties, ironically showed high levels of both lead and the pesticide DDT, banned in much of the world. Pesticides are also widely used on many of India's tea plantations. While there has been little research into its environmental impacts, tea production shares some similarities with other world crops such as coffee and grains. There have been landslides on tea plantations in India's mountainous Darjeeling district, and studies have found lower bird diversity in tea monoculture systems, where native forest has been replaced by tea crops.

Many of our favourite tea companies –

including Tetleys, Twinings and Taylors of Harrogate – now belong to the Ethical Tea Partnership (ETP) www.ethicalteapartnership. org which monitors six key areas of tea-estate life – employment (including minimum age and wage levels), education, maternity, health and safety, housing and basic rights – and covers 75 per cent of the UK tea market. If the website address appears on the pack, then the tea packer is a member of the ETP.

BUY: Buying fairly traded basic teas will help support those millions working in the tea plantations. Buying a little less but paying more will help save resources at the same time. Organic and fairly traded teas are quite easy to find in the shops and online. For organic single-region loose-leaf teas, try www.mightyleafteas. co.uk who also supply other organic teas such as the South African (and delicious) rooibos and herbal teas. www.traidcraftshop.co.uk does a small selection of Fairtrade and single-estate teas, and herbal teas. www.cafedirect.co.uk sells fairly traded African tea. www.equalexchange. co.uk sell fairly traded and organic teas, including single-garden teas, from Sri Lanka and India.

Tomatoes

OVERVIEW: Tomatoes are the UK's bestselling individual salad item – and we also eat huge amounts in cooked and processed form. British growers provide about 20 per cent of the total number of fresh tomatoes that we eat: 75,000 tonnes in all. The rest are imported, largely from Spain, the Canary Islands and Holland.

While 370 acres in this country (most of the total UK production) are covered with tomato hothouses, in fact tomatoes don't need very high temperatures to thrive and the British Tomato Growers Association (BTGA) tells me that they have managed to reduce the amount of heat used by 50 per cent since the 1970s. The BTGA's green aspirations include recycling their irrigation water (tomatoes need a lot of water); composting leaves and old plants; and using waste heat from nearby industries. They avoid the use of peat, bumblebees are used for pollination and pests are controlled using natural predators. British growers aim to use *no* pesticides and 6 per cent of the area is organic production.

BUY: Buy British if you can. Imports may be grown to lower standards than those I have described above. Imported tomatoes are sometimes flown in – if the label doesn't tell you, ask. Try to buy tomatoes that arrive here by other means. Indeed, in winter, choosing other salad plants instead of fresh tomatoes is the greenest option of all. Use canned tomatoes for hot dishes, or organic sundried

tomatoes or tomato paste. Buy loose tomatoes rather than in packs when you can. I would also consider buying in bulk during our season (local tomatoes from the farmers' market, for example) and making your own tomato sauces (simply fry up some onion with chopped fresh tomatoes for a freezable base). Also look out for unusual varieties to help keep our tomato diversity alive. British Tomato Growers' Association: www.britishtomatoes.co.uk

Vegetables and salad

OVERVIEW: For a detailed appraisal of why or if you should buy vegetables in season, locally and/or organic, see Chapters 2–3.

One of the greatest UK food market increases in recent years has been bagged mixed salads. They now outsell 'old-fashioned' whole lettuces in the supermarkets and have achieved this success at least partially because of the advent of Modified Atmosphere Packaging (MAP), which allows the picked or cut leaves to stay fresh for up to a week. Research shows that a bagged salad will last longer in its packaging than a salad cut at home and left for the same time. It's also down to our own in-built laziness in preparing items such as whole lettuces, and our fascination with the variety of leaves such packaging allows us to try for less cash than buying each type of leaf separately.

While MAP is not exactly 'natural', the gases used – oxygen, nitrogen, CO_2 – are those which make up air, but in a different combination. The leaves are also usually washed in a mild chlorine solution (or in organic fruit acids in the case of organic salads), but, the manufacturers are quick to point out, any residues are, with infrequent exceptions, well within the safety limits imposed by the EU. Vitamin levels have been shown to be similar to, or better than, standard lettuce kept for the same length of time.

My own objection to bagged salads is that often 'baby' leaves are used, which is a woeful waste of the plant – let them grow bigger and we get more food for our seed and a better taste. In some circumstances the bagged salads may create less waste than whole, dirty lettuces – we throw away much of the salad stuffs that we buy, but in theory a bagged salad has no waste. For families they may be OK, but for a single person the salad leftovers will quickly go 'off' once opened. Lastly, I am assured by Florette, one of the largest salad-bag producers in Europe, that most of the content of the UK bags is, at least from spring to autumn, British-grown near the factories, and mostly from Spain in other months. And the UK Fresh Prepared Salads Producer Group say that only 20 per cent of their bagged salads are MAP bagged anyway. When you buy, you aren't told which is the case, though.

Other vegetables, such as peeled and cut carrots, potatoes, beans and so on which you buy from the supermarket chilled counters, are also regularly MAP-ed.

Much of the salad stuff and greens grown in

this country and indeed around the world, is grown using chemicals including fertilizers, fungicides, pesticides and herbicides. Because of the nature of the food (lots of leaf area), the sprays are readily absorbed and may be present in the finished product – every year, for example, a percentage of lettuces tested by the government is found to be 'over the limit' for residues. The only way round this is to buy organic – and if you buy only a handful of organic items, I suggest you put salad and greens on the list.

BUY: The alternative is to visit the farmers' markets, where you will often find bags or bunches of mixed salad – these need using up soon. But you can buy long-life storage bags for vegetables in the fridge, which prolong the life of all types of salads, fruit and veg for a considerable time. Try www.lakeland.co.uk.

BOX SCHEMES: Salad items also come in the dozens of veg-box delivery schemes which have taken off in popularity over the past decade. Most of these companies provide organic vegetables. Their pricing and the amount and type of vegetable that you get, as well as the amount of veto you get (on items you don't like, for example), also varies a great deal, so check before you sign up. While it is sometimes nice to have a surprise, I would always go for the services which allow you to choose the contents (depending on what is available). But be aware that a box delivery doesn't mean that all the contents will be local, or even from the UK; at some times of the year much of the content will be imported. Good schemes let you know where everything has come from.

The granddaddy is Abel & Cole (www.abel-cole.co.uk) who have now expanded and sell almost anything ... but some of the best of the others are www.farmfreshexpress.co.uk which delivers local and seasonal produce in compostable bags (south-east area only); www.goodnessdirect.co.uk have a good selection of boxes and deliver to most of the UK; at www.thelocalfoodcompany.co.uk (based in Devon but deliver elsewhere) you can pick exactly what you want and items are priced individually (plus mixed boxes as well). For many more local and national schemes, try www.alotoforganics.co.uk

Water

For a discussion on water, see page 112. While some bottled-water companies seek to persuade us to buy by offering ethical incentives – including that some of the profits from each purchase go to helping communities and projects in developing countries – the fact remains that drinking tap water (with a filter if you really must) is the most green option. If these companies want to help such communities they could offer us a different product (say, something local or truly necessary for our well-being) and donate profits from that instead.

If you really must buy bottled water, at least

go for the UK brand nearest to where you live – which doesn't necessarily mean it won't have travelled around the country a bit in the bottling and central distribution process, but it might not have come that far.

Wine, beer, spirits

WINE: To save food miles and to help save the French wine industry, buy French and European wines rather than those that come from Australia, New Zealand, South Africa, California or South America. If you are going to buy a 'far-away' wine, make it a Fairtrade one (stocked by all the major supermarkets or from www.winedirect.co.uk). While some wine producers are beginning to take part in carbon-offsetting schemes to counter production and transport, I don't set much store long-term by this policy.

Organic wine: Also a good bet, since non-organic grapes are routinely sprayed and Friends of the Earth detected over 200 chemical compounds from residues in wine. However, organic wine still contains the preservative sulphur dioxide, linked with asthma and present in non-organic wine in even greater amounts. The Soil Association's online Directory www.whyorganic.org lists many organic wine producers and sellers.

Vegetarian wine: Some wine is not suitable for strict vegetarians as it has been produced using gelatine, shell, or even isinglass from fish bladders, as fining agents. Look for the Vegetarian Society symbol or 'suitable for vegetarians' on the label – these wines will have been fined using casein or albumen (suitable for vegetarians but not vegans), or bentonite or other vegan-friendly products. www.vintageroots.co.uk supplies many vegetarian and vegan wines amongst its all-organic collection. By the way, not all organic wine is suitable for vegetarians.

British wine: Beware when buying UK-produced wine. A bottle carrying the name 'British wine' is fermented and bottled in Britain, but from grape juice, usually in concentrate form, grown abroad, shipped in and tanked to factory fermenting plants. You need to look for 'English' or 'Welsh' wine from named vineyards. There are nearly 400 commercial vineyards in England and Wales, covering approximately 2,000 acres of land in total. www.english-wine.com lists most of the country's vineyards, the majority of which welcome visitors and sell their own wines in their vineyard shops and sometimes on their websites. You can buy a huge selection of English wines – some organic/suitable for vegans – at www.bestenglishwine.co.uk. www.davenportvineyards.co.uk (01892 852 380) sell white and sparkling wine online from their Kent and Sussex vineyards.

BEER: Most of the beer and lager produced for sale in the UK is from the 'big four' brewers. If you want to avoid these, you need to seek out the smaller, local, traditional ales.

But even 'English' ales with quaint-sounding names are not necessarily full of English ingredients. Many of the industry's hops now come from abroad – as far away as New Zealand. Some producers using local hops are www.westerhambrewery.co.uk (01732 864427), who make fine beers with local hops from Kent, bottles from Waitrose or mail order; Brakspear and St Peters, both of whom do organic beers – but again, one of St Peters' organic beers used New Zealand hops. Fullers Organic Honey Dew is well reviewed and available at Sainsbury's. The website www. beersofeurope.co.uk lists background information on almost all the beers you can buy in the UK (and ciders and other drinks).

PERRIES, CIDERS, ETC.: Traditional ciders and perries can be found wherever the old cider apples and perry pears grow – Somerset and Herefordshire being two counties. www. dunkertons.co.uk press cider and perry from their own trees; www.orchard-hive-and-vine. co.uk has a superb online shop selling many varieties of local and sometimes organic beers, ciders, perries and wines, including the award-winning Olivers range. www. pennardorganicwines.co.uk (01749 860393) are Somerset based and sell only produce – including cider and perry – traditionally made on their farm from their own fruits, which can be ordered online.

SPIRITS: Gin and whisky are traditional UK-produced spirits, while rum (made with sugar cane) hails from Jamaica and other cane-producing countries (see Sugar for more about the sugar-cane industry) and vodka (made with unspecified grains) hails from Russia and Poland but is now made in quantity in Britain. Brandy is made using grapes and originated in France but is now produced all over Europe and elsewhere. The grains used for all spirits will have been sprayed with chemicals unless you buy organic.

You can buy award-winning Juniper Green Organic Gin, made from organic rye imported from the EU, and organic whisky, vodka and rum made by UK Organic Spirits Company, on sale in several supermarkets, including ASDA and Sainsbury's. www.graigfarm.co.uk sell a variety of British and European organic spirits, including a small estate French cognac and a Fairtrade white rum.

Resources:
**Sources of Further
Information**

CAMPAIGNERS

www.foodcomm.org.uk
020 7837 2250
The Food Commission
– independent organization
campaigning for safer, healthier
food in the UK.

www.sustainweb.org
020 7837 1228
Sustain – the alliance for better
food and farming.

www.foodethicscouncil.org
0845 345 8574
Independent charity and think
tank, champions better food and
farming through independent
research and advice.

www.foe.co.uk 020 7490 1555
Friends of the Earth – 'inspiring
solutions to environmental
problems'.

www.neweweconomics.org
020 7820 6300
The New Economics Foundation
– 'challenge mainstream thinking
on economic, environment and
social issues'.

www.greenpeace.org.uk
020 7865 8100
The goal of Greenpeace 'is to
ensure the ability of the earth to
nurture life in all its diversity'.

www.forumforthefuture.org.uk
020 7324 3630
Mission – to find practical ways to
a sustainable future.

www.viva.org.uk 0117 944 1000
Vegetarians International Voice for
Animals; they are against eating
meat, fish or dairy, which causes
'environmental destruction'.

www.ciwf.org.uk 01483 521950
Compassion in World Farming
– campaigns for the welfare of
farm animals.

www.peopleandplanet.org
01865 245678
Student action on world poverty
and the environment.

www.isec.org.uk 01803 868650
The International Society
for Ecology and Culture, an
anti-globalism, educational
organization for the protection
of biological and cultural diversity
– with food being a major topic.

www.pan-uk.org 020 7065 0905
Pesticide Action Network (PAN
UK) – research, information and
policymaking.

www.pesticideinfo.org
PAN North America's
information website.

www.gmfreeze.org 020 7837 0642
Anti-GM campaigning group.

GOVERNMENT, EU, UN AND RESEARCH INSTITUTES

www.fao.org
+39 06 57051
(European Regional Office)
Food and Agriculture
Organization of the United
Nations.

www.defra.gov.uk/environment/
08459 33 55 77
Department for Environment,
Food and Rural Affairs
– for information on what the
government is doing to protect
the environment.

www.eea.europa.eu +45 33 36 71
00 (Information Centre)
The European Environment
Agency aims to help achieve
significant and measurable
improvement in Europe's
environment.

www.eci.ox.ac.uk 01865 275848
Oxford University Environmental
Change Institute – research
and teaching on environmental
change and its causes, including
climate change, energy and
ecosystems.

www.tyndall.ac.uk 01603 593900
Tyndall Centre for Climate
Change Research, University of
East Anglia (headquarters).

www.ipcc.ch/
Intergovernmental Panel on Climate Change website where you can read official documents and find out what the panel is doing.

www.fcrn.org.uk 020 7686 2687
The Food Climate Research Network – researches and promotes ways of achieving reductions in greenhouse-gas emissions from the whole UK food chain.

ORGANIC AND SUSTAINABLE FARMING
www.soilassociation.org
0117 314 5000
UK's leading environmental charity promoting sustainable, organic farming – includes information centre and library.

www.biodynamic.org.uk
01453 759501
The Biodynamic Agricultural Association – background and information. Also certifies biodynamic farmers (the Demeter certification).

FOOD AND SHOPPING

Farmers' markets, farm shops and pick your own:
www.farma.org.uk 0845 45 88 420
National Farmers' Retail and Markets Association

www.farmersmarkets.net
Online place to find your nearest FARMA market or shop.

www.farmshop.uk.com
01427 787076
Listing of many farm shops in the UK.

www.country-markets.co.uk
01246 261508
Lists all the member country markets across the UK. (Previously the Women's Institute Country Markets.)

www.pickyourown.info
Wide selection of PYO, farm shops and box schemes by region.

www.countrylovers.co.uk/wfs
01208 873788
Offers short-break or half-day wild food courses at their Wild Food School in Cornwall.

Box schemes:
www.green-england.co.uk
Has a good search facility for nationwide box-delivery schemes.

www.livingethically.co.uk
Has all kinds of food-delivery schemes listed by county.

Supermarket alternatives and local shopping:
www.whyorganic.org
The Soil Association's consumer site, containing the Organic Directory which lists hundreds of organic producers and suppliers across the UK.

www.bigbarn.co.uk 01234 871005
Links you with local producers in your area (no online sales).

www.localfoodweb.co.uk
Choose your own area and find local markets, farm outlets and independent retailers of a wide variety of produce.

www.organic-store.co.uk
Lists everything from shops, cafés, specialists and markets county by county.

www.FoodLoversBritain.com
0208 206 6111
Started by food expert Henrietta Green, a comprehensive guide to the best of local and regional food buying and eating out, plus an online shop.

www.foodfullstop.com
0870 383 0122
Shop online for traditionally produced foods (not always organic).

www.localfoodshop.com
Shop online for food in your area.

SUPERMARKETS

www.waitrose.com/food/
0800 188 884

www.tesco.com
0845 7225533

www.sainsburys.co.uk
020 7695 6000

www.asda.co.uk
0845 300 1111

www.co-operative.co.uk/en/food
0800 0686 727

www.morrisons.co.uk
0845 611 5000

www.marksandspencer.com
0845 302 1234

OTHER SHOPPING, SWAPPING AND DONATING

www.naturalcollection.com
0845 3677 001
Recycled kitchen goods, such as tinfoil.

www.ecoutlet.co.uk 020 7272 7233
Lots of good ideas for the kitchen and home, including manual coffee- and juice-makers and the eco-kettle which boils only what you need.

www.recycledproducts.org.uk
Listing developed by WRAP (see below) which includes kitchen utensils, bags and bins.
www.bioregional.com
020 8404 4880

www.graigfarm.co.uk
01597 851655
Sustainable UK charcoal for sale.

www.bpgaslight.co.uk
0845 607 6943
BP refillable Gaslight for outdoor cooking.

www.ethicalpartybags.com
07948 343653

www.vegware.co.uk
0845 643 0406
Picnic, lunch-box and outdoor ware.

www.carryfreedom.com
0845 456 0928
Sells bicycle trailers.

www.gumtree.com
Swap goods (London based).

www.uk.freecycle.org
Give away unwanted items (groups all over the country).

FOOD STANDARDS

www.foodstandards.gov.uk
020 7276 8000
UK Food Standards Agency
– wide range of advice on healthy eating and nutrition, labelling, and food-safety issues

www.redtractor.org.uk
020 7630 3320
Red Tractor labelling-scheme information.

www.msc.org 020 7811 3300
Marine Stewardship Council.

www.mcsuk.org 01989 566017
Marine Conservation Society.

www.fishonline.org
Find out which fish to eat and which to avoid.

www.rspca.org.uk
Information on the Freedom Food label.

www.britegg.co.uk 0207 808 9790
Information about the Lion symbol and UK egg production.

www.leafuk.org 0247 6413 911
LEAF, linking environment and
farming.

FAIRTRADE AND CONSERVATION
www.fairtrade.org.uk
020 7405 5942
Fairtrade Foundation
information.

www.rainforest-alliance.org (USA)
001 212 677 1900
Rainforest Alliance.

FOOD SOCIETIES
www.vegsoc.org 0161 925 2000
The Vegetarian Society – recipes,
information and cookery school.

www.thevegansociety.com
0121 523 1730
The Vegan Society.

www.slowfood.org.uk
01584 879599
The Slow Food Movement.

GROWING AND REARING
www.nationalsmallholders.org.uk
07989 343 559

www.farmgarden.org.uk
0117 923 1800
For city growing and farming.

www.allotments-uk.com
Online community with advice
and good forums.

COOKING
www.eattheseasons.co.uk
Information on seasonal foods
and recipes.

www.greencuisine.co.uk
01544 230720
Residential organic cookery
courses in medieval manor
house/hotel in Herefordshire.

GREEN ENERGY AND ENERGY-SAVING
www.nef.org.uk 01908 665555
The National Energy Foundation
– lots of information on different
types of green energy.

www.greenenergy.uk.com
0845 456 9550
Sells energy from renewable
sources.

www.greenelectricity.org
Provides online information on
which green electricity supplier
is best.

www.green.energyhelpline.com
0800 634 1606
Gives green gas and electricity
suppliers and comparisons for
every area.

www.est.org.uk 0800 512 012
(free helpline)
The Energy Saving Trust
– established by the government,
has a good online Q & A section
with 230 answers on energy-
saving in the home.

WASTE, PACKAGING AND RECYCLING
www.wrap.org.uk 0808 100 2040
Helps with information and
practical advice on waste
reduction and recycling.

www.greencone.com
020 7499 4344
Sells all kinds of composters,
including the Johanna.

www.wigglywigglers.co.uk
Household composters.

www.lakeland.co.uk

www.homerecycling.co.uk
Recycling bins for your kitchen.

www.tetrapakrecycling.co.uk
0870 442 6000
Find out whether tetrapak can
be recycled in your area, plus
information about postal-return
system (not free).

www.saveacup.co.uk
01494 510167
Polystyrene-cup recycling from places of work.

www.wastewatch.org.uk
Waste Watch, the environmental charity. Plenty of good information in A–Z form and details of help in your area.

www.incpen.org.uk 0118 925 5991
Industry Council for Packaging and the Environment
– the industry's own site. While naturally not anti-packaging, contains a lot of information.

OUT AND ABOUT

www.livingrainforest.org
01635 202444
Indoor tropical rainforest with animals, Berkshire.

www.organicholidays.co.uk
Hotels and holidays.

www.aboutorganics.co.uk
Hotels, farmhouses, health farms, B & B.

www.alotoforganics.co.uk
Organic eating out, sorted into regions.

www.visitlondon.com
London organic restaurants and vegetarian/vegan places (listed separately).

www.veggieplaces.co.uk
Hotels and restaurants, all shown by area and on an interactive map.

www.veggieheaven.com/uk/
Vegetarian restaurants all across the UK, all reviewed by customers.

www.vegetarianvisitor.co.uk
Hundreds of cafés, pubs, restaurants and hotels. Also sells a book, updated annually, for £2.50.

www.veggies.org.uk
Guesthouses, B & B, hotels.

www.edenproject.com
01726 811911
An excellent family day out with thought-provoking themes of nature, conservation and sustainability.

BOOKS

Issues:

Heat: How to Stop the Planet Burning, George Monbiot, Allen Lane, 2006.

Harvest for Hope: A Guide to Mindful Eating, Jane Goodall, Little Brown, 2006.

Bringing the Food Economy Home: Local Alternatives to Global Agribusiness, Helena Norberg-Hodge, Todd Merrified and Steven Gorelick. Zed Books (UK), 2002.

Feeding People Is Easy, Colin Tudge, Pari Publishing, 2007. Tudge, a trustee of the Food Ethics Council, calls for 'enlightened agriculture' and a complete deconstruction of our food system and the global corporations who run it.

A History of World Agriculture: From the Neolithic to the Current Crisis, Marcel Mazoyer and Laurence Roudart, Earthscan, 2006. Looks at how farming has influenced our development and questions how the world will feed itself in the future.

Twinkie, Deconstructed, Steve Ettlinger, Plume Books, 2007. An analysis of the processed-food industry.